Empowering Leaders

David A. Ramey

Sheed & Ward

Sheed & Ward™ is a service of National Catholic Reporter Publishing Company, Inc.

Library of Congress Cataloging-in-Publication Data
Ramey, David A., 1951-
     Empowering leaders / by David A. Ramey.
          p.   cm.
     Includes bibliographical references (p.   ).
     ISBN 1-55612-372-8 (acid free)
     1. Leadership. 2. Political leadership. I. Title.
     HD57.7.R36 1991   91-35001
     303.3'4—dc20   CIP
Published by: Sheed & Ward
               115 E. Armour Blvd. P.O. Box 419492
               Kansas City, MO 64141-6492
To order, call: (800) 333-7373

For my grandfather, Anthony Ramey,
whose life remains a model
of wisdom and leadership.

Contents

Acknowledgements

In the end all good works are a collective effort. This book is no exception. There are many who have become a "community of thought" for me in refining and maturing the work of this manuscript. To all of them I remain most grateful. My wife Mary has remained a constant companion in life and often a partner in work. Her professional insights and thoughtful editing were a true gift enhancing this book. Her loving support over many years has enriched my life and work in countless ways. I am grateful to our four children; Matthew, Paul, Andrew, and Elizabeth. They have taught me well that authentic leadership is based in a consistent care for all dimensions of life by working at love and loving work.

Mary Sullivan has been an invaluable aid to this manuscript in editing, typing, and meticulously arranging what may have been disorganized copy without her skillful help. I have enjoyed many contemporaries of thought whose colleagueship has refined my thinking and advanced my understanding of the relationship between people and systems. Bruce Kline of Kline and Assoc.; Bob Spiewak of Organizational Resources International; Fred Ziedman of Woolpert Consultants; Fred Ungerman of Coolidge, Wall, Womsley, and Lombard; and Tim Nealon of Dayton City Schools all have influenced and sharpened my perspectives in ways they may never have realized.

I am deeply appreciative of those who have read parts of this manuscript and in doing so kept me faithful to myself and my beliefs. No doubt they also saved me countless days and hours in distinguishing the forest from the trees in the process of completing this book. Charlie Joiner of Values Technology, Marianna Bridge of The Lilly Endowment, and Newell Wert of United Theological Seminary have been caring and helpful collaborators in this endeavor.

The trustees and employees of Bergamo Center have been treasured supporters of this effort in allowing time and attention for the writing of this book and consulting away from the routine of organizational leadership. Over the past ten years we have learned together what is effective, and perhaps more importantly what is not effective, in guiding a growing organization into the future.

Many consulting clients and workshop participants throughout the country have enabled me to grow and expand my conceptual base of thought and experience through their careful praise and criticism over the years. I hope they shall find these pages to be a consistent complement to our work together.

Finally, I appreciate the invitation of Sheed and Ward Publishers to write this book. The keen insight of Robert Heyer detected a need for a book which integrates leadership and values without a naive disregard for organizational strategy. Their faith in this project is an example to me of their concern for the real work of social leadership.

I hope these pages will serve as some credit to all who have made this project possible including yourself as a reader.

David A. Ramey
July 1991

Introduction

The challenge to create a more humane yet productive social order is the heart of leadership. This challenge is not restricted to political, economic, or business sectors of life. It is as much a personal responsibility for our individual lifestyles as it requires the renewal of our organizational, political, religious, and social systems. In a new decade on the verge of a third millennium we collectively face the limits of our world's capacity to provide for us without our returning the favor. Rather than being passive beneficiaries of our social prosperity, we are called to care about and nurture life both personally and socially.

Businesses struggle to become more socially responsible while monitoring the bottom line as they recognize their obligations to their employees, to the environment, and to the global community. Mainline churches seek to motivate and involve lapsed members amidst apparent declines in membership, participation and financial contributions; meanwhile, evangelical and fundamental religious communities expand their influence with easily digested messages and promises of personal salvation which neatly compartmentalize the complexities of a changing world. Families work to preserve the social structure of intimate relationships among the demands of mobile careers, multiple social and personal priorities, and an insatiable cultural dependence on technology and consumer conveniences. Structured, scheduled and personalized leisure pursuits offer increasingly comfortable but isolated lifestyles. Yet our private self-styled conveniences offer less satisfaction than our personal success has promised.

A recent television advertisement portrays a successful senior executive taking pride of ownership in his new automobile. The commercial depicts a hard-working, hard-driving manager leaving his office late into the evening for his Cadillac. As he sits in an empty parking lot, the caption reads, "The rewards of success." Can this dubious image of successful leadership truly reflect the ultimate testimony of our public contribution?

Municipal and suburban governments scramble to incorporate changing demographics that reshape their identity, autonomy, economic base, security, and viability. Overlapping and competitive local jurisdictions cause us to romantically desire a return to a simpler social fabric once defined by self-contained ethnic neighborhoods and communities. For all of the increase in layers of governance, little seems improved for the quality of life in our communities. Stabilizing basic services such as waste disposal, adequate water supply, and consistent educational quality in our schools plagues our major cities.

National and international governments seek to keep pace with the changing global character, increased population, and greater diversity of its world citizens. Formerly passive citizens of oppressed nations and repressive political regimes risk death and extinction, often through the inappropriate expression of terrorism, in desperate moves to achieve a greater political franchise. These ultimate acts of human despair and desperation reflect the longings of humanity for less economic and military vulnerability, a redistribution of world resources, and preservation of our global environment. The most sophisticated global intelligence cannot monitor the human spirit with speed enough to predict such upheavals of consciousness as the political changes in Eastern Europe of 1990 inspired by the citizens of the Eastern Block Countries.

We all intuitively sense that we live on the critical edge of social, political, and economic extinction but cannot quite grasp its significance for our collective human destiny, or even its relevance for living a responsible lifestyle. We are at the crossroads of human development. We are changing paradigms of human meaning, making a quantum leap of consciousness where everything appears beyond our control, even our abilities to control ourselves.

Yet in these times there are those who seem instinctively to know how to respond to the events shaping the course of history and humanity. Some of these leaders even create or influence the stream of social evolution and destiny in ways that engage our imagination and give us true hope. Mikhail Gorbachev initiated a wave of change in the Soviet Union, the citadel of sovereign bureaucracy where individual leadership was anathema. He has so stretched the limits of state control that he barely avoided a reactive use of extreme force in an aborted military coup of August 1991. His leadership knowingly countered generations of Soviet power which subjugated and repressed movements towards freedom. In a few years of international leadership his actions have altered decades of foreign policy for the world's superpowers and forced the beginnings of a massive adjustment to the economics of peace.

Polish patriot Lech Walesa initiated a labor movement, "Solidarity," attracting the support of governments, political leaders, the Pope, and millions of kindred souls around the world. Through the nightly media he became a living room champion reminding us of the neighbor who works with us in the assembly line and lives next door. Yet he has emerged as a world citizen capable of negotiating and brokering power and influence with the leaders of international governments. He changed the course of Polish and international history with the tools of faith and the weapons of courage and integrity. Ironically, he has accomplished these with an inherent "naivete" of the powerful moral influence of his nationalistic but symbolic actions for the international world community.

Mother Theresa has become a global celebrity through the simplest human power of compassion. Her spartan lifestyle sets rigorous standards for membership among followers. Her passion for a mission-driven life of hard and thankless work serves as a model for authentic servant leadership on the most personal level as well as on the widest global scale of social reorganization.

What is it about these people that empowers them to transcend their immediate challenges, appearing larger than life? How is it that their efforts succeed in ways that redefine the standards of success and change the course of history for millions of people beyond their immediate sphere of influence? What knowledge have they mastered and which skills have they refined to influence the course of humanity, perhaps beyond their own desires or intent? These individuals and those like them are people who have internalized the quest for leadership so completely that they have become universal champions. They transcend the expected boundaries of human excellence in ways that evoke not only our admiration but also our passion and pathos. While these leaders inspire our admiration, we also fear the consequences of following such a course of action in the context of our personal, organizational, and public lives. The standard of courage in our own lives requires no less than this same level of dedication. They have abandoned the assumed boundaries of predetermined solutions and social conditions. They understand that convention is the lowest common denominator for humanity. They apprehend "what is" yet seek to provide something better rather than leave well enough alone. They are masters of the inner challenge of leadership. They are artists of an inner passion and clarity of personal mission measured in public integrity which in turn influences others and expands a wider consciousness for humanity, a social transcendence. They know themselves with such intimate precision and personal depth that they understand the universal and collective mindset of others. When we see them, we see and fear ourselves as we might be if we could choose their courageous path.

Their techniques are as diverse as the complex interface of their personalities with their personal, social and political circumstances and experiences. The lives of these leaders bear no simple imitation. Our task is to internalize the disciplines of personal and social responsibility which they exhibit. This requires gaining sufficient self-knowledge which in turn effects a social impact in our lives beyond our expected means and available resources. These heroes do not follow the leadership of convention. Their work constantly redefines prevailing wisdom by anticipating strategies for change which widen the path for human meaning. These leaders have so integrated their inner vocation of leadership that little difference exists between finding their true inner vision and losing themselves in service to others. They are initiators who redefine our symbols, expand our relationships, enlist our spirits, and yet guide our actions with stability and order. Despite their constant change and unpredictability they give us a new sense of order and refreshing confidence. Their discipline is an internal one which provides public reassurance to others in their disarray. First and foremost they are people who have mastered themselves and learned to use the tools of their personalities, both strengths and limits, as opportunities to achieve their mission. For them there is no dichotomy of self-realization and public service. Their social responsibility to use their talents for society is their social capital of integrity, providing the security we all prize in situations of enormous risk and vulnerability. Their capacities for endurance and human excellence provide a transformative, mystical influence that accords them a special reserve and reverence. They transcend death and extinction through the memories they leave behind, as living legacies of their work for the world community. Their vision allows them to live in the future while grounded in the present, with a chilling courage that gives us hope. In the end they lead with a wisdom beyond technology and technicality which employs these tools for the true service of an effective public mission.

These enduring leaders understand that mastery of the world of people, events, power, and authority is first an inner quest to follow an original call or personal vision of life, heard only by them and answered by themselves and no one else. They know leadership is ultimately a spiritual journey of discovering and responding to each new challenge and question with the abandon of "yes" in the face of ambiguity, despair, and isolation. While busy pursuing their unique vision they unwittingly call others toward greater personal, social, and organizational competence. They demonstrate a tremendous fidelity to and faith in a transformative power spanning many traditions of belief. Their leadership is a "religious" mission in universal terms, strengthening the self-awareness and confidence of humanity in our collective ability to make a difference beyond ourselves. They live as we all might with a frightening yet peaceful self-possession.

This wisdom of leadership propelled Martin Luther King to imagine the "promised land" of human equality while we struggle yet 30 years later to comprehend and implement his message in our racially and economically divided cities. The truth of this kind of leadership allowed Mahatma Gandhi to liberate India from Britain's political dominance while we often struggle to liberate ourselves in embarrassingly small ways from our own stress of living crowded and complex lifestyles. The courage of this leadership required Abraham Lincoln to accept the deaths of half a million of his countrymen and ultimately his own. Yet he healed a broken nation's hope to sponsor life and economic opportunity for our posterity and bring unity to our divided values. The grace of this leadership allowed Nelson Mandela to arise from prison after nearly 30 years of political confinement with the poise, balance, and countenance of a nation's grandfather away from his family on a visit to a foreign land. His graced public posture bespeaks a lifetime of action born from a generation of solitude and imprisonment.

The success of these leaders is not measured in the benefits of personal comfort, nor in evidence and acclaim of immediate tangible rewards or results. This leadership is substantiated by the larger social contribution of the quality of their life to the advancing frontiers of human destiny and fulfillment. In this respect these leaders are no different from each of us: called to make a difference of character in the personal, public, and organizational contexts of our life. They model for us on a larger scale and wider stage the purpose of each of our lives to provide leadership in the context of our personal history and destiny.

This book is a reflection on the practice of leadership which contributes to personal, public, and organizational development. It is meant not only to inform or illustrate effective strategy but also to mature our consciousness in the act of leading which stimulates further insight. Its postscript will be written in the expanded self-knowledge the reader may gain in applying its contents and concepts to his or her own opportunities to lead, creating greater awareness and effectiveness for themselves and others. If successful, it will provide some testimony that leadership is a unified fabric of self expression and social contribution. Leadership is the art of simultaneously empowering oneself and enabling others toward a more comprehensive personal and collective human development.

Chapter I

The Mission of Leadership

The fundamental responsibility of leadership is to make a commitment and a contribution of lasting public value to the quality of our lives, the quality of our work, and the quality of society. The rest is technique. We have lived too long with separate realities for our personal lives, our organizational work, and our public responsibilities. There is an essential connection between the fundamental quality of our personal life and the quality of our work which creates a lasting public value for the social good of our constituencies and our wider world community.

There is a gap between our hopeful desires and our present experience. We live in a cultural milieu disconnected from the natural ebb and flow of our lives, from the lasting effectiveness of our work on both an individual and corporate level, and from the public good we are all called to enhance. Dag Hammarskjold in 1959 understood the essential connection among all of these areas as chronicled in his book *Markings*:

> What distinguishes the 'elite' from the masses is only their insistence upon 'quality.' This implies a responsibility to all and for all to the past for the future, which is the reflection of a humble and spontaneous response to Life—with its endless possibilities and its present which never happens twice.[1]

There is no separate leadership for the quality of our lives which is also not concerned with the quality of our work, and which does not perpetuate a lasting concern for the quality of our

society. No longer can we afford to run institutions, and organizations, or provide jobs or work responsibilities for individuals, in a
context that does not understand the essential connection between
these three realities. The advancing limits of our production systems to provide a lasting concern for our environment, humane
working systems for our employees, and a rich and balanced life
for all of us as citizens signals the need for a change of vision for
leadership. The fundamental responsibility of leadership is to integrate organizational, institutional, and personal values into coherent systems.

This book develops a quality-based model for leadership (Figure
1) which describes the essential ingredients and relationships
among our lives, our work, and our social commitment. These
three commitments of leadership involve corresponding vocational
(personal), organizational, and public qualities. One cannot enhance or strengthen the vocational development of individuals without making an impact on the quality of their organizations. Consequently, one cannot strengthen the quality of our organizational
life and its leadership without creating some lasting public value
for our society. The vocational leadership we exercise in our personal lives, the corporate leadership of our organizations and the
lasting effects of our public leadership in society are different expressions of the same reality. Integrating these three expressions of
leadership is our collective agenda.

Leadership Quality Commitments

Quality
of Life

Quality
of Work

Quality
of Society

Figure 1. Leadership Quality Commitments

This is not a book about heroic leadership. The lives of people on which history has bestowed that honor enlarge and embellish our understanding of leadership beyond the capacity of the written word to explain. They have begun and will continue to rewrite the meaning of leadership in human experience. If effective, this book may at times prick our motivations and serve as a counterpoint to some of the goals of personal gratification and self-indulgence often associated with our customary measures and definitions of success. In the end the amount of one's accumulated resources has little to do with the power of leadership. At best these are the physical, economic, and social endowments which make effective and lasting leadership easier.

This book is written for those who seek to lead by identifying, articulating, and actualizing the personal mission they are called to fulfill. It is for those of us who despite our ordinary attributes seek to accomplish extraordinary things. Japanese industrialist and management sage Konosuke Matsushita describes this process as developing "extraordinary qualities in ordinary people." Leadership is a relationship not only between leader and circumstance or leader and constituency but between leader and a higher power, calling us forward to become more personally competent and complete by using our portfolio of personal assets and physical resources to strengthen our social contribution.

Irrespective of our formal spiritual life or even its absence, leadership finds its source and root in the experience of being called beyond oneself. This belief in "what is not yet" is faith in action. Leadership without faith is the unfocused demonstration of technique, an exercise in self expression without lasting value. This book is for those with sufficient faith in themselves, their destiny, and humanity to master their personal, organizational, and public competence, to produce a stronger contribution to the fabric of human life over the span of a lifetime. It is for those who desire greater self-knowledge in the pursuit of helping others to learn. It is a book about the continuity of the inner journey of self-possession, inner discovery, self-direction, and self-expression with the outer advancement of human goals through social and organizational development. Leadership is an artistic process of weaving the tapestry of outward strategy, technique, and analysis with intrinsic insight, integrity, and authenticity.

The literature on the personalities and strategies of leadership is abundant. One can peruse the shelves of recent literature in government, education, business, economics, and philosophy and find a treasure of resources and experience related to the skills and models of effective leadership. This book relates leadership strategy and action to the intrinsic meaning of human development and higher purposes. Our purpose is not to define leadership, but educate others to achieve it.

Inspired by Japanese management, our Western institutions have shown a lingering thirst for models of productivity and prosperity which also incorporate corresponding social and spiritual values. Konosuke Matsushita in his book *Quest for Prosperity* speaks of the awakening of his consciousness to this necessary unity as reflected in his speech to the staff of Matsushita Electric in 1932.

> The mission of a manufacturer is to overcome poverty, to relieve society as a whole from the misery of poverty and bring it wealth. Business and production are not meant to enrich only the shops or the factories of the enterprise concerned, but all the rest of society as well. And society needs the dynamism and vitality of business and industry to generate its wealth. Only under such conditions will businesses and factories truly prosper, but their prosperity is secondary. Our primary concern is to eliminate poverty and increase wealth. How? By producing goods in abundant supply. No matter what the condition of society, a manufacturer must sustain his efforts in making available large volumes of goods. This is his true mission. . . .

> Only after there is a limitless supply of material goods as well as spiritual peace of mind will man achieve true happiness. I believe that here is the manufacturer's true mission and the mission of Matsushita Electric. I would like you all to keep in mind that the true mission of Matsushita Electric is to produce an inexhaustible supply of goods, thus creating peace and prosperity throughout the land.[2]

Sixty years later in the West we are awakening to the realization that our mission to be productive with our resources is connected to our social mission for humanity. Rather than opposites, these are two dimensions of the same reality. As leaders, we search for the potential to create continuous and compatible benefits in our lives, our work, our organizations, and our world community.

There is an inherent spirituality of leadership which anchors our motivations and our actions. The complementarity of our own interests and the public good emerges when our public and private missions are congruent. This spiritual dimension of leadership is not necessarily observed or described in religious language or easily compared to the beliefs of formal religious traditions. There is a universal faith of leadership which if real will be recognized by those who live their lives with an intentional dedication to a cohesive personal, public, and organizational quest. For the religious believer these associations and implications will be apparent. Leadership may be seen by some as a vital component not only of our specific confessional beliefs or religious orientation, but as a response to a universal call to enrich humanity. In either case leadership is essentially and intrinsically a spiritual process. It is entirely consumed with tapping, motivating, developing, inspiring or correcting the human spirit in addressing a goal or challenge.

The disengagement of strategies and techniques of leadership from their transformative impact upon people and events is similar to using technology without understanding the logic of its operating systems. Without careful grounding in an intentional and inner directed lifestyle of leadership effectiveness is limited to our present awareness and experience of trial and error. Each new circumstance or challenge calls for yet another new leadership "technique." However, with introspection and personal integration, true leaders possess a foundation of values which grounds their efforts at authentic leadership. Once the inner and outer dimensions of leadership are united in our consciousness, coherent strategies emerge to respond to the myriad of experiences and the circumstances we face. One may possess a variety of mechanical tools capable of producing good carpentry, but the real craftsman is the carpenter who can achieve great results with only chisel and mallet. Likewise the spirituality of leadership is the foundation for using the tools of management strategy and technical resources. A consistent understanding of spirituality and management strategy unlocks the resources and power of our work, and transforms our productive efforts into social value. Authentic leaders require an equally facile literacy in the languages of both human meaning and of technical competence in their occupational and career settings. Expanding the spiritual literacy of leaders is a key dimension of leadership this book aspires to enrich.

Leaders are often ordinary people with a heightened sensitivity for detecting the unspoken message and a perceptive eye for nuance in their daily responsibilities and relationships. They employ an artful self-awareness and intentional self-deployment in their activities, defining rather than being defined by their work and its results. The parent leader in the process of parenting discovers a missing element of their own childhood maturation and simultaneously teaches their children and themselves the new lesson of experience. The educator leader instructs students in the art of critical self-reflection not only to solve problems in the immediate circumstance, but also to be able to apply the cognitive process to new experiences and events in the future. The minister leader provides reflection on the scriptural message as it influences life today in ways that enlarge the believers' perspectives by helping them to acquire greater introspection, inner wisdom, and self-direction in interpreting issues of meaning and value. The physician leader assists patients to comprehend the interplay of their current physical condition with those past and future behaviors and attitudes that may contribute to the healing process. The executive leader advances strategic corporate goals by expanding the professional competence and repertoire of subordinates, who in the process learn to lead others with their new-found vision and experience.

In this sense leaders are present within many areas of life beyond the usual limits of formal authority or control. Their primary form of self expression is direct influence. These leaders conduct their affairs with a qualitative presence that imperceptibly fuses their work and their identity. They are not lost in their work without a sense of self-definition; rather their identity is so firmly secured that they exhibit a second-level efficiency in their actions. In the midst of their work they simultaneously develop themselves and others in the process of growth, both achieving immediate tactical results as well as acquiring insight and meaning for life's future endeavors. They know their work and themselves so well that they exhibit a playful sense of abandon and dispassion allowing working relationships and events a freedom of their own. They work intensely and seriously toward directed goals but possess an amazing detachment of their egos from their short-term results or impacts, concentrating instead on the long-term quality of their efforts. In this way leadership is the ultimate form of self-expression, contributing to both process (the quality of our relationship) and product (the lasting value of our results).

Quality of Life

Each of us is endowed with a distinctive vocational (personal) leadership which we are called to contribute through the quality of our lives. This contribution is more than the sum of the different dimensions of our personal, relational, and work lives. It is somehow a composite view of who we are as individuals in relationship to ourselves, our families, and our communities. This vocational leadership is the fundamental core of beliefs, of values, of strengths, of limits, and of talents that each one of us brings to the many responsibilities, demands, and tasks of life.

On a personal level, we are all challenged with the difficult responsibility to create a balance among the many dimensions of our lives. The physical disciplines, the mental disciplines, and the spiritual disciplines are essential ingredients to create an integrated fabric of life. Over-extending our lives in an imbalanced way—inappropriately stressing career pursuits over physical, emotional, relational, or spiritual pursuits—clearly leads to our disengagement from the quality of our work and has lasting negative consequences for our organizations as well as for our social fabric.

The Center for Creative Leadership in Greensboro, North Carolina, has done extensive research on the quality of life for successful executives. They describe several characteristics that are necessary learnings in the lives of successful people. The "lessons of experience" that successful leaders and executives must accomplish include: a) a recognition of personal limits, b) a sensitivity to others, c) coping with events beyond our own control, d) the balance between life and work.[3]

The research of the Center for Creative Leadership indicates that many leaders achieve these lessons and master these dimensions of personal integrity largely through the experience of hardship. They chronicle their work in the following way:

> Many rummage through their achievements and realize that while achievements brought satisfaction, only relationships brought joy. Their traumas caused them to reevaluate what was important to them. One manager

left the company to help his son work through some problems, another refused an important transfer and eventually resigned so that his retarded daughter's development wouldn't be disrupted by having to move away from the therapy center. The manager who is threatened by the angry wife realized that he could be sensitive to people without sacrificing his effectiveness in a marriage. In fact, he and others found they could increase their effectiveness by allowing the complementary lesson of their personal lives to seep more into their work. In a sense, all the lessons from traumas helped managers regain a sense of balance. Whether it was in how they reacted to fate, or how they sought to reintegrate their view of themselves as a person and as a manager, balance was the issue. They sought to regain control of their reactions and of situations and to influence how others viewed them.[4]

An expression of a well-developed sense of vocational leadership is represented by a balanced sense of life commitments throughout the quality of one's life and one's work. This is a surprising portrait of success as contrasted with the image conveyed in our popular perception. Sam Walton, once the richest business executive in the U.S., lives in the same Arkansas house in which his career began. People such as Sam Walton who exhibit a high degree of integrity do not see a discontinuity between commitment to family, commitment to community, and a commitment to deep and lasting relationships with their co-workers and their colleagues.

A recent book on the relational dimension of leadership, *Tender Power* by Sherry Cohen, takes a controversial view of the feminine dimensions of work and intimacy. She makes a convincing case of their importance for the long-term success of our personal, organizational, and public lives. She discusses the integrity of personal leadership through the imagery of the feminine dimension of management.

The feminine context depends on stirring people to produce their best work because they feel good about the organization and because they feel good about themselves. The feminine context combines firm direction along with the empowerment of others. Cooperation, for instance, as women have developed the art through the ages, is an example of power and empowerment. As we help each other to explore, discover, and ripen, we find new sources of strength within ourselves.[5]

A successful understanding of personal leadership is contingent upon a belief that we find the inner strength and the outer support for our long-term resiliency and resourcefulness in the breadth and depth of our relational lives, and the quality of those relationships which we extend to others.

Quality of Work

In the quality of our work, we are also called to exercise organizational leadership. This organizational leadership comes from an understanding of the fundamental ingredients in motivating and enlisting the capacities of others for vocational leadership in collective ways. Organizational leadership also requires us to transition our systems successfully into the future. However, often our understanding of organizational leadership is limited by one-dimensional views of tactics or strategies, short-term results, limited corporate goals, and narrow motives for profit. We cannot disengage our quest for organizational leadership and achievement from the impact on the vocational dimensions of leadership in our lives or from the public impact on the quality of our society.

Many business understandings of leadership are confined to the organizational techniques we master. Clearly the success of our private lives, our organizational futures, and our social good is partly contingent on the mastery of technical skills and abilities. However, overemphasizing either the personal qualities of leadership or the organizational qualities that are necessary to create a successful future reflects the imbalances we experience in our corporate lives. Achieving an integrated unity among the vocational, organizational, and public expressions of leadership is a hallmark of the leader of the future.

This book develops key organizational qualities which are required for the successful execution of leadership in any organizational or systemic environment. Frequently in our nonprofit or public sector community, these qualities are overlooked as merely commercial business practices or techniques. However, there are basic structures of accountability and responsibility essential for all organizations to move a mission forward in order to create lasting value for individuals, for systems, and for society as a whole.

Quality of Society

The third expression of leadership is the value our work contributes to the quality of society. Creating lasting public value through leadership depends on the internal and the external competencies of our organizations to create a better world, not just build a better mouse trap. There may have been a time in our social fabric when individuals and organizations could survive exclusively on the entrepreneurial wit and wisdom of creating a better product, increasing profitability, or establishing greater convenience for consumers. However, these short-term approaches to leadership among sectors of society are rapidly hitting their limits. The realities of our global interdependence, our complex social systems, and our environment and economic limits to support an expanding world population—all signal a need for change in respecting the three dimensions of leadership for total quality of life, work, and society. No longer will leaders be able to live in a world where they can restrict attention to only one expression of individual, organizational, or public issues. Sophisticated leaders will use all three expressions of leadership as the criteria for evaluating the decisions necessary to create a successful future. No single dimension can serve as the ultimate measure of effectiveness.

The successful future organization will be well-versed in its understanding of the lasting value it creates for its publics. Organizations are already beginning to emphasize their commitment to higher purposes and social values as an integral part of their mission. It may seem at times that these are expedient pleas to enlist the emotional support of their intended publics. However, as our organizational life matures and our understanding of leadership expands, we will see this as essential: linking our organizational futures with the survival of our society and the responsible use of our environmental resources.

In his best-selling book, *Vanguard Management,* on the future of redesigning organizations, James O'Toole talks about the higher purposes and public responsibilities of all organizations.

"The search for meaning" has become the leitmotif of modern times. Since workplaces have largely replaced the family, the church, and the community as central institution of society, more men and women have turned to their corporate employers as a source of inspiration and purpose in their lives. So a base or unelevated purpose for the corporation is inadequate. Profit maximization is not enough. And such slogans as, "Think," and, "Progress Is Our Most Important Product" are seen as hollow by the sophisticated and educated employees of today—men and women who refused to be manipulated . . . in the long term, the best employees will drift away in search of a deeper purpose and more meaningful reasons to devote their lives to a corporation.

At the Vanguard, there is commitment in word and deed to a higher purpose: these corporations exist to provide society with the goods and services it needs, to provide employment, and to create a surplus of wealth (profit) with which to improve the nation's general standard of living and the quality of life. In this view, profit is the means and not the end of corporate activity.[6]

Not only in corporate life, but also among our many nonprofit and public institutions, our future will depend upon our ability to enlist the support of our publics and provide a lasting value to society and its fundamental purposes. This includes the protection of citizens, protection of the environment, and protection of the health of our communities. No longer will an institution be able to see itself as serving a single purpose. Churches will not be able to be custodians for the spiritual life of people without attending to the fundamental issues of economic development, land use, public policy, and social responsibility. Corporations will necessarily exercise their responsibility to care for the environment, the quality of community housing, and the educational systems which support the families of their employees. Political entities are rapidly realizing the limitations of divided approaches to community development among competing municipalities. Clearly the prevailing model of future leadership is attention to the lasting public value that an organization creates among its internal and external constituencies of employees, consumers, and publics. The successful leader of the future, both individually and organizationally, will be required to master competencies to create a sense of lasting public value for the quality of society through the exercise of public leadership.

Each of us as responsible workers, family members, and world citizens will be required to learn a new paradigm of social responsibility. The three criteria of lasting value for the quality of life, quality of work, and quality of society are necessary to assess all our life choices including those related to business, organizations, communities, and individuals.

The dynamics, the responsibilities, and the interplay between these essential dimensions of leadership present an evolution in our human consciousness. Leadership is a personal requirement for being a complete individual. Despite the complexity of our social agenda for the 21st century, the need for its presence is felt on the most personal level of life. Commitment to leadership is measured in the meaning we create and express on a personal level. All of us are capable of leading in these three dimensions of life.

An illustration may help: Tom came to his job as a dishwasher after being severely disabled in a serious automobile accident. He lost 50% of his brain capacity and suffered life-threatening consequences as a result of his misfortune. His manager had sought counsel on whether or not to hire Tom; he was advised to make his own decision, but to be willing to accept the consequences however they might fall.

In the ten years since his hiring, Tom has expressed a coherent understanding of his personal, organizational, and public contribution of leadership. He sees his work and his life as essentially a devotion to service. He realizes that he is not just a dishwasher. His helpfulness is clearly represented in the care he extends to his family. He supports his working mother and her care for the failing health of his father. He has a great devotion to his two older sisters. He is helpful and considerate to co-workers and customers. Tom clearly has a sense of his inner mission not only as a utility worker but as a devoted contributor to those individuals and groups he encounters on a daily basis.

In his organization, Tom is an extraordinary worker. He has never missed a day of work in ten years, is always punctual, stays late without hesitation, participates in all employee involvement programs, and has taken upon himself further literacy training to strengthen his intellectual abilities since his accident. When he finishes his primary duties, he is often found in the kitchen assisting other employees in the preparation of food as well as the service of meals to guests. Once his additional support duties are fulfilled with his co-workers, Tom can even be found welcoming guests into the dining room, asking them about the nature of their training program, and promoting the services of his organization.

When one measures the progress and the effectiveness of the work of this individual employee, one cannot help comprehend the significance of his commitment and contribution to lasting public value in the quality of his life. He enriches the fabric of life for his co-workers, for his superiors, and for the customers whom he serves. He understands that his work is about strengthening the quality of his life and the lives of others, impacting the quality of his work and strengthening the quality of the social fabric. He creates a positive environment for all those who come in contact with him, thus demonstrating a significant understanding of the personal, organizational, and public expressions of leadership.

Tom understands the reality of leadership. In a basic way his actions reinforce a belief that the quality of life, the quality of work, and the quality of our society as essentially bound together. The gap we sometimes demonstrate in our organizational practices between these realities is a false dichotomy. His life, in a very simple and profound way, is a model for the qualities, the ingredients, and the responsibilities of leadership.

John Gardner in his recent book on leadership discusses the importance of tapping the gifts of all members of our society, of our institutions, and our families as leaders.

> Great gifts unused, even unsuspected, are hardly a rarity. No doubt there have always been a great many men and women of extraordinary talent who have died "with all their music in them," but it is my belief that with some imagination and social inventiveness we could tap those hidden reserves not just for government, not just for business, but for all the diverse leadership needs of a dynamic society.[7]

Each one of us is called to do no less, and those of us who would aspire to be leaders are required to elicit such a response among all those whom we influence, impact, and serve.

Is such a broad view of leadership simplistic and impossible to achieve? Quite the contrary. This book intends a simple but comprehensive understanding of the task of leadership. Leaders of the future can no longer attend to one dimension or one reality for the success of their organizations, institutions, or businesses. They must become adept in simultaneously evaluating short-term and long-term decisions against their impact on the quality of life, the quality of work, and the quality of society. Only in the internal wrestling with the complexity and paradox of such decisions will true leadership emerge. This task is no more or less complicated than a change in our consciousness of what it means to be a leader. Focusing on a singular dimension of organizational life, public service, or individual achievement will no longer be an adequate measure of the success of leaders. Can it be done? There is no alternative. Nuclear physicist Edwin Teller, in writing about breakthroughs in human consciousness and human understanding, describes our task this way:

> Survival of humanity must also include the survival of human dignity. I believe that no endeavor that is worthwhile is simple in prospect. If it is right, it will be simple in retrospect. Belief in action will accomplish that which does not exist, but which in the future will be taken for granted.[8]

Figure 2 outlines the basic skills of leadership which strengthen the quality of life, quality of work, and quality of society as a comprehensive reality. Each of these is a foundational ability that we are individually and organizationally required to master. The following chapters will develop this quality-based model as the full complement of leadership competencies. Chapter III will focus on vocational leadership and the personal qualities which constitute full personal development in the quality of life. Chapter VI will detail organizational qualities necessary for quality in the workplace. Chapter VII will consider the qualitative skills essential to ensure a social contribution. When we can access these three dimensions of leadership and use them simultaneously in decision-making, we will begin to understand the essential construction of the new reality of leadership for which our society and our world deeply longs.

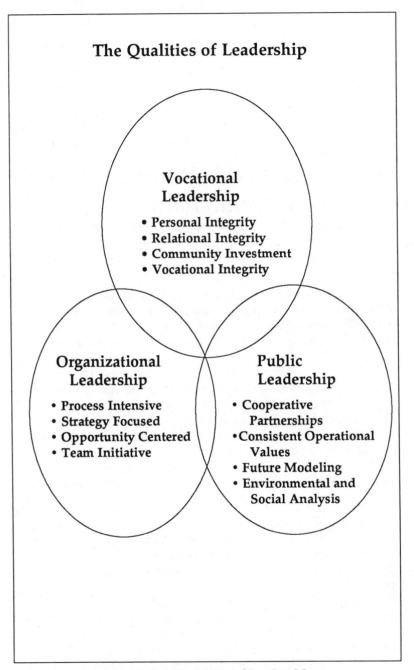

The Qualities of Leadership

Vocational Leadership

- Personal Integrity
- Relational Integrity
- Community Investment
- Vocational Integrity

Organizational Leadership

- Process Intensive
- Strategy Focused
- Opportunity Centered
- Team Initiative

Public Leadership

- Cooperative Partnerships
- Consistent Operational Values
- Future Modeling
- Environmental and Social Analysis

Figure 2. The Qualities of Leadership

Chapter II

The Cultural Challenges to Leadership

We face unprecedented complexity in the challenge to effect a contribution of lasting public value to the quality of life, to the quality of work, and to our social posterity. Recent emphasis on leadership issues in American business is in response to the competitive challenge launched by Japanese industries, with their emphasis on participative management, employment for life, meticulous hiring and selection practices, continuous employee training and development, and extensive systems of job rotation and job enlargement. In government the silent threat of nuclear disaster, the aging of our population, the escalation of the national debt, the unfavorable balance of trade, the limitation of law enforcement to address the social problems of crowded cities, and the cultural poison of drugs contribute to our dissatisfaction with the social climate.

What has dramatically changed is that leaders can no longer succeed by attending only to their chosen specialized profession or expertise. The worlds of business, government, education, religion, economics and health care are so intricately woven in our social fabric that "experts" in only one field cannot address the complexity of human problems. Consider the example of unintended pregnancies and the resulting debate over abortion as an acceptable remedy. This issue has deeply polarized our society to the point where major institutions, each espousing the goal of responsible family life, are poised as enemies in a game of enormous importance, wasting financial resources on the public relations dimension of this compelling social concern. We cannot seem to find the appropriate sector of society in which to study the issue in all its dimensions and to develop commonly acceptable alternatives. This issue transcends social sectors as we currently define them. We have not identified a trusted authority for the quality of our life capable of embracing the problem of abortion. No public institution, including our government, has gained enough public trust to develop multi-dimensional strategies which comprehensively consider all elements of abortion's consequences before advancing a solution for public consensus.

In education we witness rising rates of absenteeism and decreasing levels of literacy and basic skills. In central cities fewer graduates from our secondary school systems (partly the result of suburban flight by middle income families) and more recently the green belt escape by high technology industry both further increase racial division and poverty. Our colleges and universities threaten to once again become the resource of a privileged class to gain greater economic and social advantage, as double-digit annual tuition increases proliferate among both public and private institutions. City schools often become a convenient battleground for multiple social problems of family fragmentation, diminished community values, economic and social deprivation and the quick fix of drug proliferation to ease students' pain and deliver them from financial obscurity. It is no wonder that many a teacher has abdicated the personal mantle of leadership in favor of a complacency of survival. Each day they address a jungle of needs too enormous to comprehend and manage.

In health care inflation outraces other sectors by a multiple of two, and the economic resources among many to purchase the quality of health care they have grown up with dwindle. Our physicians and medical institutions now accept credit cards, realizing the enormity of the proportional costs on our personal and corporate budgets for health care. Keenly competitive hospital systems vie for local approval for room expansions and sophisticated technology in order to remain competitive; however, they paradoxically lower costs by pressure to expand outpatient surgery and limited stays for inpatient procedures, often weakening the quality of care. Many older Americans are overlooked in their illnesses because of the cost of providing care in relation to their advancing age; if they were younger with less risk and if their medical insurance, and Medicare and Medicaid weren't so encumbering to administer, they could receive better assistance in treating their medical conditions. All of these indicators and countless more that could be cited, from a declining global environment to the changing political economies of South America and Eastern Europe, present a complex and rapidly expanding background of social and cultural perplexity for leaders in any sector of public or private life.

Leadership in a cultural context of increased professional and technical specialization amidst escalating interdependent issues is an enormous and formidable challenge for those truly courageous enough to accept its invitation. In this chapter we will try to traverse the maze of our cultural issues and resulting challenges for leadership by examining five dimensions of our present social conditions which influence any form of vocational, public, and organizational leadership. Leadership has become a generative theme for our society as it captures our imaginations yet eludes our grasp. Perhaps the first challenge for leadership in our culture is not to scrutinize the skills or the task of leadership but to truly understand the cultural consciousness to which leaders must respond in order to create successful futures.

In our society five cultural challenges pervade the activity and awareness of leadership in any sector from family planning to global manufacturing:

1. The Limits of Technology to Solve Human Problems

2. The Accelerated Rate and Complexity of Change

3. Advanced Specialization

4. Global Interdependence

5. The Isolation of Human Values from Institutions.

These cultural pressures influence the process of leadership in ways that cannot be overlooked. For each challenge a corresponding lesson for leadership follows. In order to learn these lessons and succeed, effective leaders must overcome inertia and influence cultural forces to support the preferred future they develop with their constituents. Skillful mastery of the task of leadership and the formation of consensus among a constituency are contingent on a comprehensive understanding and response to these cultural forces which prevail.

Limits of Technology to Solve Human Problems

The power of technology to shape our livelihood has enormous impact upon our social, economic, and personal capabilities. Quantum leaps in the capacity of computing through microprocessors have enormously advanced our technical capabilities in science and engineering almost beyond our comprehension. In *New World New Mind*, a sweeping social commentary and call for a new way of comprehending global reality, Robert Ornstein and Paul Ehrlich assert:

> In computing power we are more separated from the world of the 1950's than the 1950's was from the accountants of Hammurabi. Those "mainframe" computers that housed schools and other records in the 1960's could perform fewer calculations per second than the average AT-class machine of today, now available for under two thousand dollars.[1]

Yet these technical capabilities have created unprecedented dangers not only for the quality of life, but also for its ultimate continuance. The destructive capacity of only one of our current nuclear weapons systems, the MX missile ("Peacekeeper"), provides for the simultaneous destruction of up to ten major population centers. Within 25 - 30 minutes of launch this system has the precision to target each warhead within one city block of a designated point of reentry such as Moscow's Red Square.

Technology has enabled significant positive social advances within medicine, transportation, education, politics, religion, athletics, and public communications. Yet in each of these sectors of society we face unparalleled ethical dilemmas and in some instances cultural declines despite our advanced ability to access information quickly and to develop increasingly sophisticated technical tools and resources. Without instant satellite communications the social changes in the Soviet Bloc might have taken centuries to evolve. Yet today Estonian patriots can express solidarity with Lithuanian officials by declaring national sovereignty within days of each other, aided by instantaneous communications in television and radio. The declaration of independent sovereignty might have taken months to reach Moscow a century ago. In the 1991 Persian Gulf War, the Secretary of State of our nation watched satellite commercial television accounts in order to gain current information.

In their 1950's advertising General Electric displayed a completely outfitted model kitchen equipped with their latest product innovations. The prototype featured a homemaker leisurely sitting at the table reading. The implication was that the anticipated advances in technology would create greater leisure and personal growth opportunities. Not long ago in a major metropolitan museum I saw the same display of the GE model kitchen, which brought back a flood of personal feelings and memories of a world view that no longer exists. That leisurely and peaceful home of the 1950's statistically now has one or two working parents employed an average of 50 hours or more weekly to pay for the "leisurely" enjoyment of these technological lifestyle enhancements. It seems that our technology has created greater dependence and greater complexity of lifestyle to accompany its many benefits.

A few years ago, the MacNeil-Lehrer News Hour on public television featured a special segment interviewing a prominent metropolitan attorney. His commentary was on the legal complexities created by advances in biogenetic research. He described a sobering scenario which crystallized the interplay of technical opportunity with its corresponding effect on social complexity. He asserted that to accommodate current advances in genetic capabilities in human reproduction, there are five potential legal claimants for parental rights in a court of law: a donor father, a donor mother, a host mother, and two adoptive parents. He suggested that the potential complication to the legal system could take decades or longer for test litigation to clarify relative parental rights. Not only has technology advanced our capabilities to improve the quality of life on a personal level, it has also created tremendous complexities for the quality of our social life in raising ethical dilemmas unparalleled to human understanding.

It would be foolish and shortsighted to undervalue benefits we have accrued through technical advancement. The communication process between author and reader we are engaged at this moment in would not have been nearly as feasible without the technological resources of mass printing, marketing, word processing, manufacturing, and transportation. However, the experience and expertise of authentic leadership must be mindful of the full range of consequences in relying on technology or technique to provide lasting solutions to human problems, which remains the intended goal of the art of leading.

This personal story may exemplify the impact of technology on our cultural context. On Saturdays when not travelling for professional commitments, I arise about 5:30 a.m. to drive out to the country for an early morning breakfast, some quiet reading, and a hike in a favorite nature preserve. I stop at an all-night dairy store that serves homestyle meals. From week to week my order varies little. Since there are few frequent predawn guests the employees have become very familiar with my requests to the point that an abbreviated query "The Usual?" had been sufficient. Recently the dairy introduced a computerized food ordering system integrating cash register sales with kitchen grill orders and inventory controls, similar to a "PLU" system one might find in a major fast food chain. The attendant merely pushes keys indicating preselected items to create the order. With the computerized system in place the embarrassed and frustrated waitress spent what seemed an eternity attempting to place my order into the system for the short order cook waiting impatiently no more than five feet away. After having been beeped at with an error message several times, the waitress finally yelled over the counter, "He wants his regular . . ." We all smiled at one another in instant recognition that technology has not always lived up to the GE promise of "Progress for People."

In our highly technical and integrated systems environment it is imperative for leaders not to subordinate the authentic and present human agenda to a technical applied solution without considering its corresponding social consequence. Technical resources may provide the resources for solutions to problems that leaders face but rarely does a resource comprise the entirety of a solution despite any advanced capabilities. Global as well as local leaders fail to apprehend this distinction as we gravitate toward technical solutions to the problems of humanity. Does the development of Strategic Defense Initiatives (the Star Wars technology) authentically contribute to the international management of nuclear arms? It appears only to add one further layer of technical sophistication and one more point of leverage in the nuclear equation to an already complex calculation of nuclear parity, an international issue of the greatest human proportions. On a more practical level, what impact do computerized telephone answering systems have on their operators as well as customers? This technology now takes the human contact from customer and worker changing the very nature of the direct relationship between people in this communication process.

Leaders committed to comprehensive strategies for the future must re-engage workers, customers, suppliers, and colleagues with the direct results and impacts of their labor, employing technology as a resource, not a solution.

Complexity and Accelerated Rate of Change

Leaders in almost any setting are increasingly aware of the difficulties and fears people express in relation to rapid change. This pervasive resistant stance in the face of change indicates a second deep seated cultural anxiety over the accelerated rate of change and its increasing complexity. In the midst of the frenzy of mergers, takeovers, and acquisitions in American industry a cartoon appeared in *The Harvard Business Review* depicting an executive returning to the office on a Monday morning. Before entering the executive suite, he turned to his secretary and asked, "OK, who do we work for this week?" This quasi-matter-of-fact yet inwardly cynical sentiment is fairly commonplace among employees and members of all types of organizations when dealing with pervasive change. Innate wariness with the nature of change compounds the tasks of leaders to introduce even favorable changes because constituents have difficulty investing in situations that may signal continued impermanence and transition. This cultural condition had grave implications for life in our time.

Astronomer Carl Sagan wrote a clever article on the acceleration of change in human history. He positioned events in history on a time line corresponding to a 365 day calendar year. In his model the discovery of fire occurred late in the month of December. Certainly much has transpired in our collective human life cycle in the last few days of "our year." Sociologist Morris Massey developed a series of videotapes on some of the social and evolutionary factors impacting our human development. He indicated that the equivalent to a "generation of thought," those with whom we share a common educational, social, familial, and historical base, occurs about every five years. Unlike past generations our longing for contemporaries of human experience is increasingly vulnerable to a complex set of conditions including frequent career changes, social and geographic mobility, and a pervasive feeling of impermanence. Our moorings of meaning in traditional sources of stability such as family, neighborhood, schools, and church all exhibit the cultural momentum of torrential winds of change shaping the experience of our lives. Our loss of confidence in the permanence of things silently influences our experiences almost daily, contributing to an inner doubt in the stability of institutions, leaders, events, and resources in providing any long term satisfaction.

In *New World New Mind,* Ornstein and Ehrlich develop a compelling thesis that our cultural and biological evolution is now deficiently slow in recognizing and responding to the new world challenges and issues we have created as a result of our mastery of the world's resources and of our technical skills. They imply we are almost incapable of responding to the consequences of our actions on a personal, organizational, and global scale.

The world that made us is now gone, and the world we made is a new world, one that we have little capacity to comprehend. The old world for which our perceptual systems were "designed" was one where the overall environment was a relatively stable, limited one in which threats were signaled by short-term changes and action was usually required immediately. . . . Human beings, however have changed the world more in the last ten thousand years that their ancestors did in the preceding 4 million.[2]

Not only has our perceptual system been required to adapt to an unprecedented rate of change beyond the ability of our biological and social systems to assimilate, but the complexity of scale of the events of change has increased exponentially. Early in the evolution of events in Eastern Europe, as a result of the policies of "glasnost" and "perestroika" of Mikhail Gorbachev, a cartoon appeared in the editorial section of a major metropolitan newspaper. The cartoonist depicted a diminutive George Bush and Gorbachev riding atop an enormous whale with the only control being a minuscule rein similar to a horse bridle connected to the enormous snout of the whale. As the imposing creature moved with abandon, Bush asked his compatriot "Which direction should we go in now?" It is not a comforting thought to think of international leaders of this stature and position without greater influence and control over the destinies of the nations they lead and the world they influence. For many years after the Persian Gulf War of 1991, we will remain unable to assess or comprehend the long-term social, genetic, and environmental impact of the hundreds of burning oil wells and the bombing of nuclear and chemical facilities. Our immediate-term "successful outcome" will influence decades of future changes far beyond the ability of present leaders to articulate or predict.

It is not surprising that the only American president of the last seven who completed two terms of office had the disposition of a kindly grandparent and was a literal reminder, through his acting career, of simpler days filled with images of college football heroes and the old west. Ornstein and Ehrlich illustrate the complexity of change for current generations and our leaders in graphic terms.

> Think about the rate at which we have entered this "new world" in the twentieth century. Many people who are alive today were born when the automobile was a curiosity and there were no freeways, airplanes, radios, refrigerators, dryers, paperback books, frozen dinners, tape recorders, TV's, VCR's, compact disk players, computers, antibiotics, credit cards, lasers, satellites, or nuclear weapons.

> Anyone who is fifty years old today was born into a world where a majority of the countries that are presently in the United Nations did not even exist. At the time of birth of those who are now over seventy-five, there had never been a world war, electricity and pasteurization were rarities, and one in three babies died in infancy. In 1945 only half as many people lived on the earth as there are in 1988; at the end of World War II, the gigantic nuclear arsenal that now threatens the world was nonexistent.[3]

The unparalleled rate of change in our lives and the complex scale of resulting consequences greatly limits the available options of those who lead. The diminishment of the world's natural resources and increasing demands upon them by an expansive world population make each of us less resilient in responding to the challenges placed upon us by leadership to be more public spirited and open to the requisite changes in human history. President Jimmy Carter was chastised in the press and in the subsequent election for suggesting that we will have to adapt to a world of fewer economic and environmental resources for us both individually and as a nation. Our instinctive tendency in the face of limits is to become territorial and isolated in preserving whatever economic and human equity we have achieved in real or perceived terms. We will review the psychology of change on a personal and organizational level later in this book. However, it should be presently apparent that one of the cultural conditions any leader faces in moving a constituency forward is their predisposition to resist change and their concern over the immediate consequences of change for their security.

Employment trends such as job sharing, parental leave, flextime, and working at home indicate need for coherence and personal stability by bringing the stable values of personal life to the workplace. A corresponding trend to include social and environmental considerations in our personal and organizational habits will be required. The accelerated rate and complexity of change requires leaders to create linkages of thought and action between work, personal, and social environments, creating greater continuity and stability.

Leadership in the future will be required to make the necessary linkages between the quality of one's personal life, the quality of our work environments, and the quality of our social fabric in order to supply a more comprehensive and global sense of security to assist constituents in understanding the need for change.

Advanced Specialization

We live in a historical period which may represent the apex of technical and occupational specialization. In virtually all areas of our society we witness increasing limitation in the focus of work for many individuals. In medicine we have developed subspecialties such as neonatology and pediatric cardiology, enabling children previously destined for early death to live normal lives. In auto maintenance no longer will the corner service station suffice to repair our increasingly complicated and computer assisted autos; we frequent one location for gasoline, another for oil changes, another for tune-ups and exhaust systems, and yet another for mechanical or electrical repairs. In education one trip to a university library to review the microfiche of recent doctoral dissertations will illustrate the highly complex nature of educational research in all fields of study. Recently I attended an awards ceremony for a high school science fair. A list of student projects was included with the program for parents to peruse. With great amusement the auditorium listened as the principal read the titles of award winning projects which were beyond his ability to pronounce, much less comprehend their content. His students' technical grasp of their individual interests exceeded his ability to remain conversant with their work, not at all an unusual experience of modern leadership.

In retail sales we have witnessed the rise of specialty shops, shopping malls, several levels of market-stratified discount and department stores, and more recently the concept of a "superstore" with virtual acres of goods and products. In the one product area of athletic shoes, for example, one can possess different shoes each more suited only for walking, running, indoor and outdoor soccer, tennis, aerobics, basketball, racquetball—and finally a return to an all-purpose "cross trainer." We are a society constituted of carefully researched market niches in business, sound bites in the media, and career specialties within traditional occupational fields such as medicine, law, religion, social service and education. Millions of dollars are spent annually researching ever more specialized niches in the traditional demographics of income, age, race, occupation, education, and family status. The field of psychographic marketing now attempts to match our tastes for tennis shoes with apparently related purchasing patterns such as camera equipment. Our diversified culture seeks increasingly refined ways to accomplish specialized purposes. The benefits of such a highly evolved world of work has brought tremendous influence upon society in shaping the future of humanity on a global scale. Our cultural advancements include such benefits as laser surgery, computerized learning for the handicapped, computer-assisted design in engineering, mobile communications, and hydroponic farming.

Our specialized social advancement, however, has not been without its consequences that require careful examination on the level of human psychology and social ethics. Many of our technical capabilities disengage our behavior from the long-term results of our decisions. I once toured the unclassified section of an engineering design area for a sophisticated nuclear weapons system. In the middle of the work area was a full-size prototype of the warhead, no taller than my shoulders. It was referred to by the design engineers as a "reentry vehicle." It was truly hard to comprehend that fully armed this cone-like projectile could eliminate several population centers simultaneously, obliterating an entire culture with a single decision. The capacity for psychological disengagement from our work has significant vocational, organizational, and public consequences for our life and work and therefore our leadership. In many areas the nature of work itself has been redefined to serve the technical systems which now produce what humans once did. Rather than create the production process we often manage systems which produce what we once did, such as in automotive robotics. In response, Japanese trends of job rotation, job enlargement, continuous training, and employment for life represent a requirement of the future to broaden employee capacities within their organizational settings beyond one dimensional skills. Japanese commitment to general knowledge as well as technical skill is a major contributor to their success in innovation, quality, and continuous improvement among workers.

Advanced specialization requires leaders to create greater general knowledge and skills among technical specialties to appreciate the qualitative dimensions of human work.

Global Interdependence

The highly specialized disengagement of the means from the ends of our livelihood runs counter to the critical reality of an increasingly interdependent society and world. Much of our technical specialization disengages the impact of our personal work and the quality of our personal lives from the impact of our actions on society. This further insulates us from global realities and the ethical and moral byproducts of our labors and productive advancements. Growing social awareness of the consequences of nuclear proliferation and the focus on the environment are perhaps the early warning signals of what may be a greater global consciousness correcting our isolation and estrangement from the social impacts of our specialized interests. Public awareness of issues such as nuclear winter, the depletion of natural energy sources, global warming, and the complexities of waste management increases our knowledge and perhaps our discomfort with problems that may exceed our consciousness and our present ability to effectively address them.

Global interdependence is not a remote eventuality relegated to the domain of international business and governance. It is a personal issue effecting each of us and being effected by the life choices we make and the leadership we follow or provide. Consider a personal example. At 5:00 a.m. when I awake and enter a dimly lit bathroom in the darkness of the predawn it seems surreal to acknowledge that my personal hygiene product of choice in an aerosol spray contributes fluorocarbons to the atmosphere, hastens the depletion of the ozone layer, effects global warming, and advances the melting of polar ice caps, further raising sea levels. My disengagement from this reality is conditioned by a culture that caters to my individual tastes and preferences. How can I accept the concept that such convenient specialization has global effects for tens of generations hence? Or as I think back to the day before and a delightful family picnic, a socially rewarding experience, I realize the disposable plastic tableware I purchased accelerated the depletion of the world's supply of fossil fuels at a rate faster than it can be replenished by the means we now have available. In these circumstances, I am participating in a decision of global significance by selecting personal convenience over wise social judgement. And as I look ahead to a complex day of career pursuits that will allow only a few moments to eat a hamburger in a fast food restaurant, it may offend my sense of present reality to accept the likelihood that I am consuming South American beef from a depleted rain forest cleared for feeding cattle less expensively than on a domestic Midwestern farm. My lunch is at the expense of family farming in the U. S. and the ecology of South America.

We resist or deny the undesirable and unintended consequences of our highly specialized and individualized society. Our personal and convenient social milieu has difficulty recognizing the effects of our collective work on our quality of life. Our private consciousness still falls well short of the scope of the global community we influence. We remain perceptually limited in recognizing our social impact. Yet increasingly the global community more closely encroaches upon our lifestyles in singular events but powerful images that call us to a new consciousness of leadership. We hear that major east coast cities contract with African nations to dispose of garbage in foreign landfills. Recently a study on solid waste disposal for Ohio indicated that by 1995 all existing landfills in the state will be full to capacity. Within four years we will have to develop the technology and resources to stop the advancement of a this primitive system of waste disposal, or choose the destructive course of transposing more agricultural land into dumps. Yet the Ohio legislature cannot consent to simple measures such as bottle deposits to assure their return and recycling. Ten years ago Wisconsin adopted legislation requiring residency for the purchase of major production farms, to reduce the influx of Arab wealth which was used to buy millions of acres of farmland. The irony was that most of the Arab wealth originated with American purchases of oil supplies during the energy crisis of the 1970's. We were in effect trading future farmland for current gasoline supplies, jeopardizing our future control of a major natural resource and our domestic food production capacity.

Today in the state of Ohio, Japanese ownership of business and industrial interests exceeds state and local investments. The Japanese are, in effect, heavily influencing the direction of our state economy. One of the major economic considerations in our national recovery from the drastic stock market decline of "Blue Monday" in 1988 was the confidence shown by the Japanese stock market on the next trading day by heavy Japanese investment in our domestic stock. Despite our predisposition to favor specialized and individualized solutions and decisions, most of what we effect and are effected by is based upon a highly complex network of global relationships.

Our psychological preference for local and immediate resources and solutions cannot erase the reality that the lingering impact and long-term results of our livelihood and work are global in nature. The extensive global interplay of our livelihood and social well-being, and our accompanying desire for simple and isolated decisions, present a unique cultural challenge for the task of leadership. First, the problems and issues for leaders to address exhibit a knotty complexity that overwhelms what may have been once perceived as the decisive hand of former leaders. Our nation became extremely frustrated with the apparent weakness of President Carter who negotiated for 15 months for the release of U. S. hostages in Iran. All were returned home unharmed as the result of meticulous diplomacy over several months through the involvement of many governments and unofficial mediators. After losing the national election he was not even invited to participate in the welcoming home ceremonies, despite his deployment of complex leadership and diplomacy in their behalf. His sophistication and discretion were perceived as weakness and the implication was that his deliberation might even have contributed to the hostage taking from its inception. By stark contrast President Reagan received enormous public support from most sectors of society for his bold, "decisive" invasion of Grenada to stem the influence of the Cuban military in Central America. Despite the casualties to American troops, the apparent lack of clear and present danger in the situation, and the potential international ramifications of our actions we were willing to accept this act as a reflection of popular "leadership."

Our Persian Gulf War propelled several military leaders and President George Bush to heroic status for their clear and decisive efforts. Yet the lingering political, environmental, social, and human consequences of our actions remain for history to unfold. We appear to have little tolerance for global complexity and the consequent slow, detailed, and discreet solutions to immediate circumstances. Public opinion militates against leadership that responds to the complexities of our global reality, especially when it contradicts or postpones our immediate self-interest. Yet effective leadership is hampered in its search for viable alternatives when it fails account for the ramifications of a course of action for global complexity.

Since many of the decisions we face have a complex system of relational impacts to weigh, the task of leadership is considerably harder than it may have been earlier in history. The crisis of limits has advanced into the present. Today's decision to wage war on a global scale would not take several years to evolve, with gradual assessments to abort or continue warfare based on the accumulated success or failure of successive battles. It would not even last as long as a skillful game of chess. The execution and completion of a full nuclear exchange would extend no longer than a typical commute to work for many of our citizens. The need for greater sophistication and nuance of decision-making creates frustration on the part of constituents who crave a simpler time and a one-dimensional solution to their immediate circumstances. We expect leaders to resolve major problems with expediency and a minimum of disruption to our individual systems of meaning and lifestyle. But the lesson of our interdependent world is clear for all who lead, despite their unique setting or circumstance.

Global interdependence requires leaders to stress long-term, strategic innovation and to involve workers, suppliers, and publics in evaluating the organizational, community, and global impacts of decisions.

Isolation of Human Values

In my professional work I have the occasion to work in proximity with civic and governmental leaders, administrators of nonprofit organizations, and business executives. I have benefitted by an intimate insight into the personal motivation and work patterns that govern a variety of careers and occupations. Through management consulting I have worked with the similarities and distinctions among leaders across traditional private sector, public service, and social service boundaries. Our society enforces some very clear and distinct leadership scripts for these individuals to follow based upon type of organizational setting. There exists a unique and often naive set of assumptions that each sector of society imposes on their leaders. In the nonprofit human service, educational, or religious community we seem to expect that good leaders are not driven by bottom lines or economics, are good with people, are motivated by a social purpose, and often do not possess the depth of technical management skill to survive in a competitive corporate environment. To the extent that this set of assumptions is followed in action by nonprofit leaders or imposed upon them by constituents, they are limited in their goals and techniques to develop a productive work environment that stimulates creativity and expands subordinate motivation. Many of these leaders in management coaching sessions long for greater depth in the disciplines of marketing, financing, strategic planning, and organizational development. Their "human-intensive" myths often limit them and their systems from the requirement to exercise technical knowledge and skills that allow our business community to succeed in international markets. These leaders are more prone to burnout, fatigue, or mid-career complacency. Systems of work in the public sector and non-profit community are often void of an appreciation of the benefits of tangible goals which motivate the human spirit toward productivity along with those which represent a commitment to human values. At times, a clear statement of objectives, priorities, and expectations provides an opportunity for people to become more expansive and creative under pressure. Simplistically, our bias is that these social and human systems should master the public and community side of leadership but not be integrally connected to productivity and efficiency, or demonstrated results.

In working closely with corporate leaders in upper management, I have heard numerous desires for a career change to "something more meaningful, less profit-oriented, more involved with people in all their dimensions." I expect we soon will witness a significant trend of corporate executives transitioning to the public sector and nonprofit community in second-career shifts or through midlife transitions. One high technology corporate executive confided recently:

> "Please don't get me wrong, my company (an international high technology leader) has been extremely good to me. I am paid very well, manage hundreds of people, have the freedom to develop new skills, but something is missing. It just does something dehumanizing to me and others when it seems the only motivation in the end that counts for my boss and those above him is greater corporate profitability."

His plea is one echoed innumerable times by those in American industry who have experienced the limits of their work environment to provide for career satisfaction congruent with their personal and social values.

This dichotomy between our productive systems of work and our social systems of meaning exists not only on the personal level; it is a crisis of limits of cultural proportion. In corporate business we witness the rise of a billion dollar industry devoted to the development of "human resources," compensating for prior organizational deficiencies of not creating a comprehensive environment to assist people in their integration of personal values and professional growth. Corporate resources now support efforts of day care for children and aging parents; employee assistance programs for personal problems of drug, alcohol, and family abuse; extensive career, personality, and skill testing; multiple forms of management development resources; and more recently, corporate-run elementary schools. This growing edge of employee development is in response to a decline in productivity due to excessive attention to overspecialization, unrestrained technology, and static organization theory. But as one CEO of a divisional company of a Fortune 500 conglomerate recently advised, these human resource systems will not succeed, since they exist along side of and are tangential to the main production functions of organizational life. They are parallel but not integrated systems, auxiliary in nature, which exist primarily to support the productive function of the organization. They are secondary and subordinate to our business plans. In business, human resource systems are seldom integral to the redefinition of the strategic direction of corporate goals or product development toward the benefit of consumers or society.

The same imposed artificial dichotomy of production systems and public values exists in our social, educational, religious, and public service organizations. We witness in these institutions the growing urgency to effectively manage personnel and technical resources driven by drastic reductions in traditional sources of philanthropic or governmental support. The thirst for substantive training and development is evident in the quest for improved planning techniques, measurable performance appraisal systems, and increased attention to quality control, gain-sharing, and profit-sharing plans. These indicate the need to develop well-integrated systems of work including productive goals in order to better serve human values. In the public sector it seems we have evolved an institutional mentality that has forgotten the necessity of focusing on the benefits of productive means and measures to channel human energy to achieve a social good.

In the private sector it may be that we have lost sight of the social purpose and values that production must demonstrate to advance a better society, not only a better product with increased profits. In both cases we are susceptible to the exaggerated evolution of systems of work that have lost sight of the integral need for a unified strategy of human productivity with social value and meaning. Richard Tanner Pascale and Anthony Athos in *The Art of Japanese Management* put this institutional phenomenon in a wider perspective of our cultural evolution.

> In contrast to China or Japan, western society evolved separate institutions with separate spheres of influence: the Church emerged as custodian of man's faith and spiritual life while governmental and the commercial institutions were given the role of providing for man's worldly existence. Not unexpectedly, western organizational theory evolved to legitimize this duality as a natural state of affairs.
>
> The emergence of the concepts of "factors of production" (land, labor, and capital) had revolutionary implications for the western view of humankind. Humans (the labor content) were no longer an inextricable part of the organic whole of society. Rather the person as laborer became an objectified and standardized compo-

nent of the production process. Not surprisingly, this view of labor tended to divorce man as a social and spiritual being from his productive role at work. Correspondingly this reaffirmed the lingering lesson of the centuries that one's spiritual and social life should reside outside of the workplace. This concept has persisted in Western thinking to this day, and as we will see is one of the sources of our present problems.[4]

Our evolution of isolated traditions of human work and human meaning has created an unnatural and uncomfortable distinction between these two fundamental ingredients of human development: an accomplished sense of productivity and a drive to make a social contribution. This imposes significant obstacles for the process of leadership to reunite these disparate sides to our human integrity. It also has significant implications for our capacity as persons to be healthy and happy.

Sigmund Freud, when asked over a century ago about his definition of human health, responded with the assertion that it consists of the capacity to love coupled with the capacity to work. These components of human development do not exist in a by-product or causal relationship where our capacity to produce provides the resources or material goods to consequently make us happy. Rather, there is a more fundamental process of unity where our work is an expression of our desire to contribute socially. The effects of a greater social contribution in turn provide the contentment and inner satisfaction for greater creativity in producing an expansive dedication to work. Our cultural predisposition to isolate expediency and efficiency from our values has everything to do with the process of leadership, whose ultimate goal is to reunite these lost partners.

In *Let the Trumpets Sound*, a well-documented and well-conceived biography of Dr. Martin Luther King Jr., Steven Oates chronicles the discussion among Dr. King and his aides in determining the strategy to include the cause of the Vietnam conflict in the civil rights agenda. Afraid of losing their prior success in moving public consensus toward support of their cause, Dr. King's aides argued bitterly against losing ground on public support by taking on the then controversial cause of opposing the war in Southeast Asia. In the final debate Dr. King settled the dispute simply, with his assertion that "justice knows no such convenient dichotomy." His refusal to accept the stereotype of polarizing efficiency from advancing social values was integral to his expression of leadership. The integration of these values of personal consistency and organizational behavior directed toward a socially useful and valuable goal is the distinctive hallmark of leaders. It is the ultimate reflection of leadership which contributes simultaneously to the quality of life for constituents, the quality of society for culture, and organizational health for our systems.

The public expression of commitment among constituents is perhaps one of the best measures of the presence of effective leadership in our culture. Richard Tanner Pascale and Anthony Athos go further in their analysis of human commitment and its absence.

> Splitting man into separate "personal" and "productive" beings makes somewhat artificial parts of what is the whole of his character. When we do our cultural heritage not only too strictly enforces this artificial dichotomy, but deprives us of two rather important ingredients for building employee commitment.[5]

This unification of the inwardly personal and externally social productive sides of human commitment is the focus of leadership we will discuss in the next chapter. Perhaps one final illustration will be helpful. United Theological Seminary, a regional Methodist seminary in Dayton, Ohio, has had a tradition of integrating management and leadership development topics in their curriculum for training pastors. A friend and CEO of a manufacturing firm for industrial furnaces is often invited to be a guest lecturer in a course on spirituality and management. He remarked at one particular lecture that at one time he also had attended seminary but left to pursue a career in a family-held business. During the question and answer session following his address one student asked him what had caused him to leave the ministry. Pretending not to understand the question, the CEO asked the student for further clarification. When his answer was ready to be "heard" by the student and his colleagues, the CEO patiently responded "I never have." His vocation as a business executive is coextensive with his commitment to ministry, to service in the world. This integral unity of the practice of management with the social purpose of creating meaningful work and an improved fabric of life is the true substance of the leadership that our culture yearns for and is desperate to receive. Despite the cultural complexities we face in moving our institutions forward, perhaps even as a result of them, we are faced with the unique challenge to forge new partnerships.

Faced with a social crisis of limits driven by the inadequacies of our technology to address our social problems, the rapidly expanding rate of change on a personal and organizational level, the increasing impact of global interdependence, and the institutional segmentation of our value systems, we are poised on the verge of a new consciousness in human history. The world will never be the same as it was in our infancy and it cannot afford to regress further in areas vital to our survival. The prospects for our leadership seem enormous but the benefits are greater still. We have little choice but to advance human understanding through our efforts.

We are called to bridge gaps of knowledge, experience, and skill across the public, private, and philanthropic sectors of society to provide renewed leadership.

Chapter III

Leadership and the Quality of Life

A balanced, diverse, and disciplined contribution of our gifts and talents of the many dimensions of our lives is the primary ingredient for satisfaction and meaning for leaders. We often associate the process of devoted leadership with the experience of a tragic flaw in either personal or professional life. However, recent research in the field of management, leadership development, and human development indicates that the quality of our personal lives, the effectiveness of our professional work, and the lasting public value of our social contribution originate from a coherent sense of personal integration and wholeness. It is through integration of the many dimensions of our lives where we can express both who we are as people and what we contribute as leaders through one unique vocation.

Enduring leadership involves a high degree of personal integrity based upon a structured, satisfying, and enriching personal lifestyle. Effective leadership is also supported by the consistent quality of intimacy in our lives among the personal, public, and professional relationships we establish. Lasting leadership also consists of attention to community commitments beyond our primary workplaces as the foreground for the ultimate contribution of our gifts and talents to others. Finally, leadership is contingent upon having a broad sense of one's vocation and one's distinct mission in life with a capacity to distinguish between the work of one's life apart from the task, the priorities, the activities, or the immediate responsibilities at hand. This balanced distribution of meaning across these elements of our lifestyle provides the best guarantee of satisfaction, detachment, and long-term effectiveness for leaders.

Not long ago, newspapers chronicled another story of the tragic flaw of leadership. The mayor of a major U. S. city was accused of drug abuse, an example of personal misconduct often associated with the unsavory side of high achievement. One does not have to reach far into our recent history of the United States to see this discouraging portrait of talented leadership recur. These dimensions often appear posthumously in the biographies of great historic figures. We now know that the life of John Kennedy, a man of extraordinary vision, intellect, and capability, was also marked with the inconsistency of sexual relationships which did not enhance his public stature. Likewise, the life of Martin Luther King, Jr., perhaps one of the greatest historical public figures of all times, was also marked with a degree of personal indiscretion in his intimate human relationships.

A biographical sketch on public radio on the life of Benjamin Franklin gave some insight as to why the tragic paradox of leadership so often includes inconsistent quality of our personal lives as was his experience. The editor concluded that perhaps Benjamin Franklin's "gift was too large to be given or received by anyone in his lifetime." This insight provides the clue to why we often associate the lives of significant leaders with some personal, professional, or organizational isolation. In fact, a life of personal tragedy is no more consistent with the price of leadership than driving a car necessitates an automobile accident. By careful monitoring of our own human development and the planning of our lifework we can become attentive to the appropriate road signs and dangers to the quality of our lives. It is possible to lead effective lives that are well-balanced, and make a contribution to ourselves and those we serve publicly as leaders. The correlations between the quality of personal life and public leadership among women seem less clear due to several factors. Until recently prominent leadership roles have been limited for women in both private and public sectors as compared to men.

It is my opinion that there is little gender difference of lifestyle and leadership among women and men except for one possible variable. The quality of life issues raised in this chapter are premised on possessing a cohesive intimate nurture and care for oneself, work, and others. These are traditionally associated in the literature as feminine traits. Both women and men who can combine a personal lifestyle of care and nurture for themselves and others with their public roles as an integral expression of their well-being have a well-developed sense of vocation. Golda Meir, Margaret Thatcher, Jane Goodall, Susan B. Anthony, Gloria Steinhem, Clara Barton, and Harriet Tubman stand as current and past examples. It is the ability to combine the qualities of personal and public nurture that is the critical variable in balanced leadership and not necessarily one's gender.

The paradox of leadership can probably be summarized in three unique experiences that leaders encounter which may make them more prone to isolation or difficulty in coping with the reality of having gifts "too large to be given or received." This paradox of leadership may have very little to do with the nature of leadership itself. It has to do with understanding the gap between the advanced perception, skill, and insight which distances leaders from those they serve.

First, all strategic leaders by definition possess a vision and a foresight which far exceeds, and transcends, their lifetime and often the experiences of their contemporaries. General George Patton at the conclusion of World War II could see with precise accuracy the consequences of an "easy peace" with the Russians for the next 45 years of our history in the cold war. It has taken a generation of American life to reduce the international tension of the cold war which has almost brought us to the perimeter of nuclear disaster.

Elliot Jacque, an organizational psychologist, has researched this quality of "executive vision." His contention is that people of extensive leadership capability possess a unique ability to visualize the future and imagine the impact of different strategies and actions in the present in light of their future consequences.

> I have found that "executive vision" or the ability to view scenarios in terms of an extended planning horizon is an integral part of the upper management psyche. Some top executives for example are capable of planning into 20-year time spans. My findings also indicate that the "vision" potential is an inborn trait unrelated to our other biological or socioeconomic variables which matures at predictable rates throughout life. The

discernible differences between individuals lie in their various levels of "envisioning" ability.[1]

Certainly leaders who have a high degree of success in creating a new strategic vision through their work demonstrate this capability of looking into the future and imagining the unfolding of events and how they can be influenced in the present. Konosuke Matsushita, the Japanese guru of management, developed a strategic plan for his electronics company for the "first" 250 years of its organizational life.

A second experience which contributes to the paradox of leadership is the capacity of these leaders to have a sense of "multidimensional thinking." Leaders seem to possess an intuitive ability to see a situation, an experience, or a set of relationships and their consequences simultaneously. The immediacy of this multifaceted vision can create gaps of self-confidence in the life of a leader, as well as gaps of trust among the constituencies a leader seeks to serve. Siegfried Streufert, a psychologist at Penn State University College of Medicine, refers to this conceptual quality of multidimensional integration as differentiation. For several years he has been studying highly successful executives to identify this characteristic in a behavioral fashion. *Fortune Magazine* describes Streufert's multidimensional integration this way:

> Executives display a distinctive talent for what Streufert calls integration. . . . Having picked out the salient facts, managers put them together in ways that other folks don't, posting a causal connection here, speculating on a possible analogy there. To use Streufert's term, good managerial thinking is multidimensional.[2]

A third dimension to the lives of leaders which contributes to their sense of isolation is an introspective capacity for solitude. Many visionaries, or people capable of distinctive contributions to the advancement of human consciousness, have developed an active inner life which often is refreshed by periodically retreating from the world of other experiences and relationships. W. H. Auden, translator of the biographical journal, *Markings* of Dag Hammarskjold, describes the secluded personal life of the former Secretary General of the United Nations in this way:

> To the outward eye, Dag Hammarskjold's career was from the very beginning one of uninterrupted success. He does brilliantly at college . . . he enters public gov-

ernment service, by the age of 36 has become Chairman of the National Bank of Sweden, and by 46 a member of the Cabinet. In addition to the success which his talents and industry win for him, his life to the outward eye is exceptionally fortunate. He has never known poverty, he enjoys excellent health, and as a citizen of a neutral country, he is spared the privations, sufferings and horrors inflicted by the War upon the majority of people in Europe. Inwardly, however, in spite of all these advantages . . . there is a great spiritual distress. . . . Consequently, a feeling of personal unworthiness which went very far, for it let him, it would seem, to undervalue or even doubt the reality of friendship and sympathy which must have always been offered him in plenty.[3]

In the life of Dag Hammarskjold, as for many significant leaders, the necessity to retreat from the world and take solace and comfort in solitude was a way to compensate for his extraordinary vision of reality which far surpassed his contemporaries, and perhaps even his historical times. This solitude experience can be over-expressed and lead to an insulated loneliness without contemporaries. Yet of necessity, creative leaders learn to be comfortable with their own inner worth particularly when experiencing a lack of acceptance for their vision.

Spiritual writer and mystic Thomas Merton, wrote to Robert Williams, a gifted young black musician, about the distance of vision between leaders and their historical impact:

You are right in feeling a little fear at the greatness of the task and the possible difficulties. You will certainly meet great difficulties and heartbreaking opposition and disappointment in many ways. You may, in fact, even be deprived of tasting the full fruits of success. But if you simply forget about the results and do the work with all of your heart . . . you will achieve far more than you can ever hope.[4]

As for many leaders, Thomas Merton evolved his spiritual solitude as a means of inwardly resolving this creative and lonely tension between the perceptions and experiences of others and the inner reality and deeper vision of life one perceives beyond the present circumstances.

These three elements of the paradox of leadership may contribute to a sense of isolation and loneliness particularly for leaders in significant personal or historical transitions. Their experience of vision and foresight into the future; multidimensional thinking in being able to relate disparate possibilities as inter-connected; and their capacity for solitude creates a striking discontinuity between the personal reality that they know inwardly and the circumstances they experience in daily life. It may be that under inner pressures to either conform to external circumstance or follow an inner vision, many take refuge as leaders in self-destructive behaviors. In these circumstances, many a leader may make the mistake of overextending his or her gifts by forcing their vision into the present circumstance or abdicating present realities for the sake of living an isolated, withdrawn, and potentially self-destructive life. It is clear in the lives of great musicians, poets, and artists that such occurrences have happened. The tremendous talents of artist Vincent Van Gogh and actress Marilyn Monroe contributed to their suicides. The destructive lifestyle of Wolfgang Mozart made short what could have been an enormously talented and long life of brilliant musical accomplishment.

These tragic expressions of talented lives is not necessarily a fare to be accepted by leaders. These tendencies may be more prevalent among leaders who shape enormously complex organizational or social challenges. But there are choices available to balance leadership and the quality of life. Our task is to make intentional choices among resources, relationships, and priorities to create a satisfying and meaningful life. Respecting an intense inner vision and extending meaningful influences to others are both supported by a qualitative and sound lifestyle.

The insights of Zen Buddhism and Japanese management can teach two psychological skills for the art of leadership. Creative leaders who are able to achieve an effective public contribution and maintain the quality of life have mastered two fundamental abilities. First, they are able to view situations, events, and circumstances in the present with a high degree of inner detachment or disengagement, allowing them the freedom to think critically about themselves before acting. This detachment or disengagement allows the flexibility to become aware of themselves, the situation, and the future integration of the two in order to plan their next strategic involvement. Creative leaders have the ability to step back from the circumstances at hand no matter how immense or inordinate the crisis and evaluate the paradox or difference between circumstances as we experience it and the reality of our vision as we know it before acting.

Once this experience of detachment and disengagement has occurred, leaders appear to have an extraordinary ability to reinvest themselves in the situation with a new degree of enthusiasm, resourcefulness, and a higher level of understanding. This process of detachment and engagement is very close to the spiritual disciplines of contemplation. It is based on deep understanding of the differences and the diversity between our own ego strength and the prevailing external influences.

This process of detachment and engagement is not some mystical quality available to only those highly seasoned in the spiritual disciplines. It is a very practical behavior that is learned and practiced in the quality of our lives. It is the artful process of living an alternately detached-and-involved lifestyle which balances the priorities of personal self-esteem, relational values, community investment, and vocational wisdom. This self-directed, refined, and mature detachment and engagement eventually becomes part of the disciplined repertoire of our lives.

Recent research on the lives of highly successful executives indicates that their personal values almost always follow a pattern of a primary commitment to family and core relational values; secondly, a commitment to community involvement; and thirdly, a commitment and contribution to the world of work. It may be that this diverse and balanced lifestyle demonstrated by these executives indicates that the process of detachment and engagement is a pro-active and learned approach to direct the quality of our lives by a highly intentional investment in relationships and tasks of value.

We are often accustomed to think of our historical figures as being wearisome and burdened with the responsibilities of public office. However, when one looks at the recent choices of our historical elections for President of the United States, one finds a striking continuity between the past four Presidents George Bush, Ronald Reagan, Jimmy Carter, and Gerald Ford. Each of these four men was able to demonstrate in his life a broad-based commitment to the many dimensions of personal health, public responsibility, family relationship, and leisure. We are beginning to realize the integral connection between a substantive and mature approach to our own human development and the effectiveness of our vocational commitments and leadership. There are four critical commitments which illustrate a reinforcement between the quality of our lives and the effective and lasting public impact of leadership.

Personal Integrity

A balanced and diverse lifestyle, involving disciplined physical routine, sustained intellectual stimulation, emotionally satisfying leisure activities, and a commitment to a higher purpose or spiritual values, is the key to a satisfying life and qualitative personal integrity. So often we consider the personal lives of successful leaders as neither having the time nor the place for attention to these four dimensions of life. Recent literature and research on the quality of life and our ability to make a sustained contribution to work and vocation indicates need for consistency among these dimensions of our personal lives.

Frank is a departmental manager within a medium-sized manufacturing organization. Frank has been in his current position for over 16 years and enjoys a high degree of comradery and colleagueship with his subordinates. He is a highly talented creative specialist. Frank's department has long been plagued with cost overruns and inconsistencies in service which have often been compensated for by the efforts of other parts of the organization. The turnover rate among his particular unit is much higher than the balance of the organization.

Upon appointment of a new vice president, Frank indicated that he had not intended to change his organizational practices, as they have lasted him well for the past 16 years. With thorough investigation, the new vice president realized that Frank's management problems went far deeper than his work behavior. Frank was a "successful alcoholic." In the fact his career enabled him opportunities to hide his behavior in ways that had not become apparent to many of his employees or to other peers within his organization. After repeated management counseling sessions, the vice president offered Frank one clear alternative: "participate in an alcohol rehabilitation program, or be terminated."

Upon completion of the program, Frank tendered his resignation and completely changed his lifestyle. Frank became more personally integrated, more responsive and responsible to his family and the world around of him as a result of his changed organizational experience.

Frank is evidence that there is no discontinuity between our personal lives and the exercise of our gift in professional and organizational behavior. These continuities, when reinforced, simply enrich the lifestyles of ourselves and those around us in more productive and satisfying ways.

A personally integrated lifestyle possesses the following disciplines. First, those who demonstrate a personally successful lifestyle have one clear physical routine to which they are committed. This physical routine often involves vigorous activity and exercise which may be done alone or in groups, but which is often seen as an anchor to one's daily and weekly planning. This physical routine will not often be displaced by the expectations of work or career priorities, but may be tailored in such a way to fit one's diverse lifestyle in a compact and convenient fashion. A 5:00 a.m. vigorous morning walk is the clue to a satisfying day for one successful executive. The physical endurance has a corresponding inner mental and emotional fitness.

Secondly, a personally integrated life often has a commitment to an intellectual or personal development routine beyond work that is as equally valuable as a physical routine. The experience of keeping a personal journal, spending ample amounts of time in a day for quiet, leisurely reading beyond professional pursuits, or some inner discipline that centers oneself on the higher purposes and priorities of life is a key ingredient of longevity in leadership and the quality of life which shapes its results. Developing personal lifestyle habits that combine some intellectual stimulation beyond professional pursuits gives one a sense of broad-based investment in life and the value of appreciating our contributions not only to our workplace, but to the development of ourselves and the world around us.

A third dimension of a personally satisfying and integrated life is the emotional satisfaction one takes for some investment in leisure, cultural, or hobby-related activities that may often become life's later avocations. A dedication to the arts, to a specific hobby, a unique craft, or alternate skill such as music, often characterizes the lives of successful leaders. One successful international labor negotiator finds his solitude in the original design and building of ships in a bottle. It is through this introspective ability to control a limited environment that he finds a new resourcefulness to return to and approach the wider complex environment of difficult labor management issues on a daily basis. Organizational psychologist Fernando Bartolome' describes a positive compensation that comes from the emotional satisfaction of leisure activities.

> Often this positive compensation comes through developing leisure activities. These activities have, however, a professional quality to them rather than being mere relaxation. . . .

> We can add nuance to Freud's idea that, "the main source of self-esteem and pleasure in an individual's life are work and love." Failure at work cannot be fully compensated by success in love. Failure at work has to be compensated by success in work-like activities. Only when work and love co-exist in parallel and appropriate proportion do we achieve happiness and fulfillment.[5]

A final discipline which creates a high degree of consistency in one's personal life and also contributes to one's professional behavior is the commitment to higher purposes or spiritual values of life. Many psychologists and organizational experts are uncomfortable around the concept of spirituality, a dichotomy which is quickly becoming passe in today's complex understanding of the human person. The higher purpose or spiritual dimension of life exists far beyond the commitment to any specific code of religious beliefs, practices, or denomination. Spirituality provides the fundamental grounding of who we are, our core values and our ultimate commitments in life through our personal and professional behavior. This capacity for a spiritual insight in the context of our professional life is quickly becoming recognized as a very practical value.

In the book, *Tender Power,* by Sherry Cohen, John Evans, President of Murdock Magazines describes this spiritual dimension to his life:

> Sometimes it's a question of developing something very close to the spiritual in life—and when I say spiritual I don't necessarily mean religion, he answers. To be a rounded and superb business leader, one must be able to reach out, step on an edge and put a hand out to someone in a corporation whom everyone else thinks is

a leper. To do that you need inner peace and to get that inner peace, you have to be a bit spiritual.[6]

A balanced lifestyle consisting of an active physical routine, a strong commitment to development of one's intellectual abilities outside of work; emotional satisfaction through hobby and leisure pursuits; as well as a strongly-grounded experience of higher purposes or spiritual values are the fundamental building blocks to personal integrity in one's life. These are not only a matter of personal responsibility for leading a disciplined life, they are a key factor in one's public contribution and one's successful vocational contribution of leadership. There is no discontinuity between self-care for our human development and our professional behavior. For enduring leaders, strengthening one enriches the other.

How can one make the time to create such a balanced and disciplined lifestyle? The answer is simple. Find new ways to do multidimensional things at the same time. One client executive found the following solution. After an audit of his personal values and lifestyle preferences, he identified three common values as key to his personal satisfaction: a commitment to the outdoors; the opportunity to be alone; and the ability to maintain a high degree of vigorous physical exercise. Realizing that all three pursuits were probably unlikely given the pace of his schedule, I asked him to identify an alternative where he could achieve these values at one time. The man is now an avid bicyclist, driving to the country for several hours of cycling a week in order to achieve those three values of his personal life in a simultaneous fashion. He has found the key to finding an efficient resolution to the divided nature of our personal lives by developing new lifestyle habits which achieve many inner purposes in the same concentrated timeframe and activity.

Relational Integrity

If we have a crisis of professional leadership in our public organizations, our private businesses and our religious institutions, we have an equally intense crisis of personal intimacy in this country. We tend to think of these two crises as somehow being discontinuous in nature. They may, however, be different symptoms of the same problem. Our technical and highly specialized society does not promote relationally integrated lives where we can maintain solid and lasting commitments; not only to work, but to family, to friends, and to those who will live beyond us in life. Sherry Cohen in the book *Tender Power* reports on recent research linking intimacy in men and women to organizational behavior.

A new national study, the largest investigation to date on the need for intimacy, was recently reported on in the *Journal of Personality*. Dr. Dan P. McAdams, a psychologist at Loyola University in Chicago, reports that although women seem to have a slightly higher need for intimacy, men felt the need for this tender trait almost as much. The differences lie in the way that men and women experience intimacy and what it does for them. "Women," says Dr. McAdams, "find that emotional intimacy leads directly to satisfying roles like wife, mother, or friend. Men, on the other hand, find that emotional intimacy and a sense of closeness is not as directly related to personal relationships as it is to their sense of resilience and confidence in the world around them—the same confidence and resiliency that makes for achievement in work."[7]

The crisis of our commitments both to work and to relationships reflects an inner need for a deeper relational integrity among the different dimensions in our lives. In *The Art of Japanese Management*, Richard Pascale contrasts the discontinuous nature of our relationships in the West with the integrated nature of relationship lives in Japan by using the image of concentric circles to describe a Japanese world view of relationships. Each segment of Japanese cultural life is a deepening circle of intimacy with inter-relationships and familiarity among the various components of personal, family, friendship, and organizational lives. Japanese employment, for example, is considered a lifelong commitment between an individual and organization.

Peter was a participant on a leadership wilderness experience for the top divisional executives of a major multinational corporation. Peter is a tough-minded, hard-nosed, and intellectually astute leader. In his late fifties, he has achieved all he has set out to do in his life. He was responsible almost single-handedly for the presence of his company's markets in approximately one-third of the United States. He is known to be an impeccable, hard-driving task master, perhaps due to his former Marine experience. But now, as he approaches the end of his career, he sits around the campfire for a discussion with his colleagues and reviews his desire to raise their work together to what he calls "a higher level of play."

Peter describes the higher level of play in this way. "We are all competent people, all have achieved much in our careers. We also work well as a team as our lives depend on one another. Yet, there is a deeper level of intimacy or relationship that we must acquire. We must begin to understand one another in terms of our strengths and our weaknesses and how those contribute together to make not only a satisfying corporation, but also a meaningful contribution to our families and the world in the future. I wished this week we could have our spouses and our families with us to share in this experience of bonding and unity. There is more to life than the experience of success. The quality of our lives together and the value of our relationships and our concern for one another are key ingredients to not only our personal, but also our organizational future." Peter has come to understand the connection between the intimate personal relationships of his life and the intimacies and commitment necessary to maintain a satisfying and lasting career. These are not seen as divided dimensions of a human person, but as a unified lifestyle of personal commitment to the priorities one values, including all of the primary and secondary relationships of our lives.

To achieve a lifestyle of relational integrity, three commitments become essential. First, in each of our lives there must exist those primary familial relationships, be they within a household or not, where we are accepted and accept others unconditionally for who we are beyond what we produce. Many family lifestyles have become another extension of the workplace where we provide and exchange needs to one another almost as goods in a common market. Many families are "managed" on an efficiency model coordinating diverse professional, relational, and recreational priorities. We must restore a sense of congruence and acceptance to our family lives which becomes an extension of intimacy and values to the workplace rather than an expression of our workplace values of efficiency projected upon these primary relationships. These primary relationships are characterized by close intimacy which gives us the freedom and the flexibility to discuss not only what we do, but the quality of our relationships and who we are with one another.

Secondly, diverse experience of colleagues in work life are key to our long-term career satisfaction. The experience of constant demands, priorities, and pressures of individual, highly-specialized work careers requires support of both the general acceptance and personal appreciation that comes from families as well as from contemporaries of professional experience. Professional friendships and colleagues who provide a base for professional challenge, acceptance, and care characterize the successful leaders of the future. An intentional approach to developing one's personal relationships is needed which includes core people such as family and friends who understand our personal lives and accept us for who we are. But our career satisfaction is also supported by those who have a sense of our professional competencies and abilities. So often in management coaching sessions I experience clients using that professional relationship as a temporary substitute for professional colleagues and contemporaries. Actively choosing friends and colleagues who provide encouraging professional relationships can create a sense of deep satisfaction and relational integrity for our lives and for our leadership. There is an abundance of recent literature on the "feminine dimension" of leadership highlighting this theme. Workplaces and leaders benefit by developing co-workers who support our individual career development as well as organizational priorities.

A third quality of relational integrity is the capacity to mentor or sponsor other leaders for the future. As careers mature we begin to understand the limits of our own ability to make a contribution of lasting public value. A key ingredient of our relational integrity is satisfying mentoring and sponsoring relationships where we provide the appropriate guidance, discipline, and distance to those we lead. Strengthening the inner abilities and confidence of others to lead in the future is a key relational attribute of good leaders. Successful leaders report in career counseling how they have found others willing to gain from their experience. This process of mentoring another individual contributes future success and lasting value to both mentor and protege.

Relational symmetry among these different dimensions of our lives brings a sense of coherence and commitment to all of the dimensions of our lives rather than exercising one at the expense of another. The continuity between our deepest intimacies of life and our workplace commitments and productivity is a key element of relational integrity which shapes our positive commitment to leadership and the quality of life.

Community Investment

In addition to leading personally disciplined and integrated lives and possessing relational symmetry among the different intimacies of our world, it is important to demonstrate public commitments to the community beyond our work. A diverse public contribution of leaders on a personal level contributes to a sense of satisfaction and well-being especially during times in our careers when the immediate circumstances of our work can no longer provide the necessary professional satisfaction to which we aspire.

Alice is an extraordinarily gifted executive. She has led two organizations in their total transformation and renewal through the development of new services for the nonprofit community. For each organization she has created innovative and different strategic plans from their organizational past. Alice is a fast tracker. In each organization she has received successive promotions in a short time span. In her most recent setting, she has received three promotions within a seven-year period and now serves as the Chief Executive Officer. Alice is an especially gifted person both conceptually and relationally. At times, the sheer power of her gifts are perceived by others to be intimidating. She reports in management counseling that she doesn't understand how a person of such integrity, honesty, and high commitment to ideals can be so frightening to others. Alice approaches her work as she approaches all of her life with a high degree of intensity and discipline. She lives a very balanced and committed personal life, structures time in her daily and weekly routine for intimate relationships with friends and colleagues, but invests the majority of her professional life in the immediate job responsibilities and priorities at hand.

Alice's comprehensive vision is far too intense for the immediate professional circumstances and her colleagues to comprehend and digest. Alice needs time to diversify her gifts and broaden her contribution, giving others the time to literally catch up to her vision and her priorities for the future. Alice added great value to her personal and professional life by investing time and energy in community activities. Prior to career counseling, Alice was a single-focus work person. Her total commitment was to the job and the position at hand, with full loyalty dedicated to the organization, working 60 to 80 hours a week. Alice is still a highly productive individual, but she contributes approximately 20 hours a week to civic, voluntary, and professional associations of which she is now an active member. Not surprisingly, Alice has also taken on leadership roles in these circles, noted for her strategic planning and conceptual ability. Interestingly enough, Alice has developed a great deal more intimacy, connection, and empathy for the people with whom she works. She is no longer seen as a hard-driving, demanding executive. In fact, she has become a well-accepted and beloved leader of 100 employees.

What is the key to Alice's professional maturity? She has chosen to invest her intensity among a diverse portfolio of community involvements which bring her life satisfaction and enrich not only her professional work but the community and the world around her. Alice understands the value of community investment as part of the long-term success among leaders concerned for the quality of life for themselves and others.

Strong community investment through leadership in each of our lives could include the following avenues to effectively contribute lasting public value. First, involvement in professional associations with colleagues often gives us the opportunity to gain perspective on immediate problems and priorities which plague us from day to day. In "executive roundtables" people report a sense of ease and comfort with previously dreaded organizational responsibilities and assignments as they find others in similar circumstances. These experiences of professional support groups often provide the necessary forum to experience the wisdom of one who has met the same challenge once before. We often gain the simple ability to laugh at ourselves in order to bring a sense of congruence and balance to our lives as leaders.

Secondly, organizations are becoming increasingly aware of the value of the public service of their employees to the community of civic, arts, and educational organizations. We see in corporate industry the tremendous trend of partner-in-education models which exist in major metropolitan cities. Corporations adopt nonprofit organizations (and in particular, schools) to share leadership, technology, and organizational vision to enhance the success of a public system which contributes lasting public value to society as a whole. Many corporations contribute much expertise and talent to the improvement of the quality of life in a community by strengthening a school district or an individual school. Organizations realize that this public service also enhances the confidence of their employees to remain in their local communities in the future.

This principle holds true for individuals as well. Contributions of time to public organizations which provide for the aesthetic, educational, and environment is an important ingredient not only for the community, but for our personal success. Those of us who may not be financially well endowed can create a sense of personal philanthropy for the future by the contribution of our time and energy as human capital to the lasting public value of these institutions.

Thirdly, many talented people may be hesitant to commit personal time for voluntary manual activities which require less than our professional talents or capabilities. However, it is important for all of us to stay grounded in the basic human values that constitute the quality of our social lives and the fabric of our communities.

Tom is a very successful banking executive. Most of his work is spent in the world of ideas, finance, sales, and personal and organizational planning with his clients. Tom wanted to make a personal contribution of something very hands-on to the world around him. Tom became a volunteer in a local overnight shelter for the homeless. Tom put aside his executive business suit and put on his blue jeans and tennis shoes and washes the clothes, prepares the food, and makes the beds, assisting people who are far less fortunate. He now sees the continuity of caring for the posterity of his clients through banking as the same caring for the posterity of individuals who are less fortunate than he in this homeless shelter. He understands the benefit of personally volunteering for tasks that are more mundane or physical than he is accustomed to as a benefit to his life. For him "love is work made visible." In the work at a homeless shelter he finds new analogies to interpret and bring meaning to his professional vocation.

These three dimensions of community involvement, including active professional associations and colleagueship, commitment to public service, and the personal volunteer time we spend in simple tasks may serve as benefits and resources to our understanding of leadership and the quality of life. In living a complete life through this expression of social responsibility, we become not only one-dimensional leaders in the professional arenas of our lives, but we become multidimensional leaders, seeing leadership not so much as a task, an activity, or an organizational responsibility, but as a total commitment to the quality of life by investing in our communities. We see our lives as a devotion or vocation.

Vocational Integrity

For many, our professional lives consist of a contribution to one organization, a particular role or set of assignments, and one professional responsibility. Our sense of vocation is often eclipsed by a singular career or occupational focus which at times confuses our personal identity with the work that we do. This is a dangerous experience for most, putting us at risk not only of changes in our organizational lives, but in fearing the inability to progress through our professional careers with a sense of diversity, balance, and broad skill developments. Vocational diversing is also a core expression of living a satisfying and complete life.

Terry is a brilliant young market analyst. She works for an established investment firm in a major metropolitan area. Terry has earned several key clients, and is seen by her colleagues and the partners of the firm as a "board certified genius." She has been warned on numerous occasions, however, about several unsavory personal behaviors and dress that contribute to her lack of monetary success and mobility in the firm. In fact, upon a recent performance review, she was told that unless she can change some disagreeable dress, lifestyle, and personal etiquette habits, she will no longer be considered for management.

Upon careful career counseling, we find that Terry exhibits a rare connection between failure and success. She perceives the next level of success as fatal if she fails. Terry must minimize her vulnerability in making a singular professional commitment only to the investment firm. We encourage her to diversify her professional pursuits, realizing that Terry's unsatisfying personal habits perhaps have little to do with changing them on the surface level. Terry begins extensive reading and research in the field of investment banking, her greatest interest. Her corporate firm is persuaded to allow her to conduct public seminars beyond the practice as part of her professional development and teach in the local community college. We also encourage her to write extensively in professional journals in order to strengthen her broader sense of vocation.

Terry realizes "the difference between her lifework and the works of her life." As this awareness matures she will achieve a balanced appreciation of success in various components of her life so that no single source of career satisfaction can recreate the personal vulnerability she experiences from one source of self-esteem and personal value.

Like many of us, Terry is prone to a single professional approach to vocation and personal leadership. Maintaining a balanced and diverse approach to one's professional development and a sense of vocation is an important resource to one's career and professional life. In essence, understanding the difference between the vocation (what we are ultimately called to contribute through our work) and our immediate job assignment is the key insight of vocational maturity.

There are many diverse ways that individuals can express their wider professional vocation beyond their immediate job or occupational priority or task. Many organizations now see the benefit in allowing employees the opportunity to do some limited consulting work beyond their responsibilities. Corporate executive loan programs are increasing to the public and nonprofit sector. This often provides an alternate professional experience, allowing people to exercise their talents and abilities in a new way, bringing new resourcefulness to their original workplace. Certainly professional reading and writing and research provide the same type of satisfying enrichment on a professional level that one's immediate occupational tasks also contribute.

Finally, within one's workplace, the diversification of priorities becomes important to a leader at any level. All leaders should be involved in a certain amount of project development, supervisory activity, and extended planning to contribute healthy satisfaction to one's work effort. The successful CEO is unlikely to be one who spends his or her entire week in efforts of strategic planning envisioning the future without having some short-term, concrete operational or activity responsibility to complete and some guidance, support, and direction for direct reports. These are important dimensions of our own professional lives that cannot be overlooked and replaced by a one-dimensional approach to the tasks of work or leadership at hand. Diversifying our vocational interests is a great resource to the stresses of our immediate leadership task. A diverse sense of the works of our lives also brings multidimensional satisfaction to who we are professionally and a new sense of resiliency and resourcefulness to the primary tasks and work responsibilities we possess in our organizational roles.

Throughout this chapter we have concentrated on four dimensions that contribute to leadership and quality of life. We have stressed the importance of a personally disciplined lifestyle with behaviors that contribute to the physical, intellectual, emotional, and spiritual enhancement of our well-being.

Secondly, we have concentrated on the relational dimensions of our lives, seeing the intimacies of our personal lives tied to the intimacies of our work lives in a new way. These two dimensions of intimacy are not opposite competitors in a game for our attention; they are collaborative partners in strengthening our ability to maintain human commitment.

Thirdly, we have discussed the importance of a broad-based community investment creating a lasting public value, not only for our immediate organizations, but also within our communities which provide for the health of our citizens and our populations.

Lastly, we have stressed the importance of a broad-based understanding of vocation within our careers and our occupations. Many potentially successful people become derailed by gaining a singular understanding of who they are and equating it with the immediate job, work assignment, or role responsibility they currently possess. Each of us has within us the ability for diverse professional contributions far beyond the immediate role or primary assignment for our attention.

Quality of Life Assessment

At the conclusion of this chapter, we have included three individual exercises which may help you assess the quality of your own life and its impact upon your organizational and public leadership. Figure 3 outlines Phase I of a quality of life model. This model describes several behaviors which participants in career counseling indicate as resources for their balanced distribution of their time and attention. This balanced portrait of personal, professional, and relational pursuits often contributes to a greater sense of well-being and quality within one's life. The reader is advised to look at these behaviors and identify which of them is a current priority in his/her life at the present. Further, the reader is encouraged to identify which of these behaviors exists for them as future priorities that they would appreciate building in their life structure.

Realizing that all instruments are limited, the reader is advised to identify which of these priorities simply does not apply to his/her life structure and bears little contribution to his/her self-understanding of leadership and its relationship to the quality of one's life. Changing the relative behaviors of our lives is a difficult proposition. We are all entrenched in behavior patterns that often keep us from implementing new priorities on a sustained basis. One strategy that has worked successfully in career counseling is to focus upon only one behavior at a time until an established and satisfying life structure consisting of new behaviors replace some old habits which, for most of us, die hard.

One executive recently reported that after two years he has totally replaced time mindlessly watching television with leisurely reading of personally and professionally satisfying literature. This one behavior change has taken two years to accomplish. The importance of this exercise is not the number of behaviors that we can modify, but the quality of those behaviors in impacting our lifestyles and ultimately our leadership and contribution to others.

In Figure 4, Phase II, you are encouraged to develop your own quality of life model once you have reviewed your current and your future priorities. Please take the basic elements of your life structure, including those which constitute your personal integrity, your relational integrity, your extended community investment, and your vocational integrity and outline a projective view of your life for a week in advance. Most of us consider behavioral change by looking back with regret upon what we have not accomplished. Once you have found a satisfying life structure which supports the quality of life in a planned fashion, use this plan on a weekly basis to identify those behaviors in advance to which you will devote time and attention in that weekly timeframe. Once a consistent pattern of comfort and desirability is established, the routine will now exist in your life habits.

This type of projective quality of life plan often keeps us from derailing through "guilt" by looking back over our past experience and identifying what went wrong. This plan gives you the opportunity to look ahead on a structured basis, week by week, to identify those behaviors most important to you in building and establishing a strong and lasting quality of life.

Figure 5 outlines a final step in planning quality of life goals. This step should be undertaken after several weeks of experimentation with the quality of life plan. It gives you the opportunity to set some established goals for the future modification of the quality of your life which contributes actively to your experience of leadership. After several weeks of experimentation with the quality of life plan (Figure 4), you should begin to identify those behaviors that bring a sense of resiliency, resourcefulness, and new energy to your leadership and total life satisfaction. Please establish some goals which creatively can influence the interplay between the quality of your life and your professional leadership in the future. We encourage you to share these goals with a partner or friend as a learning contract and source of accountability in the future.

All of life change requires a commitment to behavior, but behavior must be rooted in our fundamental values. The focus and purpose of this chapter has been to identify those critical life values essential to understanding that the quality of our lives as an integral and fundamental ingredient of the quality of our work and our lasting public contribution to society. There is no greater misfortune than for a leader not to appreciate the benefit of his or her work on the world around them. To achieve that we must first appreciate and understand ourselves.

Quality of Life Model: Phase I

Please take some time by yourself to review your life priorities based on the following Quality of Life Model. Identify areas of current priorities (C), areas to strengthen or refocus your future priorities (F), and those areas unrelated to your life at this time (U).

	Current Priority	Future Priority	Unrelated Priority

Personal Integrity

Solitude and
time alone

Contemplation, self-reflection,
life planning

Creative expression
(i.e. photography, music, art)

Health and nutrition, diet

Exercise (i.e. tennis, running,
aerobics, swimming)

Nature, outdoors, recreation

Self-expressive time (i.e. leisure,
reading, creative hobby, journal)

Relational Integrity

Time for shared family/core relationship activity

Time alone with spouse/intimate friend(s)

Time with children individually

Contact with extended family and relatives

Personal support for unique interests of _____

Unstructured fun or leisure time with _____

Figure 3. Quality of Life Model: Phase I

	Current Priority	Future Priority	Unrelated Priority
Community Investment			
Participation in professional associations or peer groups			
Communication with individual professional friends and colleagues			
Professional contributed service			
Community involvement and volunteer activity			
Vocational Integrity			
Expanded life skills in diverse "lifework projects"			
Public expression of career skills (writing, correspondence, consulting, public speaking)			
Career enhancement of others, mentoring			
Broad professional development			
• project development			
• supervision with others			
• peer learning			
Professional reading and research			

Figure 3, continued

Week of ____	Quality of Life Plan: Phase II

From the Quality of Life Model you have analyzed, rewrite your own preferred priorities for your future personal development. Keep them behavioral in nature and based on your existing priorities and future goals. This model should be used by you weekly to plan your life structure until you have internalized a desired change in your lifestyle.

                               Projected Activity   *Completed Activity*

Personal Integrity

Relational Integrity

Community Investment

Vocational Integrity

Figure 4. Quality of Life Plan: Phase II

Quality of Life Goals   Phase III

As a result of your Quality of Life Plan, formulate some real goals you will commit to accomplish, strengthening the life structure of your personal development. Share these goals with a partner as a learning contract and source of accountability. Your goals should be behavioral in form.

Week 1

Week 2

Week 3

Week 4

Month 2

Month 3

Month 6

Month 9

Month 12

Figure 5. Quality of Life Goals: Phase III

Chapter IV

Vocational Leadership

One's personal vocational mission in life arises from a coherent and intimate appreciation of the comprehensive quality of personal wholeness, relational integrity, community investment, and clarity of calling. This distinctive vocational mission is expressed in a full and active life which combines meaningful and challenging work with personal and social values, along with a corresponding contribution of the gift of one's life to society. To truly develop leaders is to develop the whole person.

Despite our cultural predisposition towards increasingly specialized and compartmentalized lives, human development is a continuous process. Our life structure integrates our knowledge, expands our skills, and completes our abilities over our lifetime. The prevailing direction of institutional life and cultural value stresses the increased refinement of knowledge and the narrow focus of occupational tasks. This can isolate human meaning and creativity from the productive results of our efforts on both personal and organizational levels. Living separate personal and professional lives often arrests our realization of our unique human vocation to be simultaneously productive and nurturing. Our dichotomous organizations and social systems actually impede our human development and the realization of our individual vocations. They further distance the constituents, consumers, and publics we seek to influence from those who develop and create the goods or services they require.

This mechanical and fragmented view of work has built to a crescendo since the Industrial Revolution, with significant impact for our personal and organizational ability to promote and achieve human development. A materials engineering specialist may only vaguely comprehend the full impact of her research in composite fibers and polymers used for the development of the "shroud" or surface skin of a missile reentry vehicle with multiple thermonuclear warheads. These missiles are capable of eliminating major population centers within minutes of launch, yet she may have given little thought to the potential result of her work. In the absence of this self-awareness and social insight she is less developed as a person and less capable of positively impacting her world by providing leadership.

In response to a growing uneasiness with advanced specialization and its encroachment on our personal, relational, and organizational lives, many of us have an instinctive desire to reunify the personal, social, and organizational dimensions which bring unity and meaning to our lives. Movement away from the fast-paced, highly specialized and disengaged aspects of work and careers is increasingly prevalent in our society. We are witnessing the growth of a whole industry of personal growth and human potential services and activities seeking to restore balance to our lives. Health spas, recreation and wellness centers, diet and nutritional products and services, sports clubs of many varieties and a host of physical improvement and psychological growth aids seek to restore a sense of inner harmony to the excessive overextension and chronic stress many people experience. Depression and stress are the cultural symptoms of fragmentating the various naturally integrated dimensions of our lives. These "holistic movements" are beneficial, yet follow the prevalent social convention of treating isolated components of human development in an attempt to achieve a sense of having life "together." Conceivably a well-balanced person could have a psychological therapist, career advisor, nutritional specialist, spiritual director, health club trainer, and several physicians all assisting him or her in living a more integrated life. It appears ironic to pursue more personal and relational balance through increased specialization.

On the career and professional front we are seeing organization dropouts in increasing numbers as our creative work force seeks alternate career paths in consulting, small businesses, and the growing trend of cottage industries. One 1990 study on this phenomenon indicates that 25% of our current available work force now make their livelihood through "homesteading," working out of their homes. In addition to providing a cost-effective benefit by delivering services efficiently and economically in many sectors of society, these deinstitutional trends are also a movement to create greater congruence and balance among our personal vocations, public values, and organizational systems. We crave more complete human development by controlling the environments that influence our work. The balance many seek is the opportunity to put together in a meaningful way a productive and satisfying life structure where the traditional dichotomies of work and leisure, efficiency and values, and personal and public contribution are blended in a healthy form of self-expression. Max DePree, President of Herman Miller, describes our task well in his book, *Leadership is an Art.*

> For many of us who work, there is an exasperating discontinuity between how we see ourselves as persons and how we see ourselves as workers. We need to eliminate that sense of discontinuity and to restore a
> * sense of coherence to our lives.[1]

The commonly held notion that there must be an essential discontinuity between the inner and outer successes of leading a quality life (which contributes to quality in one's work, thus advancing the quality of society) is erroneous. One's vocational mission in life is a comprehensive integration beyond one's career or occupational specialty. It also includes one's total commitment and response to life, expressing the quest for human meaning, relationships, values, and contribution to future society. Vocational development results from a critical self-awareness of the deepest dimensions of human personality, where knowledge, skills, abilities, and experience give expression to the core direction or unifying purpose in life. This fundamental direction may include a career or occupational focus but is usually a broader form of self-definition with career, job, or role as only one dimension of lifework. Beyond the role of school principal the educator perceives herself as "contributing to the advancement of culture through learning." The library scientist understands his vocational mission as a "trustee of cultural wisdom." The business executive understands her lifework as a "builder." This is not just a simplistic notion of marketing easyspeak. This clear statement of fundamental life orientation results from integrated self-knowledge, an inner understanding of one's personal vocation, and one's commitment to society and community and their futures.

The homemaker devoted to child rearing and family management claims his or her role as a "contributor to the relational fabric of human community." The concept of vocational mission is no mere facile slogan for one's daily activity stated in other words. It emerges from a fundamental and comprehensive self-knowledge, an inward detachment from the immediate activities and work setting at hand, a clear vision of the fundamental purpose of one's life. It involves a precise awareness of the unique contribution to human destiny that each of us is capable of achieving. Only through the lifelong process of discovering and actualizing one's vocational mission does one make a substantive and enduring contribution to leadership. Conscious awareness of this vocational mission, and its active pursuit, is a fundamental requirement for the consequent effectiveness of public and organizational leadership.

Leadership and Human Development

Leadership unifies the maturity of inner development with one's public and organizational contribution to the social advancement of others. This inner unity is the developmental process of leadership. Without this developmental maturity we are likely to live fragmented lives never quite fulfilling the unique gift to human history each of us is privileged to carry. Without the integrated involvement of our vocational mission with our public and organizational influence, all of life—including our most intimate personal relationships and our work environments—is far less productive and fulfilling than it was meant to be. Our ability to unify an inner sense of vocation with our public values and organizational behavior consistently advances the quality of life not only for ourselves but also for society in proportion to our ability to give ourselves well.

This vocational mission is an inward process of achieving greater individualization, growing in our capacity to refine our knowledge, skills, experience and values or personal competence. It is also a simultaneous external process of achieving a greater social effectiveness. As we expand our identity we also become increasingly aware of the ways our talents can be used in service to the communities we are part of and the society and world we live in. The vocational dimension of leadership consists of two fundamental concepts that illustrate its relationship to a well developed identity. First, vocational maturity is the basic *inner* core of self-understanding and self-expression in our development. Second, there is an *outer* contribution of vocational leadership which characterizes leaders who express their mature human development in their public actions.

Leadership is rooted in an expansion of self-awareness by becoming more universal in both self-understanding and social consciousness. Understanding the vocational dimension of leadership and its connection to our personal mission requires us to step back from many preconceived notions we have about the externalized skills and techniques of leadership. It is more an artistic mastery of inner knowing, reminiscent of the discipline of detachment of Zen Buddhism. Only by a thorough inner knowledge of the strengths and boundaries of our unique capacity for personal and social effectiveness can we come to realize the full measure of leadership in our lives. Richard Tanner Pascale retells a parable that reflects this inner logic (Zen) of leadership in *The Art of Japanese Management*.

> One day a famous Japanese business executive paid a visit to a well known Zen master to discuss Zen's relevance to management. Following Japanese etiquette, the master served green tea. When the cup of the visitor was full, the master kept pouring; the tea overflowed. The executive was startled. "The cup is full; no more will go in." Said the master, "Like this cup, you are full of your own thoughts. How can I show you Zen unless you first empty your cup?" Let us proceed, then, noting how hard it is to "empty one's cup" even if one wants something else poured into it.[2]

Mature leadership is an expression of a well developed and defined sense of vocational integrity. Marsha Sinetar in her extremely insightful and popular book *Do What You Love, The Money Will Follow* devotes considerable attention to the concept of "vocational integration." She describes vocational integration as growing in self-understanding and power from an intimate knowledge of one's correct life work or "right livelihood."

> This added power is gained when the individual sees himself as he really is, understands what drives him, what motivates him to act—or to back away from things—when he knows what he wants to live for (per-

haps even die for), and then consciously chooses to enact that knowledge in everything he does. Naturally, his work falls into place as the correct thing for him to be doing ...

The vocational integrated person is able to choose to risk all and to surrender to the truth of himself as he exists within himself in that most private and sacred core of self, and this choice is the beginning of the dissolution of his egocentric former life.[3]

Her concept of vocational integration captures the essential continuity between one's unique personal competencies and the natural expression of vocation through dedication to one's work in the broadest sense. The vocationally mature see work itself as at once self-fulfilling and contributing to the social fabric. It is this continuity of quality of life on a personal as well as a public level that constitutes the root of authentic leadership. Through leadership the circumstances at hand, the events or challenges faced, the triumphs and the discouragements experienced are understood with a detachment that internalizes them as opportunities to discover and express one's unique mission in life. This clarity and unity of life purpose may be misunderstood by others as a disengagement from the moment; however, it represents the ultimate wisdom of perspective that gives meaning on both a practical and a symbolic level. Consider the phrase of St. Augustine, "Love God and do what you will." It is only with a full sense of one's vocational maturity and unique mission in life that such wisdom can be lived in its true intent. Only the highest form of intimacy with oneself along with the most profound insight into our abilities, talents, skills, and limits allows such clarity of action and freedom of thought.

There are several common elements across many disciplines of human development that point to the concept of a unique and personal vocational mission and its relationship to the process of leadership. 19th century German psychology developed a discreet concept described as a "Fictional Final Goal." This theory held that each individual life has a unifying purpose for existence that is largely subconscious or unconscious but drives all behavior and action into a common direction or life force. The assertion that this "Goal" has to remain unconscious to the self is secondary. This early expression of the later psychological concept of life project in cognitive and gestalt psychology provides evidence that each person has a distinctive contribution to share with human history if it can be discovered, matured, and shared. Leaders of true stature have been able to comprehend and express this inner mission which is uniquely theirs. This intimate self-knowledge gives them the courage to face impossible or even absurd conditions in order to succeed. Is it this inner confidence that allows Nelson Mandela an almost timeless serenity after 30 years of imprisonment for his opposition to the social structure of apartheid in South Africa? Did this conviction of personal destiny provide the basic courage of Robert Kennedy to run for president of the United States despite his brother's assassination for espousing a similar social agenda?

Yet another psychological source, Erik Erikson, in his classic theory of the Eight Ages of Man, describes the developmental task of the middle years of adult life as one of "Generativity vs. Stagnation." The task of mature life in his framework calls for the efficacious care and nurturing of one's posterity and of society after one has mastered the basic competencies of adult life.

Mature man needs to be needed, and maturity needs guidance as well as encouragement from what has been produced and must be taken care of.

Generativity, then, is primarily the concern in establishing and guiding the next generation. . . . And indeed, the concept of generativity is meant to include such more popular synonyms as productivity and creativity, which however cannot replace it.[4]

In the thinking of Erikson there is an essential connection between a meaningful interior life and care for posterity, which is reflected in the exterior values of care and nurture. Productivity is represented by Erikson as an expression of care for the good of the future rather than as the means of self-fulfillment or acquisition of wealth in the present. This generative care for nation, society and perhaps even humanity hurls Mikhail Gorbachev through history with singular dedication to a radical social agenda in the Soviet Union despite the immediate hardships to his constituents and precipitous political risk to himself.

Psychologist Abraham Maslow developed the hierarchy of human needs, indicating that as our most basic need for safety, survival, security, and comfort are met we instinctively pursue those higher needs for human meaning and ultimately for self-actualization. He described those who have mastered the continuum of human development as being fully "self-actualized." Self-actualized people are primarily inner-directed toward a unified purpose in life, maximizing the use of their gifts and talents to serve others. For both Erikson and Maslow, the capacity of the human species to exercise social concern as a result of personal development reinforces the essential connection between a commitment to the quality of life both on a personal and a collective scale. The separation of personal development from organizational behavior betrays a mistaken view of presumed separate realities for advancing people and systems.

In the field of adult learning, Allen Tough of the Ontario Institute for Studies in Education documents the motivations and learning patterns of adults cross culturally. Despite national or ethnic background, economic resources, or educational experience the average adult spends at least 100-500 hours per year on defined learning projects. These projects are self-chosen and often self-directed to expand an adult's knowledge, skill or experience in an area of practical value to their lives. Through his research Allen Tough asserts that the learning motivations of adults illustrate a desire to gain pleasure, grow in self-esteem, or expand in relation to others either by being rewarded or by giving service.[5] His adult learning research ascribes important characteristics to the natural human tendency to develop and expand one's personal competence. First, the majority of adult learning is related to some aspect of self discovery (knowledge, skill, experience, or values). Secondly, adult learning is practical or purposeful, leading to some present or future application in life. Lastly, adult learning is also motivated by some relational goal with regard to others. The continuity of the human quest for self-improvement throughout the life cycle leads to a greater sense of public expression and relational competence, or leadership. There is a developmental link between continuous learning and leadership that almost all theorists ascribe to the lives of leaders. In the process of leading, the capacity to learn and become more humanly complex and complete may be motivational in itself, inspiring leaders to greater and expansive agendas. Warren Bennis and Burt Nanus describe the integral connection between leadership and developmental learning in this way:

> If the leader is seen as an effective learner from the environment, others will emulate that model, much as a child emulates a parent or a student emulates a teacher.

The leader and the organization nurture each other, guiding the process of creative self-discovery by which each learns how to be most effective in a complex and changing environment.[6]

There are both theoretical and practical connections between human development and the natural capacity for commitment to the quality of life for oneself and others. Our vocational mission is the vehicle for expressing the deepest wisdom of self-knowledge in action for both work and society.

James Fowler proposed a refinement of developmental theories which incorporates psychological, cognitive, social, and faith dimensions of vocation. In his theory faith is not an expression of religious belief as much as it is an expression of one's comprehensive picture of human meaning and values. For Fowler faith is a way of knowing, valuing, and relating to the world, oneself, and others that expresses our core self. It is a form of vocational leadership.

Faith has to do with the making, maintenance, and transforming of human meaning. . . . Faith is a mode of knowing and being in which we shape our lives in relation to more or less comprehensive convictional assumptions about the limiting conditions of our lives. It composes a felt sense of the world as having character, pattern, and unity.[7]

This pervasive core of human meaning is the source of a proactive vocational leadership which permeates all of the decisions and actions of one's life. Living life with this heightened sense of oneself and others, our social awareness becomes an active expression of a personal leadership that truly expresses who we are. Fowler describes a stage of faith similar to a global and unified commitment to the quality of life, work, and society in which all choices and actions work together harmoniously for a higher order. His description replicates the coherent expression of vocational leadership presented here.

Persons of universalizing faith are "contagious" in the sense that they create zones of liberation from the social, political, economic, and ideological shackles we place on human futurity. Living with felt participation in a power that unifies and transforms the world, they are often experienced as subversive of the structures by which we sustain our individual and corporate survival, security, and significance. They are often more honored and revered after death than during their lives. The persons who may be described by this stage have a special grace that makes them more lucid, more simple, and yet somehow more human than the rest of us. Their community is universal in extent.[8]

Mature human development within oneself results in an active concern for the universal development of others through public and organizational leadership. The vocational dimension of leadership expresses the full awareness of one's distinctive mission which pervades one's life and personality. It requires full mindfulness of one's innate abilities, skills, talents, and personality as well as work which has a significance that far transcends the boundaries of a singular career, occupation setting, or tangible immediate results. Work becomes a more complete expression of a satisfying and meaningful life through maximum extension of our personality in our relationships, social settings and occupational tasks. In our work or vocation, we freely express our creative ability partially because we are so self-possessed that we have much to share; and partially because we know that in the process of giving of ourselves through work and through the benefits we produce for others we become more whole. Marsha Sinetar offers the following description of a "vocational integrated" person.

> Work becomes a devotion, a labor of love, and indeed—whatever the person himself might call it—a spiritual exercise because the individual's concentrative powers, his choices, actions, and values, are motivated, prompted and fueled by love, and his service, as it were, is simply the enactment of this positive life force. His being or essential self lives in all he does.[9]

Leadership which finds its source in the vocational expression of our innermost self is able to transcend the sense of tedium or burden that can be associated with leading. This does not mean that leaders who are conscious of this vocational dimension do not become tired or burdened. It does, however, imply that the traditional boundaries between personal growth and public service, between rest and work, between action and reflection become less relevant. It is not the external rewards of success or the leisurely pursuits of life that rejuvenate this wider sense of leadership through one's lifework or vocational mission. Consciously recomposing the insights we gain by assessing the reciprocal impact between our immediate activity and our lifework gives us greater energy and motivation to move ahead. The symbiotic relationship of influencing our world through the unique expression of our gifts also provides sufficient sustenance and animation to continue our unique quest of vocation.

The lack of coherence between our external works and our inner work or vocational mission is the true source of our occupational "diseases." The widening chasm between the works of life and our lifework diminishes the capacity to lead. One of the frustrating experiences of counseling people in career transitions is the inflexibility of our work environment to accept commonly applicable leadership skills across different occupational specialties. Somehow organizations give the impression that to be a marketing executive in electronics has little to do with leadership in other product-related or service-related industries. This pigeonhole mentality is limiting. It seems foolish to think that one's assimilation of inner knowledge and experience cannot be applied to new learnings among other industries or services. Consequently, we create the necessity for people to identify themselves in a very narrow sense with a particular product, service, or industry, to the detriment of their comprehensive human development and their ultimate expression of leadership.

Leadership and Vocation

Vocational leadership is an expression of mature human development. This results in an inner coherence or integrity which brings unity to the diverse elements of the quality of our lives, the quality of our work, and our contribution to the quality of society. Marsha Sinetar describes vocation integration as possessing a sense of ultimate purpose in life which results from knowing one's "right livelihood."

> Also, in corresponding with and personally interviewing actualizing people I heard them repeatedly refer to themselves as having a kind of integrity in doing their work. People meant different things by this word. Some referred to themselves as having integrity because they saw themselves acting out of what they felt was best in themselves. They saw themselves as honest, as

trustworthy, as reliable or courageous because they had
the good fortune or tenacity or the risk-taking skill to do
the work they love. Others use the term "integrity" to
mean the values which they found inherently in their
work. They saw a certain tightness or beauty or truth in
the work, or they sensed that their work had meaning
in relation to the whole of mankind and helped them
understand the whole world or universe better, even
though they knew it was just part of the whole.[10]

Her concept of vocational integration captures the essential continuity between one's unique and comprehensive quality of life and
the natural expression of vocation through dedication to one's
work in the broadest sense. The vocationally mature see work as
at once self-fulfilling and contributing to the quality of our own
and others' lives. It is this integrity of vocation on a personal as
well as a public level that constitutes the root of authentic leadership.

To conclude our analysis of leadership, there are four common
attributes among those who exhibit a profound inner sense of vocation which is rooted in their appreciation of a diverse quality of
life. These characteristics among the vocationally mature mark
their capacity to lead themselves and others towards greater potential in appreciating and realizing their gifts.

**First, vocational leadership demonstrates an understanding of
one's lifework beyond the works of life.**

Among the vocationally mature the activities, tasks, events, circumstances and roles of work are part of a tapestry or mosaic of
their ultimate life purpose which contributes to a broad sense of
one's distinctive and singular life project. The career of artist,
homemaker, executive, chemist, botanist, computer analyst, etc.,
comprises only a small role in the vocational integrity of one's lifework. The responsibilities of a job, position, or organizational role
may be major vehicles for the expression of our lifework but these
are not to be understood as comprising the whole of our developmental character or plan of work in life. An artist may see her
lifework as a vocation of "advancing a sense of the harmony and
beauty of life." In this framework she works not only in the active
use of her chosen media. She also works in the walks in nature
that formulate her concepts of environment and form. She works
in the technical reading and research in technique that shapes her

craft. She works in the observation of the artistic achievements of others. She may work in the discovery of analogies of creative design through the experience of the performing arts, engineering, architecture, or science. She may work in staying attuned to the rhythmic breathing of her daily jogging, creating greater inner harmony. She works in the teaching of her craft to others by exhibits, shows, lectures, and contributed community service enhancing appreciation of the arts. She works at her lifework in the intimate discussion with friends and family of her work and the encouragement of analogies in their own life for seeing their "works" as forms of creative expression. In this expanded concept of lifework she both is humanly developed and develops others by increasing the integration of the various strands of "work" in her life. Through this view of one's lifework, the individual immediate circumstances of productive or profitable periods, or active or inactive periods of sculpting, bear less weight and are held in perspective and balance. Understanding of the full contribution of one's work is enlarged so that each element is seen for what it is, a contribution to one's vocation despite its immediate impact. This detached identity from the singular works and episodes of one's life yet intimacy with one's overall lifework or vocation is a major characteristic of the innovation and creativity of leaders. This expanded sense of lifework or vocation enabled Martin Luther King to take hope and further inspire his followers and the nation in his "Dream" rather than accepting despair in the limited realization of its promise within his lifetime.

Secondly, vocational leadership is understood as an expression of one's own quality of life.

Almost 15 years ago I had the opportunity to hear Mother Theresa of Calcutta speak at a university in Chicago. A person of few words and deep insight, she reviewed why she often rejected American volunteers who wish to join in her work with the marginalized poor of the streets of Calcutta. She indicated those who come in order to "do good" rarely can tolerate the conditions of work and spartan livelihood presented in the impoverished missions of the Third World; yet she herself found a great deal of personal enjoyment and almost pleasure in what many would find a highly stressful and discouraging occupation, because it grew out of her own milieu. On her own terms her lifework was a means of further advancing the quality of her life and her unique talents and abilities, unusual as they may appear. The symptoms of career stress and "burnout" may be due to more than the circumstantial elements of dissatisfaction with our work—what more draining activity could one do than attend to the few among countless sick and dying on the streets of India? Our stress may be more deeply rooted in our disengagement and the lack of intimate connection between our individual works and our lifework of becoming more truly who we are intended to be. Real efficacy and efficiency are characteristics of those whose leadership also nurtures the emergence of their true personality and maturity. How often we remark at the energy, drive, intensity, and motivation despite formidable circumstances of those we emulate. Their spirited work is a reflection of the quality of life they experience, resulting from their efforts to give their gifts well. In leading others they become more truly who they are.

Thirdly, vocational leadership demonstrates an intimate association of one's personal values with the public impact of one's work.

The re-engagement of a sense of personal commitment and stewardship with the effects and results of one's labors has been the major thrust of recent trends in business leadership. Such concepts as total quality, value-added benefits, and quality assurance programs are attempts to restore the necessary relationship and sense of involvement and identification among workers with their products or services and their publics. The root of these organizational values is the active association of the personal values of employees with the public value of the product or service. For those with a well-developed identity and vocation this concept is far beyond a technique or strategy but an integral ingredient for their sense of personal leadership. The active expression of vocational leadership blends the pride of the work of the creator with what is created into a satisfying and meaningful result. To behold the clay pot is to know the potter.

Finally, vocational leadership demonstrates a perception of success and failure as positive contributions to one's growth.

John Gardner in one of his popular essays on leadership concludes that "anyone who ever achieved anything of significance had more hope than the facts justified." Leadership that results from an inwardly driven vocation which has transformation as its goal is no stranger to the experience of resistance, failure, or rejection.

Those with a mature vocation may deeply despise, regret, and struggle against adversity but at the same time they recognize a benefit or opportunity in these experiences capable of advancing the level of sophistication of their efforts. In their book *The Lessons of Experience: How Successful Executives Develop on the Job*, McCall, Lombardo, and Morrisson describe the results of their research through the Center for Creative Leadership on the career paths of corporate leaders who experience long term success. Much of their book chronicles the benefits of experience-based versus training-based development and the enhancement of oneself through complex decisions, adversity, failure, and tough assignments. The key ingredient in these advanced forms of leadership may be the capacity to extract future meaning from difficult present action to discover ultimate benefit even in misapprehension and failure. There has been recent research in developmental psychology that indicates some correlation between strong ego development, later leadership, and early experiences of adversity or hardship in childhood. Popular notions of success seem to promise a smooth path towards our human growth and development. Many theorists even propose prosperity as a result of leadership. However, among true leaders success is not measured by the relative degree of public reward or outward achievement but in the inner benefits we derive from all of our experiences. Vocational leadership is a reflection of the wisdom one is able to appropriate from both successful and unsuccessful events in achieving our life goals and fulfilling our lifework.

Conclusion

Leadership need not be a burdensome, single-focused, or isolated life devoid of meaning and satisfaction. In fact, it should represent the full extension of our human personality and expression of our gifts and talents in many areas of our lives. Much of our past educational systems and occupational career paths have led us to believe that our gifts and talents should be directed in specialized, highly focused, and singular dimensions of our lives. However, it is only in the broad-based extension of our gifts and talents into the full expression of a quality life that we fully realize our human potential. Our personal, relational, community, and organizational investments all are key ingredients to achieve a sense of lasting public value.

The four dimensions to the quality of our life outlined in Chapter III also contribute significantly to the realization of our unique personal vocation. This sense of vocation is derived from the satisfaction gleaned across the many dimensions of our lives rather than from the singular contribution of our solitary work or primary skill or expertise.

There is a true efficacy in contributing the primary work of our lives in such a way that it represents a broad understanding of the values and meaning of all of the dimensions of who we are as people and what we contribute through our work. No longer can we settle for educational systems and organizational environments that stress one-dimensional development of human persons. It is only in the full expression of who we are and the broad development of our talents and abilities that the unique and distinctive marks of our lives can be given in a way that they can be both received and accepted by ourselves and by others for the good of all.

Chapter V

Developing and Empowering Leaders

A leader's strength of character for effective leadership and the social advancement of others is based in the realization of his or her own inner human development. The capacity for increasing one's ability to integrate complex life experiences into one's quality of life has the corresponding benefit of strengthening the quality of one's work and one's public contribution to the quality of society. We have concentrated attention on the intimate link between interior human development with the exterior process of public and organizational leadership. The classic rhetorical question about leadership now remains for our consideration: "Are leaders made or are leaders born?" Both individual and collective leadership can be developed. Through a deliberate process to internalize thinking and acting, one's vocational leadership (inner capacity to lead) can be sharpened with precision, creating an expansive awareness of one's lifework, enabling one's vocational leadership to gain wider expression.

If we could gather the common experiences, values, behaviors, and knowledge about vocation gained by leaders into a learning model for empowering ourselves and others, we could maximize the realization of our capacity to lead. This chapter will provide a learning model for leadership development. Correspondingly, the same learning model could be used to design group or organizational leadership strategies to promote the formation of a "consciousness of leadership" among our diverse constituencies. For purposes of illustration we will condense several steps and sessions of a vocational counseling process to highlight this Cycle of Leadership Development.   This developmental learning model provides a basic image for the growth of leadership through vocational maturity on a personal and collective scale.

While the following case study is a one-to-one vocational planning process, the maturation of human development and vocational leadership follows these stages whether applied to group, organization, or individual growth.   The process of human development is universal.   Maintaining consistency in our developmental approaches is important to avoid the error that group, organizational, or individual changes are different in kind, although they do differ in scale and proportion.   A divided approach to personal or organizational development is precisely the source of our original dilemma separating the personal, public, and organizational dimensions of leadership.

The Cycle of Leadership Development

Figure 6 represents a model for understanding *The Cycle of Leadership Development*.   It portrays five elements to internalize experiences and information about our vocational capacities, our public values, and our organizational behavior in order to intensify our unique vocational mission and expand our capacity to lead.

The Cycle of Leadership Development

Organize Experience

Critical Awareness

Integrated Decisions

Mindful Action

Intentional Planning

Figure 6. The Cycle of Leadership Development

Organize Experience

Human development requires that we use our experiences in the past and present in order to create some expectancy models for the future. What we think, see, hear, feel, know, and experience provides a powerful source of information about ourselves inwardly as well as about our capacities for the public expression of values and organizational behavior. Individuals, groups, and systems benefit by ordering their experience in some coherent fashion so as to internalize its significance, test its boundaries, and comprehend its benefit for future challenges. Unfortunately, for many of us experience is often viewed as a linear string of episodes from one situation to the next without consistent themes or patterns to interpret life and to draw parallels or lessons from the past and present to apply to the future.

Some even experience themselves and their social and organizational life as random and unpredictable, unaware of their inner power to shape, avoid, or interpret situations with new frames of reference. Those in the position to develop and expand leadership in others must provide models or paradigms to name and organize experience, assisting others in making coherent judgements about their experience that may be useful in the future both for their inner knowing and outer behavior. Providing strong cognitive models or processes for constituents to organize their experience is a valuable first step in the process of maturing leadership.

Our example is a middle aged human service worker who appears very depressed amidst a career change. He has moved randomly and frequently in the last several years geographically around the Midwest and situationally through fairly diverse career settings of health care, education, human service, and religious organizations. When asked if he has a sense of that innermost work that makes him happy and productive, he responds tentatively and vaguely, "to help people find meaning." He seeks external situations as the only way to find and validate his identity. Lonely, without close colleagues, he is seeking work again, desperately hoping something will come along to restore energy and enrichment to his life. He has consulted a therapist and spiritual advisor but cannot seem to put together the direction of his lifework to feel productive, caring, and cared for in both the personal and professional dimensions of his life. He now finds life depressing and boring. He cannot sort out the maze of his experiences to distinguish his true calling and unique opportunity for leadership. He works at half of the level of compensation his career and skill should provide, which further constricts his options for growth and exploration and also erodes his self-esteem. His last position was with a small rural social service agency where he had hoped the solitude of the country would give him the space to put it all together; rather, it had heightened his isolation. He comes for help, frightened after phoning a friend who lovingly confronted him with the challenge of being in the same place he was five years ago.

Our strategy will be first to help him organize his career experiences into some perceptual categories to lift him out of an emotional morass, to observe his behavior, and later to make judgements about his past choices in light of a preferred future. We start with some simple questions to help him locate the right place and vocational path that will be satisfying to him for many years to come. When asked about his timeline for a new work, he presents a working timeframe of one year. Already he has shortened the five year angst into one year of proactive searching, a boundary we shall later reinforce.

Now we test some other perceptual boundaries of experience to define his thinking and internalize control rather than "scanning the newspapers for a job that is interesting." We ask if he has geographic boundaries to search; he fears but loves metropolitan areas, particularly in the Midwest, and one in particular ten years later he still feels is home. We inquire about institutional boundaries and find some decided preferences among the types of systems he has felt productive in. We ask about relational boundaries, about the types of colleagues, he enjoys: "a few to work with intimately." Our inquiry proceeds along a deliberate path of testing interests, relationships, organizational settings, income ideals, clients enjoyed, and responsibilities desired. When we get too close to testing his vocational self-knowledge he is defensive. He leaves with a further assignment to organize his search for a lifework.

Since we find he likes introspective writing but does it randomly without organization, he is asked to write five future scenarios of his lifework in detail, each as diverse as possible. We suggest he write them as if he were ten years into the future, imposing another cognitive construct of "projected time": imagining himself in a preferred future rather than in an aimless present. In each scenario he is instructed to consider a complete view of what life will be like, including the risks, rewards, and challenges in getting there. For each scenario he is to write the specific steps it would take to achieve the situation, from now to the ten years hence. Lastly he is to bring to our next session 8-10 key criteria for his vocational satisfaction that are behavioral in nature, taken from the insights of his scenarios which most engross him. Specifically he is told not to generalize (as in "to make more money"), rather if it is a value to him he is to specify how much and by when. Nor should he indicate he wishes "to have good co-workers;" rather he should indicate, "I'd like to manage a work force of 100" or "work intimately with 2-3 project specialists." He gets the drift and leaves smiling, because he now has some organized models to interpret past experience in a useful fashion to search his way back to the future.

Critical Awareness

The second dimension of the leadership development cycle is to engage others in critical analysis and reflection on present challenges, to understand the significance of past experience for desired future action. Different educational theorists describe this process in various ways, but it is a common element among developmental models for enriching insight and critical thinking among adult populations. Paolo Friere in his book *Education for Critical Consciousness* describes this ability for introspective analysis upon one's life experience as "conscientization." Friere contends that those capable of naming their reality gain power over it. In his methods of literacy education among the poor of Brazil he was acutely aware that he was teaching not only the skills of reading and writing to his constituents but the inner ability to accurately "read" reality, and therefore transform it. In a more recent scholarly work in professional education, Donald Schon in his book, *Educating the Reflective Practitioner* discusses the importance of critical problem-solving and internalizing models for analysis among professions by means of graduate education. He calls for greater attention in higher education to teaching the skills of reflective analysis in situations, events, and problems. Ideally, this critical analysis occurs in the present circumstance; often it happens in retrospect as a reflective tool to create meaningful and more satisfying experiences in the future. Leaders must internalize this self-supervisory ability to diagnose and assess current and past events and experience. This inner insight is most effective when based upon some formal models or images of reality in order to understand a present circumstance to make use of it in the future. This second dimension of developing leadership requires the ability to stand outside of our experience and review the interplay between ourselves and the immediate circumstance, in order to increase insight and meaning for future decisions and to redirect future actions.

In subsequent coaching sessions with our client we help him engage in critical analysis of his five future scenarios and his several behavioral criteria for vocational satisfaction to help him gain further insight for his future plans. Our questioning and inquiry should probe and help him consolidate his insights to give him more confidence in his ability for critical self-analysis and his ability to control his reality. If the process is successful, he should demonstrate more clarity about his distinctive vocational mission and be able to define more precisely a career path that will satisfy his quest.

In subsequent sessions our client acts more in charge of himself. His dress indicates more pride in his appearance and stature. He leans forward in his chair and begins the session by proudly reviewing his five scenarios. We ask about the various criteria he has developed for his future vocational satisfaction; he seems articulate and clear on their definition, even a little surprised with his own insight. He comments on how far his present circumstance is from meeting his objectives. We also probe for consistency among his vocational criteria for success and they seem in synch with one another—he doesn't expect to make $100,000 annually as a social worker!

We now ask him to evaluate his five scenarios against his criteria for vocational satisfaction, to narrow the courses of action for his future investigation. Quickly two of the scenarios are eliminated as being merely extensions of past experiences which are comfortably familiar but not ultimately satisfying. He rules out returning to health care as he finds it has lost much of the personal touch and influence with others he values, and it would require further formal education which he is not prepared to undertake. He dismisses a similar scenario in mental health as a therapist. While he would be open to more formal training, his future economic security would require private practice and doctoral studies; this process would bring him to the age of 50 years and he finds that time frame for change unappealing. His critical self-reflection about vocational preferences are working together well to help him weed out previously circular and unrealistic thinking.

Three of his scenarios show promise and creativity. One of his key criteria is to be involved in the public advocacy of human welfare. Another is to have exposure to many people while working closely with a few. His first scenario is to become director of public relations for a school or school system. (We encourage broadening the application of this scenario to include fundraising or student recruitment at a secondary or college level.) He also expresses interest in a sales or customer relations position for a socially responsible product or business service. His final scenario is as a counselor for returning students at a technical school or college. He seems more critically aware of his pragmatic and personal limits in developing these scenarios and he is comfortable with his criteria for vocational success ten years from now. He has developed some cognitive structures to work within. He has insight into the relationship among his abilities and limits, his past experience, his future priorities. We ask him to redefine his vocational mission in light of the assignment, returning to the ultimate question of self definition and future leadership. He seems more clear about this lifework in responding, "I am most myself when I am advocating for the quality of life of others." The act of critical self-reflection is an essential dimension of leadership development.

Mindful Action

Taking tentative actions and effecting new behaviors within acceptable levels of risk is the next step of our developmental cycle. Once constituents can see their experience, themselves, and their present and past choices with new clarity, it is important to take tentative steps toward new behaviors. The process of enlarging one's comfort zone is best done gradually. This behavioral reality-testing helps evaluate future choices based on increased experience and exposure to new events, new people, new environments and circumstances. Exploratory steps of "acting with a new mind" helps assess the congruence of one's insight with both the practical reality of life and events as we may imagine or desire them to be. It also helps reinforce insight and values by solidifying a sense of accomplishment in behavior and confidence in a new way of thinking. For many, further insight into themselves and changes in feelings often follow new experiences which may be very uncomfortable at first. Overcoming that initial resistance to new ways of self-expression is better accomplished with gradient stress rather than with total immersion in new circumstances. Knowing that actions and insights are tentative may give an individual or group confidence in their ability to try innovative or diverse approaches to the present situation or problem. We call this tentative self-expression "mindful action" to highlight its continuity with new cognitive perspectives rather than with past experiences.

To go back to our career planning process, we help the client identify new behavioral efforts to further test his career scenarios and vocational criteria for success. Our goal is to have him act differently to increase exposure and awareness of the potential life choices he is making, without a premature judgment of "accepting a new job because it was offered" or "the money was right." The emphasis is on tentative behavioral strategy removed as yet from a direct job search or inquiry. The focus of this coaching session is to define a series of actions that will clarify his preferred career scenario and his criteria for future vocational satisfaction. We return to his expressed boundaries of a city, within a day's drive, similar to the one where our client felt most at home. We find two within a hundred miles. In each city the client will do some research on a college, a university, a school district or secondary school, and a business which contributes to the quality of life. In the latter case our client has identified one publisher and one regional bookseller to contact. Since the emphasis is on a planned inquiry into career options, we ask our client to pre-arrange visits with the public relations director of a school system and one university. He will also arrange a visit with a fundraising director for a small college and with the marketing directors for the publisher and bookseller. Finally, he arranges a visit with the director of continuing education for the university to discuss a role in career counseling for returning adult students.

We coach the client not to use these visits as job interviews; rather to think of his contacts not as "prospective employers" but as "prospective colleagues" who do the type of work he may aspire to. The focus of his discussions is to assess the satisfaction these colleagues feel with the work they do. He is also to be cognizant of his criteria of vocational success, listening for indicators of these in his discussions with prospective colleagues. Some final coaching on carefully positioning these discussions in order to benefit from the experience of others rather than to seek a job will help him avoid rejection in arranging appointments. We suggest two final behavioral assignments. Since he seems headed for the public relations and marketing field we ask if he would consent to some skill testing, which he does. Finally, we ask that he keep a journal of his experiences in order to continue his critical self-reflection on making the right career choice. For each journal entry we ask him to review three steps: he should describe the experience in some detail, then evaluate its significance for him by identifying what he has learned for his vocation, and finally he is to identify what specific follow-up actions he should pursue in his vocational search. He has six weeks to begin by placing himself in these new settings and roles. His task is to try out some new actions to further his insight into choosing his true path of vocational leadership. Our goal is to help him glimpse how life might be for him in the future by tentatively acting more mindfully in the present.

Intentional Planning

We tend to think of planning as some linear representation of our future laid out in hard copy. Planning has become a goal when it is better used as a means. Planning is a far more integrated and introspective function of human development than the resulting public document or written representation of our ideas. Developmentally, a plan is the involvement of a constituency in the process of consistently thinking and acting in the same direction at the same time around the same priorities. That is the true source of a plan. It is also why planning is so tedious and difficult for many of us. Mustering the individual or collective commitments necessary to move in a clear direction together simultaneously is the true measure of a plan's success. The resulting documentation is just words on a page, only as effective as the shared commitment to a course of action that these tools and techniques of planning symbolize.

Planning in this sense is a critical ingredient in any developmental action for the future. It is a means for an individual or institution to solidify, clarify, and project their future commitments of resources to achieve a vision. Without a plan there is little chance of a vision of the future. A lack of vision begets no clarity for leadership, which results in decline rather than future development. It has been popular in recent years to diminish the importance of planning in light of rapidly changing markets and environments. While the contents of a plan are subject to constant change, the act of planning is the requisite discipline for any future vision of leadership whether on a personal level or on an organizational scale. Our task in the cycle of leadership development is to lead constituents to articulate and commit to a preferred future vision, based on their tentative experiences with new ways of thinking and acting from previous stages of the leadership development cycle. This is the commitment phase for mature leaders. Whether leading an individual toward vocational clarity and integrity or advancing a group's history and priorities, the formality of planning is a core value for the leadership process.

Returning to our career development scenario our goal is to assist the client in consolidating his insights into an intentional long term plan of action. That plan should represent and solidify his commitment to several new insights and behaviors about his vocational mission. His intentional career plan should support a vocational mission unique to him that motivates him to leadership. His plan should incorporate the perceptual boundaries of geography, setting, colleagues, income, and security which he has previously identified. Ideally his career path will also reflect the previously named criteria for vocational satisfaction he has specified. Lastly, his plan should be based on a clear appraisal of his abilities from externally validated sources as well as the experiences he has gleaned from his tentative career observations with prospective work sites and colleagues.

We begin the final planning process by asking him to redefine his unique vocational mission based on his experience. He indicates, ". . . a real call to enrich the quality of life for society by promoting education." His successive statements of vocational mission have shown increasing clarity and conviction since the process began some four months ago. Next, we ask his assessment of his recent investigations into work settings and career priorities in the two cities. He misses education (having begun his career as a teacher and school principal), but he focuses now on a desire to work for a secondary school system or institution of higher learning. He is intrigued with a community affairs or public relations role, but demonstrates interest in the challenge of fundraising as having clear measures for future productivity to hold as objectives. On the outer edges of the vocational continuum, he is less comfortable with a counseling role for adult students as being too diffuse. He likewise resists a direct sales role for a product even in the publishing world; he finds this too limited. His reasons seem well grounded in the criteria for career satisfaction he had previously developed. He is motivated now to focus his career plan on the search for a position in public relations or fundraising for a secondary school system or in higher education.

We return to his original timeframe of one year and ask him to develop a plan to locate an entry level second career choice in this new field within the next eight months. We also ask him to develop a second plan identifying his action steps toward professional proficiency in three to five years, even if it includes moving to a different system after two to four years. We help him identify several target Midwestern cities that meet his criteria for a comfortable home, and several specific educational institutions and systems he may find compatible with his values. We help him structure the plan by defining types of career contacts needed, publications to read, further training to gain, and a timetable for gaining interviews, and offers and acceptance of the second career role. For the next several months we assist him in refining, monitoring and developing the plan. We also try to reinforce previous dimensions of the cycle of leadership development by having him keep a vocational journal to continue to clarify his lifework and experiences.

He has created an intentional plan for the future of his livelihood but with deeper personal significance than just a job search. He has a new vocational clarity and will more likely meet with success and satisfaction by providing greater leadership for himself and for others. In the process of strengthening his own insight into human development he is favorably disposed toward the creative expression of vocational leadership "by enriching the quality of life for society through education."

Integrated Decisions

Throughout this chapter we have stressed the continuity of the inner process of human development with the outer expression of leadership. The greater the continuity of one's human development with one's leadership role the greater the generative impact on the qualitative fabric of our systems and those we serve. In this sense vocational leadership is a fundamental ingredient for the effective exercise of our organizational roles and public values. These three dimensions of leadership create the paradigm for renewing and reuniting the productive and personal dimensions of life and work. To echo Sigmund Freud, they are the tools of creating personal and organizational health by enhancing our ability to love and to work. There is no inherent discontinuity between the individual and the social system or organization. There are, however, institutions and individuals who ignore clues or are unaware of the long-term interdependence of both. All comprehensive decision-making for the future of leadership must engage our vocational integrity with our organizational behavior and public values. In our quest for expediency and closure we often divide the essential unity and coherence of vocational, organizational, and public dimensions of leadership by choosing personal and corporate options which respond to only one dimension of reality.

In our career development case study, our client locates his new career as a public relations director for a community college. His immediate choice is important to his livelihood but more significantly he has managed to create a new model of career decision-making. He sees his work not only as a job for an institution. He sees his career choice as a complementary match of vocational leadership with institutional mission. He is rare, for in the words of Paolo Friere he has developed a "subject to subject" rather than "subject to object" relationship with reality, in this case his work. The capacity for shared human development on personal and institutional levels is present in his new choice. On the surface it may seem that he has made an ordinary career change. More substantively, he has captured new meaning in his work by unifying his quest for personal relevance and meaning with "enriching the quality of life for society by promoting education."

His quest for a new vocational integrity mirrors the essential connection between human development and leadership. Finding the essential link between our vocational mission and our organizational and public opportunities for leadership is the glue for a consistent commitment to quality of life, work, and society. This process does not occur accidentally. The skillful leader can apply the principles of human development to the task of developing leadership among others. To the extent leaders can act with greater intentionality in the process of serving constituencies, our lives, our organizations, and our communities will fulfill their capacity to effect human advancement for ourselves and others.

Organizational Strategies

The process of developing leaders both personally and organizationally consists of not only a conceptual framework as outlined earlier in this chapter, but also a series of organizational strategies and behaviors that provide the context for other leaders to emerge. Our conceptual model of leadership development is supported and enhanced by the practices of empowering leaders. Beyond the slogans and the catch words that have become popular parlance to empower leaders, this process requires attention to several key variables which skillful leaders employ to develop the leadership capacity of others. The strategies for empowering and enabling the leadership of others consists of the following:

- Develop the capacity for critical self-reflection

- Create environments for continuous learning

- Interpret present action through a larger vision

- Create present symbolic models of the future

- Understand and use the authentic power of influence

- Emphasize action and outcomes as the expression of commitment

- Understand that leadership is personally and collectively transformative.

Among organizations that thrive on the enhancement of their members, employees, and, stakeholders as leaders, these practices prevail. Illustrating these seven strategies in organizational settings will expand our conceptual model for developing leaders.

Strategy #1: Develop the Capacity for Critical Self-Reflection

The fundamental skill for strategically analyzing present activity in light of desired future results is our capacity for critical self-reflection. This is the fundamental skill of being able to act and simultaneously to observe ourselves acting in order to redirect the course of our behavior and our organizational priorities to create new perspectives as well as more effective solutions to the immediate circumstance. Several theories of organizational development and educational leadership describe this same skill in a variety of ways.

Donald A. Schon describes this capacity as the process of reflection and action. In his book *Educating the Reflective Practitioner*, Donald Schon indicates that the fundamental skill of professional excellence consists of this process of reflection in action. He also indicates that teaching this skill is a fundamental responsibility of those that seek to educate others for professional leadership. This capacity for critical self-reflection enables leaders and those they serve to be able to analyze actions in the midst of activity, in order to find a higher ground of meaning, purpose, and strategy. Donald Schon describes this process of critical self-reflection, or as he calls it, reflection in action, this way.

> Whatever language we may employ, however, our descriptions of knowing and action are always constructions. There are always attempts to put into explicit, symbolic form a kind of intelligence that begins by being tacit and spontaneous. Our descriptions are conjectures that need to be tested against observations of their originals—which, in at least one respect, they are bound to distort. For knowing-in-action is dynamic, and "facts," "procedures," "rules," and "theories" are static. When we know how to catch a ball, for example, we anticipate the ball's coming by the way we extend and cup our hands and by the on-line adjustments we make as the ball approaches. Catching a ball is a continuous activity in which awareness, appreciation, and adjustment play their parts. Similarly, sawing along a penciled line requires a more or less continuous process of detecting and correcting deviations in the line. Indeed, it is in this on-line anticipation and adjustment, this continuous detection and correction of error, that leads us, in the first place, to call "activity" intelligent. Knowing suggests the dynamic quality of knowing-in-action, which, when we describe it we convert to knowledge-in-action.[1]

Donald Schon suggests that the capacity for reflective leadership is contingent upon this internal process of readjusting our perspectives and priority in the midst of actions. It represents a stance towards life and work that provides for simultaneous contemplation and action, allowing us to observe and act with the skill of choosing more appropriate solutions and priorities for the tasks at hand. This skill is reminiscent of a story from Gestalt psychology that represents the difference between leadership based in reflection and action and leadership based on reactive approaches to life and work. Three umpires were interviewed as to how they call a baseball game. When the first umpire was asked this question, his response was simple: "Some's balls and some's strikes." The second umpire, a bit more sophisticated in strategy, responded to the same question as follows: "Well," he said, "some's balls and some's strikes, and I call them the way I see them." The third umpire, far more sophisticated in viewpoint, illustrates the difference in a critically self reflective stance towards reality. His response was, "Well, some's balls and some's strikes, but they ain't anything until I call them."

This capacity to stay detached and disengaged from the immediate priorities and circumstances of the moment, allowing for adjustments to strategy, perception, and action, is critical self-reflection. This skill makes a fundamental difference in our approach to life and work, as being proactive versus reactive. It is representative of the philosophy of life experience of Dag Hammarskjold, former Secretary General of the United Nations, who wrote, "None of us is permitted to choose the frame of our destiny, but what we make of it is ours."

Leadership often has little to do with controlling the circumstances of our life and work. It has everything to do with responding to those circumstances in such a way that they are lifted to a higher plane of activity and priority, transforming leader, circumstance, and constituency to new levels of self-awareness. The skill of critical self reflection can be summed up in an organizational and personal strategy of leadership which always asks the question, "What are we called to do differently as a result of our experience?" It is this capacity to stand apart from the immediate circumstances which gives us new opportunities for more comprehensive, effective, and appropriate practical strategies to organizational, personal, and public leadership.

Donald Schon describes this process of rethinking as a result of critical reflection in this way.

> In such cases the practitioner experiences a surprise that leads her to rethink her knowing-in-action in ways that go beyond available rules, facts, theories, and opera-

tions. She responds to the unexpected or the anomalous by restructuring some of her strategies of action, theories of phenomena, or ways of framing the problem; and she invents on-the-spot experiments to put her new understandings to the test. She behaves more like a researcher trying to model an expert system than like the 'expert' whose behavior is modeled.[2]

Leaders who empower others to engage their imaginations and discover their own leadership capabilities invite their colleagues, constituents, and employees to engage in the process of critical self reflection.

Strategy #2: Create Environments for Continuous Learning

The quest for lifelong learning is integral to the process of developing leaders. Leaders are measured not in the knowledge or expertise they possess, but in their capacity to learn from the unknown, the unexpected, and the unexplored. The task of leadership requires the courage of conviction to venture beyond our comfort zone of existing knowledge and experience to discover new and alternative ways of thinking, acting, and behaving to lift our organizations and ourselves to greater levels of accomplishment.

Almost universally, books on organizational theory describe the process of continuous learning as an essential ingredient of leadership. A fast-tracking IBM marketing executive embarked upon a strategy to develop a national campaign to market one of IBM's new computer products. Given the opportunity to exercise his entrepreneurship, he went full bore into the effort and failed dismally, to the tune of more than a million dollar loss. With both head and letter of resignation in hand, he visited his divisional vice president. Without flinching, the divisional vice president looked him in the eye and said, "Why would we choose to fire you now, we've just spent over a million on your education!"

It is this courageous and exemplary attitude that represents an environment for continuous learning essential to the process of empowering leaders. When employees, constituents, and colleagues fear the consequences of failure, they are unable to transcend traditional organizational boundaries to rethink new solutions. The capacity for organizations and individuals to succeed is greatly diminished. An emphasis on the learning environment which encourages exploration, tolerates failure, insists on new learnings, and advocates personal and organizational challenge to untested assumptions is the hallmark of organizations that will succeed in the future.

A recent work by Peter Senge entitled *The Fifth Discipline* devotes an entire book to understanding "the art and practice of the learning organization." Peter Senge contends that the foundation of organizational development in the future is far less devoted to traditional modes of organizational behavior than it is to an organizational culture based upon new enterprise through learning. He states his premise this way:

> To practice a discipline is to be a lifelong learner. You "never arrive;" you spend your life mastering disciplines. You can never say, "We are a learning organization," anymore than you can say, "I am an enlightened person." The more you learn, the more acutely aware you become of your ignorance. Thus, a corporation cannot be "excellent" in a sense of having arrived at a permanent excellence; it is always in the state of practicing the disciplines of learning, of becoming better or worse.[3]

Peter Senge verifies what most successful leaders have learned in practice. The process of providing answers is far less effective than the process of engaging our colleagues and our organizations in the fundamental questions of leadership, "What are we called to learn from this now?"

Most organizations, however, resist the internal challenges that are presented by the quest for learning. Learning implies error, error implies uncertainty, and uncertainty implies a commitment to chaos. Not unexpectedly recent organizational consultants such as Tom Peters have built their legacy on advocating "organizational chaos." This is not a commitment to an incoherent approach to organizational design, it is a tacit recognition of the need for organizations to constantly extend their boundaries in favor of new learnings. Peter Senge describes "organizational disabilities" as the collective resistance to environments of learning. He discusses the issue by reviewing the theory of Chris Argyris, organizational consultant and Harvard University faculty member.

> Argyris argues that most managers find collective inquiry inherently threatening. Schools train us never to admit that we do not know the answer, and most cor-

porations reinforce that lesson by rewarding their people who excel in advocating their views, not in inquiring into complex issues. (When was the last time someone was rewarded in your organization for raising a difficult question about the company's current policies rather than solving urgent problems?) Even if we feel uncertain or ignorant, we learn to protect ourselves from the pain of appearing uncertain or ignorant. That very process blocks out any new understandings which might threaten us. The consequence is what Argyris calls, "skilled incompetence"—teams full of people who are incredibly proficient at keeping themselves from learning.[4]

An authentic commitment to empowering leaders conveys a passion for learning in both life and work for themselves, their colleagues, and the publics which they serve.

Strategy #3: Interpret Present Action Through a Larger Vision

The third strategy of empowering leaders is the capacity to interpret present actions, no matter how unfavorable, in light of a larger vision and future dream. This skill is based in a leadership ability to reframe present difficulties as growth points for longer term goals and priorities, imagining success in the midst of complexity, uncertainty, or failure. This behavior was graphically demonstrated to me in a capital building campaign for a large midwestern blue collar church community. Churches, like all other organizations, follow the same patterns of organizational development and decline which other public and private organizations exhibit. The newly appointed pastor was given the assignment from his regional jurisdiction to build a new church. During the late 1980's in this particular midwestern community, the economy was failing, and the congregation was largely populated by families requiring most of their income to meet day-to-day expenses. In building a new physical plant, he hired consultants to handle the technology and the techniques of fund-raising and architectural design. He concentrated his strategy on articulating a vision of fulfilling the dream that had been created 25 years earlier upon the founding of the church. Repeatedly throughout the fund-raising campaign he emphasized the fulfillment of this dream. He also allowed for the possibility that fulfillment of the dream could take shape other than in the building of a new physical plant.

When the estimates of the fund-raising executives came due for the goal of $1 1/2 million, the members of the congregation were somewhat taken aback in the face of this challenge. At no time during the process of building the new physical plant or in raising the funds did the pastor ever solicit funds directly. He simply focused his own position and strategy on what it meant to fulfill an organizational dream with a life history of 25 years. At the conclusion of the campaign, members of the congregation had supported his vision by exceeding the stated financial goal by 25 percent. This capacity to present current challenges and priorities in light of future visions and actions is characteristic of leaders who are able to inspire and empower others to higher levels of consciousness and action.

Perhaps the most memorable contemporary example of a leader who empowered his followers by interpreting present actions in light of future and larger dreams was Dr. Martin Luther King. In his famous "I Have a Dream" speech delivered at the Lincoln Memorial on August 28, 1963, Dr. King exemplified the ability to interpret present disappointment, despair, and discouragement in light of future hope and opportunity.

> So I say to you, my friends, that even though we must face the difficulties of today and tomorrow, I still have a dream. It is a dream deeply rooted in the American Dream that one day this nation will rise up and live out the true meaning of its creed—we hold these truths to be self-evident, that all men are created equal. I have a dream that one day on the red hills of Georgia, sons of former slaves and sons of former slave owners will be able to sit down together at the table of brotherhood.
>
> I have a dream that one day, even the state of Mississippi, a state sweltering with the heat of injustice, sweltering with the heat of oppression, will be transformed into an oasis of freedom and justice.
>
> I have a dream that my four little children will one day live in a nation where they will not be judged by the color of their skin but by the content of their character. I have a dream today!

I have a dream that one day, down in Alabama with its vicious racists, with its governor having his lips dripping with the words of interposition and nullification, that one day, right there in Alabama, little black boys and black girls will be able to join hands with little white boys and white girls as sisters and brothers. I have a dream today!

I have a dream that one day every valley shall be exalted every hill and mountain shall be made low, the rough places shall be made plain, and the crooked places shall be made straight, and the glory of God will be revealed, and all flesh shall see it together. This is our hope. This is the faith that I go back to the South with.[5]

Dr. King's imagery of a dream empowered a generation of leaders to emerge who later took on significant active roles in public service, the civil rights movement, and many national reform movements. His empowering leadership has significantly influenced the direction of this country. His capacity to interpret present circumstances in a larger vision was a key ingredient of his ability to enable leadership among others.

Perhaps the most famous image of this capacity to transform difficult, even tragic, circumstances in the present into future hope is the eloquent, simple, heartfelt Gettysburg Address delivered by Abraham Lincoln. Lincoln demonstrated this capacity to look at present adversity, suffering, pain, and despair yet offer a larger vision of meaning to galvanize future action.

But in a larger sense, we cannot dedicate—we cannot consecrate—we cannot hallow this ground. The brave men, living and dead, who struggled here, have consecrated it, far above our poor power to add or detract. The world will little note, nor long remember what we say here, but it can never forget what they did here. It is for us the living, rather, to be dedicated here to the unfinished work which they who fought here have thus far so nobly advanced. It is, rather, for us to be here dedicated to the great task remaining before us—that from these honored dead we take increased devotion to the cause for which they gave the last full measure of devotion—that we here highly resolve that these dead shall not have died in vain—that this nation, under God, shall have a new birth of freedom—and a government of the people, by the people, for the people, shall not perish from this earth.[6]

It is not so much the capacity for such statesmanlike eloquence that is essential to this quality of enabling leaders. It consists of our devotion and dedication to the process of enlarging the focus of the vision of our organizations and personal priorities which transcend the immediate circumstance no matter how successful, unsuccessful, or uncertain they may appear. Leaders who strive to enable the leadership of others to emerge seem always capable of inviting others to ask the question, "How does our present experience represent our dreams for the future?"

Strategy #4: Create Present Symbolic Models of the Future

Most effective organizational change results from our ability to imagine larger possibilities than our present circumstances reveal. This can be done symbolically and practically by developing examples, models, and prototypes of future strategies in the midst of present priorities. One example of this skill is the risk that Ford Motor Company took in the mid-1980's with the prototype of a teardrop-shaped car introduced with the Ford Thunderbird. This symbolic image or model became the standard for aerodynamic and aesthetic design for the automotive industry over the next several years. It even significantly influenced the previously square-shaped design of our Japanese competitors, whose automotive technology had outstripped our American capabilities. Prototypes for future action often symbolize through practical example new priorities, issues, and strategies for the future in ways that empower our publics, our employees, and our colleagues to think differently about their present behavior, priorities, and circumstances.

I was reminded again of this skill recently at a conference for a cross-section of hourly and salaried employees of a divisional company of a Fortune 500 conglomerate. The program was intended to promote teamwork and personal commitment to quality throughout the organization. After 200 employees had been involved in this personal educational commitment process, the divisional vice president took a strikingly symbolic action that galvanized people's personal responsibility and commitment to the values which the conference was intended to elicit throughout the plants and facilities of the organization. Typically, at the close of the program, the divisional executive would return for the last few hours in order to receive and respond to the individual commitments of his work force. One conference schedule made it impossible for him to attend this event, in his stead he sent an eloquent and articulate technical hourly worker who had distinguished himself for his personal leadership abilities earlier in previous conferences. He sent this hourly leader to officially represent him in receiving the commitment of his co-workers. Little had to be said concerning the vice president's commitment to a team approach for a shared organizational future and shared values. The presence of this hourly worker spoke volumes more than the conference ever could have. This experience has become a symbolic story and event signaling future change and commitments throughout that division of the large corporation.

A further example of this ability to create symbolic models of future values in the present was demonstrated by a midwestern nonprofit conference center which sought to expand their mission and agenda to include a comprehensive approach to lifelong learning to the public. Rather than choosing a future strategy of being "facility-driven," subject to the flux in the economy as a training facility hosting the educational events of other organizations, they adopted an ambitious strategic plan to create their own training opportunities not only for regional organizations and professional groups but also for individuals and families in their local market area. They developed a new direction for the organization under the umbrella of a center for lifelong learning. When presenting this strategy to the board of trustees, the management team was hard-pressed to find examples across the nation of such an ambitious endeavor. However, in their strategic planning process they had defined two prototypes for the future to serve as symbolic models of their future commitment to lifelong learning. One was the development of a daycare center, and the other was a joint venture with a hospital for an older adult day care facility. Immediately when these two priorities were presented to the trustees as representative examples of program priorities of the future, the concept of "lifelong learning" took hold. Far beyond conceptual abilities to imagine new strategic opportunities, these two practical program priorities embodied the image of what a center for lifelong learning could, and would, be for this facility.

Leaders committed to enabling and empowering their constituents to develop their own leadership capabilities insist on asking the question, "How can our future vision be modeled in the present?"

Strategy #5: Understand and Use the Authentic Power of Influence

The subject of power and authority is integral to the development of leadership among others. Often the power of position, expertise, or personal charisma blocks the expression of leadership among others particularly as they tentatively seek to discover, refine, and focus their own sense of perspective and priority. Skillful leaders, dedicated to the process of enabling and empowering the leadership of others, rely primarily upon the authentic power of influence.

Several years ago I had the opportunity to attend a management seminar at the University of Michigan. I shall never forget the opening address by one of the main presenters of the conference. He used a striking analogy to describe the role of power in effective organizations. He indicated that when we achieve the position of authority over others we are given an imaginary bag of power chips which sits on our desks. Power chips have rules, the presenter explained, but there are only two. Whenever you use them, you lose them; and when they are gone, none can be replaced. His point was clear: that the exercise of power in a direct and authoritative way diminishes the capacity for others to develop their own ability to lead.

Spiritual writer Henri Nouwen tells a story about spiritual leadership which aptly applies to our discussion. The story describes three leaders who were sent to a remote agricultural community to lead them to a new consciousness. The agricultural community was surrounded by a patch of watermelons. In the story, the community had an innate fear of watermelons since they did not plant them, nor were they able to control their growth in the environment. When the first leader was sent to the rural community, noting the fears of his followers for the watermelons, he quickly had the fields destroyed and burned. He was celebrated as a heroic leader until next year when the watermelon vines grew back again after the spring rains. His people's fears were heightened since it was his direct use of the power of fire that had destroyed the watermelons. They drove him from their land.

The second leader who was sent to this agricultural village decided to demonstrate his leadership abilities by consuming mass amounts of watermelons himself. Leading the community to the edge of their village, he demonstrated his capacity to consume and enjoy watermelons without ill consequence. However, after several months had passed, the fears of the community members grew again, and they developed the belief that his consumption of the watermelons would cause him to internalize the evil and become evil himself, so they drove him from the village.

The third leader who was sent to the village, upon observing the fears of the community for the watermelon patch, asked them questions in order to understand, to refocus, and to get behind their predisposition and anxieties. After several months of discussion and communication, he brought them to the watermelon patch, led them into the maze of vines, and one by one, invited each of them to consume the watermelons together. Their fears were transformed collectively, through the joy they found in the sweet taste of watermelons.

While this is a simple representation of the authentic use of power, it conveys a message that true leadership is not about being stylistically directive or nondirective, or advocating authority in the face of resistance to change, or necessarily asking others to change their vision. It is an invitation to others to express and exercise their own use of power in transcending their present boundaries, enlarging their comfort zones, and examining their fears. Leaders who understand and use the authentic power of influence to empower leadership in others always ask themselves and others the question, "How can I develop the power of others to choose the behavior and action I seek to engender?"

Strategy #6: Emphasize Action and Outcomes as the Expression of Commitment

The process of developing and empowering leadership has often been reduced to some elusive or magical properties of charismatic individuals. But the true measure of developing and empowering leadership is measured in our ability to effectively demonstrate personal, public, and organizational actions and priorities that reflect new levels of commitment to the future. Behavior is the truest measure of commitment and values. Organizations and individuals who seek the process of change or renewal are committed to demonstrating in practice new behaviors which reflect their values, their meaning, and their personal and public priorities. The old adage, "actions speak louder than words," may be rephrased, "actions are the only expression of our true commitments."

Not long ago I was part of a consulting team hired by the Texaco Corporation to work with a cross-section of employees throughout the organization to engender a commitment to individual entrepreneurship and a passion for quality. As a result of one of the conferences, participants left very emotional with their new sense of authority, responsibility, and expectation to demonstrate new commitments in their individual work priorities.

Their newfound strategy of personal commitment to quality was tested in a rather dramatic way. One of the plants within the sponsoring division was installing a new computer regulatory system for natural gas production. The line workers preferred the product of one vendor, while management preferred the product of a more prominent national vendor. When hearing about the conflict in the contract process, the prominent national vendor took their marketing strategy directly to the Chairman of the Board, who had a personal relationship with senior management of the vendor company. Plant employees feared organizational pressure would be created on the local plant to purchase the product of the prominent and recognized vendor. As a result of their conference learning, a team of management and non-management personnel in the plant took it upon themselves to pursue the matter further. They were convinced that while the product of the national vendor was worthwhile and had been the lowest bidder, greater capabilities for the future lay in the less prominent and more service-oriented second vendor.

Considering this purchase was a relatively small contract for a large corporation such as Texaco, it is amazing that such intensity and involvement was created around this symbolic action. The divisional vice president flew into the plant to meet with the local work team to understand and assess their views. Based on this meeting, he asked them to develop a strategy that he would take to the corporate officials of Texaco in order to advocate their viewpoints. As a result of their efforts, the plant workers were able to convince the divisional vice president, who convinced the regional president, who convinced the Chairman of the Board that the choice of vendor of #2 was a more valuable contribution to the plant at this time in their organizational history. What is even more striking about this example is the influence of those plant employees to get this commitment changed in the face of stated policy to accept low preferred bidders, which the nationally prominent vendor represented.

The impact of this one commitment in action far transcended all of the training and consulting our group had provided to influence a personal commitment to quality in the Texaco Corporation. The story of this event quickly was passed through the ranks of employees, both management and non-management, as an example of their quality process in action. The positive ramifications of this perhaps far superseded the direct benefit of the new purchase of technology.

Leadership is a performative virtue. The act of leading is directly involved in demonstrating behavioral commitments that reflect our new values. In this case, the commitment of the Texaco Corporation to the personal process of quality at the rank and file level was put to the test and successfully matured. Leaders dedicated to empowering and generating leadership among others are consistently asking themselves and others the question, "How can we act consistently to represent our commitments and values?"

Strategy #7: Understand That Leadership Is Personally and Collectively Transformative

The relationship of individuals to organizations is a far more comprehensive riddle to address than this book can ever master. However, the greater organizational complexity we face in our leadership roles, the greater our experience and awareness of personal limits becomes. In the face of adversity, most leaders fail in the overuse or overextension of their strengths. Wise leaders come quickly to the realization of personal limits. In the face of present inabilities, we often seek to push harder in what we have already learned, failing to take into account learnings that come through our inadequacies and our limitations. In the face of this necessary dilemma of leadership, the learning for leaders involves relying on the skills of others to accomplish new goals, strategies, and priorities. This process of personal transformation is integral to the maturation of leaders. Once our careers have advanced to the point where we have experienced the full extension of our gifts and talents, we begin to quickly realize the skills that brought us to our present success are not the skills that will lead us to future experiences of reward, satisfaction, and achievement. It becomes necessary then for us to rely on the abilities of others to achieve our goals.

The greater the organizational challenges, therefore, the greater the opportunities for personal growth and leadership. Our human development is enhanced by the experience of limits which corrects our perceptions, transcends our strengths, and requires us to rely upon the ability of others in order to succeed. Mahatma Gandhi was once asked who had been the most formidable opponent that he had ever encountered in his political challenge to liberate India from Great Britain. He thoughtfully replied, "I have met no greater adversary than the demon within." Gandhi understood that the limits of our own strengths and our personalities are perhaps the greatest obstacles to moving forward in leadership. This process of developing our undeveloped side is a necessary ingredient to enabling leadership among others. It is when the skillful, competent, expert leader relies upon the judgment, expertise, and experience of his or her subordinates, peers, and colleagues that the process of transformation occurs. Leadership, therefore, is a personal and a collective transformative process. In the end it should be unclear whose ultimate efforts were required for the organization, group, or person to succeed. Leadership is by nature a collective effort of personal and group transformation. In the face of complexity, difficulty, and uncertainty, effective leaders rely less on their own skills and abilities and seek to draw on the process of enlisting the abilities of others through the process of inquiry. This process helps us develop our limitations in ways in which they become strengths.

For example, the skillful strategic CEO who is capable of imagining new visions and opportunities for his organization may require the experience of a much more stable and well-grounded administrative chief financial officer to counterbalance his innovation, drive, and enthusiasm. The process of transformation in leadership brings both leader and constituency to the quick realization that the purpose of leadership is not only to achieve the goal or purpose at hand, but to become more whole and complete in the process. Leaders who seek to enable other leaders to develop their skills and abilities are willing to be subject to this process of personal and collective transformation. The willingness to examine our own limitations of perception and ability and to extend our trust in others for the success of our organizations in the future is a fundamental ingredient of empowering leaders. Skillful leaders who seek to enable and empower others in the process of leadership continuously ask the question, "How does our present experience bring us closer to knowing ourselves?"

In this chapter we have examined a conceptual model for the development of leadership among others. In addition, we have suggested several fundamental organizational strategies which summarize the literature of many volumes in describing behaviorally the strategies which empower others to lead. In the end, the process of empowering leadership brings together the two fundamental drives of human energy: our desire to be competent and effective at work and our desire to be accepted and loved in relationships. The process of empowerment is no more or less than the commitment to develop not only the circumstances and strategies at hand, but the people involved in the process of leadership. Once a skillful leader decides to adopt these two agendas as his immediate priority, the process of empowerment becomes far less a technique or a tool and more of a life commitment to genuine human transformation.

Warren Bennis and Burt Nanus in their creative book *Leaders, Strategies for Taking Charge* summarize well the activities and strategies of leaders who empower their followers to greater service.

In all of this, the role of the leader is much like that of a conductor of an orchestra. The real work of the organization is done by the people in it, just as the music is produced only by the members of the orchestra. The leader, however, serves a crucial role of seeing that the right work gets done at the right time, that it flows together harmoniously, and that the overall performance has the proper pacing, coordination, and desired impact on the outside world. The great leader, like the great orchestra conductor, calls forth the best that is in the organization. Each performance is a learning experience which enables the next understanding to be that much more effective—"more right" for the time, place, and instruments at hand. And if in the long the organization succeeds, it doesn't all detract from the quality of everyone else's work to suggest that it was the leader who made it possible for the organization to learn how to perfect his contribution.[7]

The art of developing and empowering others to lead is a simple commitment and dedication to the personal, relational, and organizational development of those we serve. It is only when we master these three priorities simultaneously that we can truly claim a commitment to the empowerment of others in finding their skills, abilities, and visions to serve as leaders of the future for our organizations.

Chapter VI

Organizational Leadership: Productivity and Prosperity

The purpose of organizational leadership is to create cultures of commitment versus cultures of complacency. In essence, this means focusing on what is essential to the development of an organization and its future. The secret of organizational leadership requires focusing strategic attention on the variables that are often intangible in order to achieve what is essential. Cultures of commitment are largely built upon highlighting discreet elements of building organizational strategy and the commitment to them by key organizational members, publics, and employees. This approach to organizational development suggests paying far more attention to the variables which create organizational commitment than to the static variables which create organizational complacency.

As a child I can remember spending hours walking down sidewalks focusing my attention on the cracks in between the neatly layered boxes of pavement. This memory is illustrative of the necessary ingredients for creating cultures of commitment. It is the points of interface—involving a high attention to process, communication, networking, strategic thinking, the development of our organizational missions, and building of team strategies and initiatives—that creates enthusiasm, innovation, and excellence for our organizational futures.

Figure 7 illustrates four essential organizational qualities needed to create cultures of commitment:

- **Process Driven**
- **Strategy Focused**
- **Mission Centered**
- **Team Oriented**

These four qualities create high degrees of synergy and organizational vitality indicative of organizations which have achieved expertise in their field and distinguished themselves among their competitors and their colleagues.

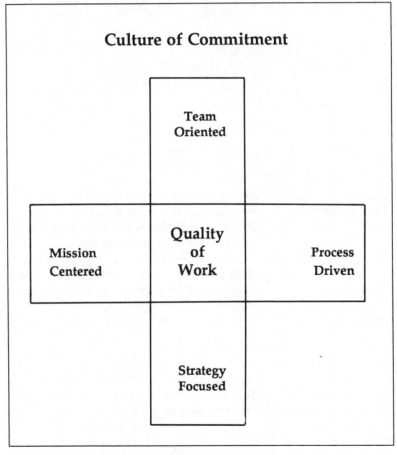

Figure 7. Culture of Commitment

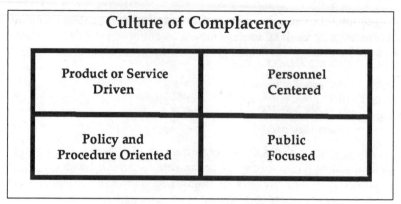

Figure 8. Culture of Complacency

Figure 8 identifies the traditional ingredients which usually constitute the fundamental areas of focus for a culture of complacency. They include:

- **Product or Service Driven**
- **Personnel Centered**
- **Policy and Procedure Oriented**
- **Public Focused**

These four static components to an organization are the major focus of attention by key leaders in a complacent organization. The problem with leading through these well-paved areas of organizational life is that we traditionally hire other employees with specialized expertise to manage these organizational dimensions. The key skill then of organizational development, and therefore strategic leadership, is not so much to duplicate these areas of attention, but to carefully orchestrate their interface, communication, and mutual enhancement in the advancement of our organizations.

We are inundated with recent literature in the field of management development and leadership education which continually has a bias in favor of one or more of these four elements of a culture of complacency. Product driven or service driven organizations are those which pay intense or exclusive attention to their output. This view of organizational development is represented by strategies that indicate the need to pay attention to "measured" quality at the expense of other variables in organizational life. While we do not intend to suggest that quality is an unimportant variable in organizational leadership, inordinate attention by top leaders to the product or service which an organization delivers sends a signal to employees and constituents that measuring or quantifying value is the driving force. This reinforces doubt among the work force in their inherent skills and abilities to produce, develop, and manage products and services with autonomy and innovation.

A second dimension of a culture of complacency is organizational leadership which focuses inordinate attention on the management of personnel. This organizational leader works too intensely at the personnel systems, role definitions, and personal dynamics of leadership. One university department with which I was recently consulting went to great lengths to describe in minute detail the various strengths and limits that they had demonstrated in a personality profile leadership assessment. This concentrated attention to the personalities and personal dynamics of personnel in an organization creates the impression that the motivating criteria for excellence is smooth, human communications and mutual understanding above all else. Once again, while these variables are important to organizational development, they are not central for strategic leadership since they ignore the interface of the organization team with other elements of organizational vitality. Does a harmonious university faculty automatically teach better? Could a university department of diverse and occasionally conflicting views stimulate learning more effectively?

A third emphasis of organizational leadership which contributes to a culture of complacency is overarching attention to policies and procedures. Policies and procedures in any healthy organization are continually out-of-date! As quickly as they are formulated they become antiquated. While not to suggest that policies and procedures are unimportant in the development of an organization, we have the benefit in most cases of technical experts who are able to assist us, both internally and externally to the organization, in formulating our basic principles and assumptions into these structured constructs. Undue attention to these management systems by key strategic leaders sends the message to an organization's constituency that stability, order, and structure are the prevailing values.

A fourth, highly visible dimension of organizational leadership that has received heavy attention recently is intense attention to an organization's publics. This has been often represented in phrases such as "market driven" and "customer focused" organizational development. Focusing intense attention and understanding an organization's constituents, customers, and employees is vital to service standards. However, it is important to recognize that attitudes, preferences, and priorities change regularly and are greatly influenced by current conditions in the economy, prevailing public confidence in politics, and the trends of other providers of our goods and services in addressing the very same needs we seek to satisfy. Great leaders and strategic organizations actually anticipate or even create needs and demands among their constituents. Strategic leadership identifies and responds to the unspoken or unexpressed need that represents true inner value to their public. An overemphasis on responding to immediate public perception or public acceptance can serve as a detriment to lasting and effective organizational development.

The purpose of this chapter is not to suggest that these four traditional lenses of viewing organizational leadership are inappropriate. In fact, they are important to the health, vitality, structure, and maintenance of any system of influence. However, leaders intending to move their organizations to greater levels of consistency, excellence, and dedication cannot afford to spend undue time and attention focusing on only these four quadrants of organizational life. Instead, organizational leaders who intend to create greater "cultures of commitment" must focus on those qualities that *integrate* these four quadrants of organizational development.

Organizations which appear to rise above the tide of present conditions in their environment seem to have leaders who are:

- **Process Intensive**
- **Mission Centered**
- **Strategy Focused**
- **Team Oriented**

These elements are prevalent among cultures of commitment within all organizations in both public and private sector businesses, as well as social service organizations.

A cultural blindspot of organizational thinking contends that business leadership and public leadership require different spheres of influence and different areas of attention and management. This is indicative of a complacency model of existence (placing undue attention on the product, the personnel, the policy, or the individual public or market). These characteristics are organization-specific centers of influence which do change from one organization to the next. However, the fundamental and enduring qualities of organizational leadership are those which transcend these limited variables and therefore are consistent, effective, and creatively implemented in all organizations. Consequently, we will use examples from both public and private sector organizations to illustrate these four principles of cultures of commitment in practice.

Process Intensive Organizations

Process intensive organizations understand the shared impact of the many variables that coalesce to form an integrated approach to philosophy, service, and organizational commitment. These variables have to do with managing the dynamic relationships between the product or service the organization provides, its external publics or customers, its staff and employees, and its organizational procedures. *Managing the process of interface* among these variables is one of the fundamental ingredients of organizations with a high commitment to process.

Jorgenson Honda in East Clarendon, Vermont is an organization which has received the number one rating in New England and the number six rating in the United States for service as a Honda dealership. Jorgenson Honda was recently reviewed in an unpublished case study by Organizational Resources International concerning their philosophy of organizational excellence. Robert Pye, Service Manager, illustrates their attention to the interface of the key variables of product and customer by describing a new reality for his attention as an organizational leader.

> Finding the real problem is not always as easy as you might think it would be with a car, too. Quite often there will be specific trouble, a mechanical thing that is involved with the car, but that necessarily doesn't mean that's what the customer needs to be fixed. You have to fix the customer as much as you do the car. That all happens because there is confusion on what the prob-

lem is. It may not be a problem. It may be a perception difficulty. It may be a problem with how something is supposed to operate. So you really have to hear what the trouble is, and it might not necessarily mean that there is something wrong with the brakes. It might be that Mrs. Jones doesn't understand or whatever. So, you really have to be sure you are addressing what the person is concerned with . . . not necessarily get the car in the air and identify a specific mechanical compromise. You have to fix what is wrong![1]

A second skill of organizations which have a high commitment to process intensity is the energy in which they invest in developing *conceptual models for thinking and analysis.* Conceptual models can include commonly held processes or technical resources such as approaches to problem solving, planning, and strategic thinking that can be employed by members within an organization in order to better understand the immediate circumstances in the task at hand. They can also include symbolic but practical working images that represent an organization's values. One of the practical images conveyed by Clarence Jorgenson, owner of Jorgenson Honda, is that each employee should "place themselves or one of their family members in the position of their customers in problem solving the immediate circumstance." Brian Fothergill, a mechanic, illustrates his application of this personalized conceptual model with the following example:

> The first year I worked here I had a job I was doing where a little 30-cent plastic door clip was missing, and the Parts Department didn't have one. And nobody would ever know if it wasn't there or not. And I told him (Jorgy) about it and I said, 'who's ever going to know?' And he said, 'I will.' So he asked the woman to come back and spent an hour taking the door apart and putting in a 30-cent clip. It gives you the underlying idea that's the way things are going to be done. You're part of the crew, that's the way you're going to do it. Everybody here's the same way.[2]

Brian Fothergill was able to analyze an acute need in his immediate job priority by calling forth the image of placing himself or his family in the place of a customer. This conceptual image or model instilled in the work force by the owner of Jorgenson Honda has paid valuable dividends to their success in customer service.

Conceptual models include analytic tools that can be used consistently in an organization to find a common language or nomenclature for group problem solving. Many successful techniques for total quality management teach common structured approaches to problem solving, planning, and strategic thinking at all levels of an organization. This serves to break the language barrier between different units of an organization by finding common vehicles for communicating their problems, concerns, and interests in the future development of the organization.

A third element of process intensive organization is the role of *senior leaders serving as facilitators and animators* versus technical managers and experts. Clarence Jorgenson demonstrates this facilitative approach to senior leadership in discussing his role in the organization.

> I think, and the whole industry agrees with me, that there isn't any other automobile dealer in the country who wouldn't rather be selling Hondas. It's an outstanding product. There's not a car in the world that's a better automobile than this at any price. It just blows my mind with the quality and attention to detail in our product. It's just hands down superior to anything you can buy . . . so we've got that.[3]

But Clarence Jorgenson doesn't attribute success of his dealership to the product alone. He attributes it to his organizational philosophy which he developed working in a cement company in Detroit in his youth.

> Every human being, whether a sweeper or on the kiln room floor or president of the corporation, in his own house, in his own environment, was king! And nobody has a right to give him any shaken confidence in his ego. He may not be as wealthy; he may not be as intelligent; he may not be as capable; but in his personal environment, he is the king. . . . I think that success of any business, the most important resource that any company has, is people. So essentially I've tried to staff my organization with people who share my philosophy toward this kind of morality and dedication to quality. And I was able to do that.[4]

Clarence Jorgenson gives little attention to the specific product lines which his organization provides; he knows they are superior.

Also, while he is attentive to the personnel in his organization, he doesn't focus exclusively on organizing or managing human systems among members of his organization. Jorgenson spends little time speaking of his customers or their changes in market priorities, interests, or consumer tastes. He concentrates his energy and attention almost exclusively on process intensive values. Jorgenson Honda is an example of an organization with a high commitment to the interface and synergy among product, public, employee, and organizational procedures and philosophy. It is this mix of organizational elements and their influence upon one another which he considers his primary commitment. Secondly, Clarence Jorgenson has been able to develop simple and practical images and conceptual models for common understanding and evaluating immediate circumstances and problems which have infused the thinking and behavior of his employees. Thirdly, Clarence Jorgenson sees himself as a facilitator and animator of excellence in his organization. Other senior leaders focus the individual dimensions of product line, market, customer service, and personnel. Jorgenson Honda is an example of a process intensive organization paying far more attention to what falls in between the cracks than focusing on the boxes of traditional organizational development which are always present.

Mission Centered

A second quality of strategic leadership among organizations that create a high culture of commitment is their insistence and passion for focus on the core expression of their mission. These organizations have a consistent propensity to make decisions about their immediate priorities, plans, and future expansions which support and strengthen their original mission and basic purpose for existence. Organizations which have a high priority on mission centered decisions demonstrate four skills in their organizational practices. First, they are consistently *focused on their core expertise,* undiluted by immediate financial concerns, resource-driven opportunities or unplanned innovation. Secondly, they are *aware of their distinctive contribution* which other organizations, competitors, or collaborators are unable to match. Thirdly, they are able to *articulate the enduring value* of their contribution which transcends the generations of its history and tradition. Lastly, organizations with a high commitment to a mission-centered philosophy are able to create a *pervading passion for goals* among their internal and external constituents.

St. Vincent Hotel in Dayton, Ohio was founded in December 1985 by the Dayton District Council of the Society of St. Vincent De Paul. The organization opened its doors to the public to serve the homeless of the Dayton area and the surrounding environments. Its stated mission is as follows:

> To provide emergency overnight shelter services to homeless men, women, and children during the period of their crisis in order to assist them in regaining their rightful place in the community. All are served regardless of race, color, creed, age, or sex . . . staff and volunteers alike treat the guests with the dignity and respect which is their due as children of God . . . to convince them of their importance as individuals and thereby to improve their self-image and their self-respect. Ancillary services conducive to and supportive of physical and mental hygiene are provided. Among these are counseling, distribution of free clothing, and purchasing of prescription medicines.[5]

St. Vincent Hotel has been the recipient of enormous public recognition and attention in only six years of its organizational history. This recognition is a result of their high commitment to a mission centered philosophy which pervades their organizational leadership. The first element of mission centered philosophy which St. Vincent Hotel demonstrates is its *consistent focus on its core expertise.* St. Vincent Hotel exists primarily and fundamentally to provide temporary emergency shelter for the homeless. In the growing years of its early organizational success, St. Vincent's has avoided opportunities for expansion into broad ancillary social services such as education, job training, case management, and extensive mental health and therapeutic services. Despite the opportunity for outside financial assistance in providing these additional services, St. Vincent's staff and administration have stayed close to their core priority of serving as a homeless shelter, working in partnership with other established organizations to address the human needs of their clients. They have avoided the temptation to dilute their mission by directly addressing these broader social needs themselves.

Secondly, St. Vincent Hotel demonstrates its mission centered philosophy in its intense *commitment to its unique and distinctive contribution.* While there is a need for permanent housing and semi-permanent shelters for many homeless people, St. Vincent has adhered strictly to its philosophy of temporary emergency shelter. It has resisted the temptation in its organizational development to provide continuous shelter for its homeless guests. Its policies and procedures assure that homeless individuals return to the street each morning and may not continue their stay beyond several consecutive nights in order to reinforce the message that their service is intended as temporary shelter and that the rightful place for their clients is to become active and contributing members of society once their immediate economic, social, or psychological needs are addressed. While this may appear to be a spartan delineation, it is an excellent example of a commitment to a distinctive contribution in adopting a mission centered approach to organizational development.

St. Vincent Hotel has struggled during its organizational evolution with self-awareness of its *enduring value and purpose for existence.* St. Vincent's Hotel sees itself as a permanent organizational contributor to the well-being of society in Dayton as a whole as well as its neighborhood community. It once resisted attempts by a large prestigious university to take over its prime downtown spot for a local campus expansion. Part of their "political success" in avoiding relocation is the public recognition of its enduring value to society and the economy of Dayton which no other organization is capable of fulfilling in the same way.

Expansion opportunities for St. Vincent Hotel have been many. However, its staff and administration have consistently returned to their primary focus of expertise when they assess such options. One recent expansion, which failed, was the attempt of St. Vincent Hotel to become a recycler of paper products in order to employ guests of the hotel and generate revenue for the hotel's operation. In retrospect, the administrators admitted they had expanded beyond their original purpose in this new enterprise. However, they have succeeded very well in starting a second level emergency relief service, working in conjunction with outside organizations to provide a community living experience for people who are in transitional work settings while they learn new occupational skills.

In the first case of recycling, they over-extended themselves beyond their primary purpose and perceived public value of providing shelter to the homeless. Other organizations can, and do, provide the service of recycling. In the second case, St. Vincent's Hotel stayed close to its original purpose and public value of providing emergency shelter. They cooperated, however, with other agencies to provide a temporary community living situation while job training was provided by others. Staying close to their enduring value and primary purpose of existence has contributed to their success in this second venture while the first venture failed.

The remaining element of mission centered organizations is *the pervading passion for their goals* they are able to create among their internal and external publics. St. Vincent Hotel provides services based upon multi funding sources. It is able to receive financial assistance from local community agencies; direct contributions from a vast pool of donors; an enormous resource bank of volunteer efforts including technical professionals in mental health and medical fields; and the sale of donated clothing by their original sponsor, the St. Vincent De Paul Society.

During consultation with members of the staff of St. Vincent Hotel, it became apparent that a critical issue in their future organizational development would be managing a pool of volunteers which far exceeded the demand and the requirements for their service. The capabilities of this organization to generate unsolicited funds from the community, as well as high commitments of contributed services and volunteer efforts indicates their ability to create a pervading passion for their clients and their services. Interviews with their staff reveal that each one of them sees their work at St. Vincent Hotel not only as a personal work of service, but as an opportunity to fulfill their own commitment to humanity as a professional within their chosen field. Staff members can be found to serve their guests with equal pleasure in cooking a meal, making a bed, providing short-term counseling, or referring them to a mental health service in the larger community. It is this passion for their mission which is indicative of an organization able to stay focused and centered on its primary mission and purpose as the foundation of its existence.

St. Vincent Hotel demonstrates the four hallmarks of an organization driven by a passionate commitment to its mission. First, they are able to focus almost exclusively on their core expertise of providing emergency shelter for the homeless. Second, they remain aware of their distinctive contribution by providing emergency shelter without diffusion into other human services or extended residential treatment of their client population. Third, they are able to represent to their public the enduring value and purpose of their existence and achieve their commitment to the total human health of their client population. This enduring value of their efforts is developed through volunteer contributions of time and effort—through networking with other community agencies—and through partnerships in projects in which they provide their expertise in housing management in support of the expertise of others, such as job training. Fourth, St. Vincent Hotel is able to generate a pervading passion among its internal and external constituents for its mission to the homeless. This is demonstrated in its extraordinary ability to generate funds from diverse private and public sources, as well as to develop a volunteer core which far exceeds their need for resources. They are an excellent example of an organization able to transcend the immediate circumstances of diminished resources for social concerns by staying centered on their mission and its public value for society.

Strategy Focused

Organizations and their leaders who are capable of creating a high degree of intensity and commitment in their organizations are able to remain strategy focused. These systems have a capacity to focus not only on their current conditions and their future expectations, but to identify the relationship between current experience and future expectation that must exist in the present in order to succeed in the future.

There are three critical skills which contribute to an organization's ability to maintain its focus on strategy. The first is *proactive planning*. Proactive planning involves the capacity of an organization and its key strategic leaders to accurately identify and synthesize the immediate needs and conditions of an organization (among its publics, customers, suppliers, and employees) with the expected future priorities of the organization for success. Proactive approaches to planning differ from reactive and projective approaches to planning. Reactive planning is content to satisfy the immediate need of the customer, the client, or the consumer at hand. Reactive planners are consistently "chasing the market" or identifying what the client needs now in order to provide their services. As pointed out earlier in the chapter, the problem with this expression of organizational leadership is that it creates a victim-oriented cycle of leadership responding to external organizational conditions which are often beyond their control. This is particularly debilitating in human service organizations with a high reliance on external sources of funding for support: they lose their autonomy and self-determination.

Projective models of planning have equally problematic consequences for organizational leadership. Projective planning is so consumed with the future vision that it is unable to focus on the immediate circumstance and develop the necessary links and strategic plans to assist an organization in the interim steps necessary to succeed with future goals. Projective planning is highly speculative, entrepreneurial, and focuses on a "what if" approach to organizational development with high risk, small chances to succeed, and often an underestimated assessment of the immediate consequences of failure. However, proactive planning is committed to linking an organization's present circumstances and priorities with its future vision in strategically sound ways to arrive at a secure future.

The second characteristic of strategically focused organizations is their ability to *identify extended timeframes for accomplishment.* This skill has to do with the art of projecting expected deadlines for future scenarios to be successful in completing organizational plans. The concept of defining clear timeframes for accomplishment is important in order to build confidence among employees and the internal and external publics of an organization. It is obviously important to know when a new product, service, or enhancement of the immediate priorities of an organization is due to succeed. This forecast for future accomplishment and the ability to accurately anticipate these timeframes is a key ingredient of strategically focused organizations.

The third dimension of strategically focused organizations is their ability to *expand existing resources* in order to fill anticipated internal and external organizational requirements. This commitment to expanded resources is demonstrated in the ability to name in the present desired techniques and technologies that will be helpful to mark and measure future success.

Donald L. Runkle of General Motors/Hughes Technology is an excellent example of a leader who was able to demonstrate a strategy focus for commitment in the acquisition of Hughes Aircraft by General Motors. His vision for General Motors/Hughes Technology was outlined in a presentation on November 7, 1989 to employees and technicians formerly of Hughes Aircraft. His remarks illustrate the three elements of strategic focus: *proactive planning, extended timeframes for accomplishment, and resource expansion.* These characterize successful ventures for developing cultures of commitment in organizations.

Donald Runkle demonstrated *proactive planning* in his assessment of the future conditions concerning the takeover of Hughes Aircraft and their future contribution to the automotive industry. He developed the following scenario for employees of Hughes Aircraft:

> Now I recognize that most of you in the audience are from the aerospace industry. So let me give you my perspective of some of the realities in the car and truck side of the business these days and some thoughts that might help guide your thinking about cars and trucks. First, it seems that the nature of the defense business that you are experts in is changing and going towards less defense. The world is tired of fighting. At the same time, the car business is increasing in its complexity, its quest for technology, and its competitiveness. Again, you are experts in these kinds of things also. So I think you need to decide what the 'new' Hughes looks like in light of a declining defense budget and an almost desperate need by the parent GM for increased capability. I think you need to invest your money and people in the car business; it's exciting, it's got lots of opportunities, it's growing world-wide, and it's big.[6]

In his representation of the existing market conditions of the automotive and defense industry, Mr. Runkle created a proactive relationship between the present conditions of Hughes Aircraft and the future opportunities that existed for them within the General Motors Corporation. He did so, however, by linking them in the present with the key strategic action. His challenge created an expectancy to be proactive in applying their past and present skills and technology to future challenges and opportunities. This link of a new application for existing experience represents the proactive planning necessary for organizations to be strategy focused.

Second, in the evolution of his philosophy for General Motors/Hughes Technology, Donald Runkle was able to identify the *necessary future timeframe* for the accomplishment of the present vision. When his presentation was given in 1989, he projected a timeframe for the future success of Hughes Technology of five years. He did so in the following way. "You need to think about timing in the car business. Our timeframe is five years, not twenty-five years. Five years is a skirmish to you, to us it's the war."[7] Donald Runkle went on to describe his proactive visions of "romancing the car" which illustrated his immediate vision for the opportunities which existed for employees of Hughes Aircraft. In order to create a graphic urgency for employees of General Motors/Hughes Technology, Mr. Runkle distributed an imaginary "excerpt" of *Fortune Magazine* which he wrote the *day* of his speach in 1989 but dated November 7, 1994 in order to galvanize the future vision of the extended timeframe for accomplishment. The article began with this headline.

GM'S VISION FOR HUGHES CLOBBERS THE COMPETITION.

General Motors/Hughes Aircraft Technology, hooked up to General Motors cars and trucks has sent the competition packing. General Motors proves, once again, that in the car business, the best car wins.[8]

In the fictional, futuristic article, Runkle went on to describe the vision for General Motors cars which he challenged the technicians at Hughes Aircraft to complete. The article continues in this way:

It became clear that General Motors had one advantage that no other competitor had . . . Hughes Aircraft. Ford didn't have Hughes, Toyota didn't have Hughes, Honda didn't have Hughes, Nissan didn't have Hughes, and Fiat didn't have Hughes. They felt that fact should make GM cars different than all the competition. How different? Well, they decided that GM cars wouldn't have accidents, and GM cars couldn't be stolen, and GM cars would drive themselves, and GM cars wouldn't have nights, and that GM cars could see through the fog.[9]

In his imaginative scenario, Runkle was able to extend not only a timeframe for thinking about the transition of Hughes Technology into General Motors, but also to create an inspiring vision of proactive planning by anticipating specific accomplishments and resources that employees of Hughes Technology could bring to the General Motors family.

He concluded his visioning session with representatives of Hughes Technology by demonstrating the third element of strategically focused organizations—*resource expansion*.   In present challenges and opportunities, Runkle was also able to identify concrete resources and expectations to utilize the immediate skills and expertise of employees of Hughes Aircraft in addressing General Motors strategic vision.   He went on to conclude his presentation by describing the following technology requirements which would represent "the perfect car."   He suggested that these elements are the desired technological benefits and advancements that Hughes Technology could develop for General Motors.

In Search of the Perfect Car, by D. L. Runkle

- GM cars don't have accidents
- GM cars can't be stolen
- GM cars know their master
- GM cars display information when needed
- GM cars drive themselves
- GM cars don't have nights, but night vision
- GM cars see through the fog
- GM cars avoid traffic congestion
- GM cars work as offices
- GM cars like their owners
- GM cars call for help automatically
- GM cars are quiet
- GM cars don't fail
- GM cars are nice to listen to
- GM cars are comfortable[10]

Under each strategy, Mr. Runkle outlined specific technological resources that Hughes Technology could develop, such as radar accident avoidance, night visions, lane follower cruise control, electronic navigation systems, and so on. His futuring scenario of 1989 for the integration of Hughes Technology into General Motors was an excellent example of leadership which is strategy focused. In his presentation and consultation with the engineers and design specialists of Hughes Aircraft, he was able to create models of proactive planning by linking their present expertise with future opportunities in the new parent organization. Secondly, he was able to clearly identify a timeframe for success and some specific accomplishments and enhancements to the automotive industry that the design technologists of Hughes Aircraft could provide. And, thirdly, he was able to be specific in identifying unique present opportunities for the extension and expansion of resources by members of the Hughes Aircraft family to the General Motors Corporation and their customers.

These three elements of proactive planning, extended timeframes for accomplishment, and resource expansion constitute the strategic focus necessary for organizational leaders to develop cultures of commitment among their internal and external publics.

Team Oriented

Leaders capable of maintaining a high commitment to organizational development and the full expression of leadership within their systems have a deep-seated focus on team-oriented initiatives for change. Team leadership is a very popular concept brought about by the revival and insistence on quality in organizational life. In the main, quality-oriented initiatives adopt a team focus in order to bring greater unity between individuals or groups responsible for producing a product or service and the "finished results" of their efforts which are distributed to customers, constituents, and clients. However, many team-oriented development strategies focus on the motivational dimension of team building. This addresses the characteristics of group communication and relationship but often ignores the tactical and tangible skills necessary for teams to succeed.

Hands-on and functional skills of team-oriented strategies for building commitment involve *project-directed work groups* which focus on specific goals in limited timeframes to demonstrate their accomplishments and results.

Secondly, team-oriented initiatives in organizations that have a high degree of commitment often involve a *matrix involvement of responsibilities and skills* on work groups. This matrix of leadership often includes both employees and outside resources representing an inter-disciplinary expertise and multiple levels within the organization on the same task force.

A third component of team-oriented initiatives which contributes to a high commitment is *issue- and value-oriented work teams.* Focusing on isolated and specific departmental or divisional priorities is a common flaw in quality management or quality circle employee involvement systems. Many organizations have a commitment to involve team-oriented approaches to leadership, but allow teams to function primarily "within their existing comfort zones." They rely on established areas of expertise focusing exclusively upon a departmental priority or strategy rather than using the expertise and advice of interdepartmental teams working towards common issues which define quality, service, or excellence in an organization's environment. This third skill requires an organization to define its fundamental values for quality or service or value before formulating team work groups in order to complete a task or assignment. For example, in order to assess what constitutes quality care in a hospital or mental health facility, the organization in conjunction with its employees and management must define the standards of quality which will shape the work of project-related groups in developing specific improvements to address these organizational standards. One issue- or value-oriented work group might be "medical ethics," a concern for all health care units, whereas a "medical records" quality team would just perpetuate existing organizational boundaries and priorities. The absence of these value- or issue-driven organizational standards for quality contributes to the failure of team-oriented efforts. When work groups are involved in replicating expected organizational patterns of expertise they may be unable to imagine alternate or expanded standards or values that would represent success.

Effective team-oriented approaches to organizational leadership employ these three skills of *project direction, matrix involvement, and issue orientation.* Metropolitan Central School for the Arts is an inner city magnet school devoted to the education of its general students in art appreciation and to the identification and training of talented students who may desire further career development in the arts. Because of its capacity for innovation and the high level of commitment among its administration and faculty, Metropolitan Central School for the Arts was chosen as a strategically positioned school to experiment with an employee-oriented approach to site based management in the school environment. Their site based management process is a three-fold effort to provide employee training on organizational leadership, employee involvement in daily management of the school environment, and strategic planning for the future of Metropolitan Central. Site based management processes are parallel concepts to industry oriented quality management initiatives.

Since Metropolitan Central was selected as a unique experimental environment, it is interesting that most educational innovations were projected for the school by outside sources. Many initiatives in education have come from the district level and senior administration within Metropolitan Central. After several years of this intensive leadership, highly motivated and innovative teachers began to experience a culture of complacency because of their resistance to other directed innovation and ideas which on the surface were intended to enhance their team involvement. However, this created an environment of externally directed leadership in the instructional process for which teachers were the experts. This is the core motivational issue of many public institutions. The site based management consultation was intended to balance this process through a bottoms-up approach to leadership and innovation in the school.

This process has yielded many challenges to the basic assumptions about managing a school system. It became apparent that the problem with education in this city school, which may be illustrative of other city schools throughout the nation, is not the competence of the teachers but ability of the teachers to control their environment. Teachers at Metropolitan Central School for the Arts, as well as in other schools within this school district (and perhaps in many other districts throughout the United States) have little control over the allotment of their time, the content of their curriculum, or the standards of performance for their students. Teachers at Metropolitan Central have no control over the standards for their own teaching performance and have little influence over setting the expected results for pupil scores which are external indicators of success set at the district and state level. They have limited ability to effectively influence the school environment as they are constantly bombarded with announcements and inter-disciplinary innovations projected upon them by district level administration. And lastly, because of the innovative nature of the magnet environment, teachers have little control over the scheduling of their classes and the frequency of pupil attendance since students are often called out of class to attend other special programs and assignments of specialized learning.

This school is not atypical of traditional approaches to team-oriented involvement. Directives are given from above as to the nature of the initiatives, the standards of performance, and the expected criteria for success. The consultation effort with Metropolitan Central School of the Arts has been directed towards reversing this process in developing project-directed work groups of teachers to structure greater control over their instructional environment.

Under the guidance of a skillful building administration, the experiment, still in progress, is working with members of the faculty on the three elements of team-oriented leadership. Teachers, parents, and students were invited to identify the constellation of issues and improvements in their educational environment that they felt was necessary for the school's successful future. These were distilled into a series of 12 project initiatives which were further subdivided among work teams for the development of future improvements for the academic community. Teachers were invited to self select into work groups in order to participate in project-directed activities focused on their immediate concerns about increasing their control and influence over the educational environment. These *project-directed work groups* have resulted in several initiatives which now have changed the prevailing direction of innovation which was district level to administration to teacher to student. Now the reverse process occurs. Students and teachers who have to produce the desired results have more control and self-determination over the innovation process. This creates greater ownership and acceptance.

Secondly, projects under examination in this site based approach to leadership involve teachers, administrators, parents, and students collectively working on shared issues in the school environment. This *matrix approach to involvement* contrasts with the traditional view of working within departmental groups at the level of administration and teachers only in order to improve immediate problems in the school environment. This matrix approach to leadership, involving people with interdisciplinary expertise at all levels within the organization, has made for more lasting solutions by anticipating problems in implementation before new initiatives are launched. Previously, new initiatives were often later rejected because they failed to take into account the consequences upon another department within the school or another level of involvement beyond the immediate group of initiators, which was often the administrative staff.

The future of the site based management process at Metropolitan Central School will be based upon a strategic plan with an organizational structure to institutionalize these work teams in order to continue to focus on bottoms-up approaches to problem solving in the school environment. The traditional approach to strategic work teams, however, has been to align them along traditional lines of the existing organizational structure. The approach to organizing these work teams at Metropolitan Central will be based upon identifying six or seven key "qualities of excellence" in education within the school environment, which will then each be championed by one work team. Rather than work teams focusing exclusively on the interest of a specific department (for example, Math, English, or the arts), work teams will focus on specific values or standards within the environment which constitute excellence in education; for example, instructional delivery, student achievement, parent satisfaction, or interdisciplinary learning. This *issue- or value-oriented approach to team initiatives* maximizes employee, student, and parent motivation by focusing on commonly held standards of excellence in analyzing an immediate circumstance or problem. This value- or issue-oriented approach to team initiatives creates movement beyond immediate problem solving and invites a cross section of organizational publics to be involved in determining the future standards and values for the school's success.

Organizations and their leaders have the capability to expand their standards of excellence and their immediate organizational boundaries to create increasing cultures of commitment. However, these cultures of commitment have little to do with staying bound within the traditional boxes of organizational development focused on the product, the personnel, policy and procedures, or the marketplace. These four static elements of organizational life, while important, are not the driving energy which empowers strategic leaders to succeed. It is through the establishment of a culture of commitment that organizational leadership can raise the level of expectancy, performance, reward, accomplishment, and success among the various employees, clients, publics, and markets served by an organization's purpose. Cultures of commitment rely upon those elements or ingredients of organizational development which fall between the traditional cracks in our organizational plans and priorities. The higher the level of responsibility a leader holds within an organization the more accountable he or she becomes for these four qualitative elements of strategic leadership. It is only in letting go of our traditional securities and reliance on the static ingredients of organizational development that we are able to achieve higher levels of commitment among our employees and publics. The four elements of *Process Driven, Strategy Focused, Mission Centered, Team Oriented* organizations are characteristic of those systems and leaders which engender and inspire greater leadership among those they serve.

Chapter VII

Public Leadership: Our Social Legacy

Our devotion to public leadership is measured in the consistent expression of responsible care for our social welfare as demonstrated in our businesses, our organizations, and our personal lives. In our highly specialized and institutionalized culture since the industrial revolution, we have delegated responsibility to various organizational jurisdictions for specific elements of our public good. Separate institutions of government, education, business, health care, social welfare, and religion all have contributed to an isolated and independent view of human life, segmenting different dimensions of a common reality of our social legacy. However, with the advancing realization of a "one world mindset" we are beginning to realize that the long-term success of our organizations, our institutions, our families, and ourselves is contingent upon a consistent ethical leadership which transcends our personal, organizational, and public boundaries.

The globalization of even the most isolated elements of our lives pushes us closer to recognizing the need for an interdependent world view. We face the rapid expansion of the world's population. The explosion of available information for decisions is almost instantaneous. The accelerated reliance on technology creates enormous options for growth. We recognize that the scope of our environmental problems especially conserving our natural resources, has outstripped our local solutions. All of these factors indicate the need for a new understanding of our individual and corporate responsibilities to public leadership. Despite our recognition of these needs as global systems issues, we are slow to adopt business and organizational practices to support these systemic solutions. We often see the "social conscience" as an individual rather than corporate responsibility. Only system solutions will resolve systems' problems. In the deepest crevices of our consciousness we are rapidly dissolving the myth of social isolation and independence in favor of a more comprehensive and interdependent approach to life. This impacts even the simplest dimensions of our lives, such as the recycling of disposable goods in our homes. The previously held perceptions about the fine lines which distinguish our private rights and our public responsibilities, as well as those which isolate who we are as people from our social requirements are rapidly diminishing. The limits of our current institutional and segmented approaches to society leave us with knotty problems that cause us anguish in discerning the appropriate course of action for such compelling social and moral issues as the raging debate on abortion and for unanticipated moral challenges such as the right to die.

In our businesses and institutions, both in the public and private sector, the clear demarcations that have distinguished the rights of private enterprise and the responsibilities for society have greatly diminished. We find government taking an increased interest and regulatory role in all dimensions of institutional management: employment, health care, safety, and the environment. This governmental and legislative response to our social issues is perhaps not the ultimate or most effective solution for a lasting social legacy. However, in the absence of a broadly held public commitment to responsible organizational life forms, the government may be signalling or previewing a change in our consciousness that will evolve in the decades ahead.

Hopefully, gone are the days of disconcerting and discouraging organizational decisions that separate the bottom line of business and organizational priorities from our social welfare. The ethical environment which accepted the classic case where executives of Ford Motor Company chose to pay lawsuits and death benefits rather than repair faulty gas tank systems in the late 1970's models of the Ford Pinto is fading. Effective bottom line management in all sectors of society requires a comprehensive view of not only the purposes of our business, but the lasting influence of our products and the employment practices of our society.

No longer can we assume that various elements in our social welfare stand apart. Schools are bombarded with a variety of social agendas including day care, nutrition education, education for the arts, special responsibilities for the handicapped and cultural minorities, as well as health care. In addition to their increasingly demanding educative role for the basics of reading, writing, and arithmetic to keep our population competitive internationally, school administrators are inundated with a variety of social agendas that makes their efforts all the more complex. No longer can we assume that the educative and social functioning of our children is a responsibility for schools alone.

We need a shared social agenda for all of our cultural institutions. Cross-culturally we also see an enormous drive pushing the boundaries of our previously held assumptions about the segmentation of our organizations and institutions, and in the way we can and will be able to conduct our business. Global markets have dramatically expanded options in employment, the production of goods, and the distribution of services. New York City law firms are able contract secretarial work in London through the technology of fax machines at a cheaper, lower rate than they can within their own municipal boundaries. What ethical and social responsibility do we have in this case alone for employment in our own cities? This type of organizational decision creates even more reason to assess the impact of our private, personal, and organizational decisions on our public lives.

The rapid spread of our technological capabilities across previously prohibitive market boundaries has allowed small electronics manufacturers within our country to sell military parts to world powers who are a threat to our own national security. It is a strange twist of history to realize that arms sales to the Middle East created a formidable technological force for our opponents in the recent Persian Gulf War, which was in part due to our business practices in the West. With the advancing global realization of the public impact of our private and organizational lives, we also realize the disequilibrium of human and technological resources on a global scale. While we are rapidly converting midwestern farmland for business and private sector use, we are also becoming increasingly aware of the exponential rise in demand for food and supplies, the shortage of food in eastern European countries, and the extensive famines which continue within Africa and Asia. As the world population expands further, do we have the responsibility to consider the impact on the American family farm and on our world food supply in our economic development?

There is little room left for a personal or an organizational viewpoint that allows us to stand apart from the public impact of our decisions on our social agenda. The future success of our institutions, businesses, governments, educational agencies, religious organizations, and our entire social welfare is dependent upon our collective capacity to generate a commitment to public leadership. This commitment will be measured in a clear assessment of the impacts of organizational behavior on individuals and communities. It will require us also to assess the results of our organizational behavior, not only on our global economy, but on our global agendas of environment, health, safety, and distribution of human and technical resources.

Finally, the future of our public agenda will require us to assess in organizational practice the social impact of our private and institutional decisions for our public legacy. The results of our radioactive waste, our excessive use of diminishing natural resources, our increased reliance on technological approaches to solve a human conflict, and our continued evolution of the gap between the have's and the have not's in the world community, all will play a role in determining the success and failure of our institutions, our private lives, and our governmental agencies. There will be no standing alone in the face of the compelling social requirement that public leadership become a norm for all sectors of society and that all people claim the responsibilities and priorities of leadership.

Consistently throughout this book we have intentionally blurred the lines between the different contexts and priorities among governmental, business, educational, social, and religious institutions. The barriers and distinctions in our organizational practices are less compelling in the future as we face a common social agenda and a global mindset. In fact, our institutions have far fewer differences in the practice of leadership than much of the literature has represented to date. It is the contention of this book that authentic leadership transcends institutional boundaries and segments of society. Authentic leadership is a unitive whole in the comprehensive expression of the care and concern we share as individuals and as organizations for our private, public, and organizational futures.

There are four dimensions of public leadership represented in Figure 9 which are incumbent upon all organizations to demonstrate in their practices. Organizations sensitive and responsive to a long-term future for themselves and society demonstrate a commitment to:

- **Cooperative Partnerships**
- **Consistent Organizational Values**
- **Future Modeling**
- **Environmental and Social Analysis**

These will be evident in day-to-day decisions and strategic priorities of organizations demonstrating responsible public leadership.

Figure 9. Qualities of Public Leadership

Cooperative Partnerships are strategic alliances which transcend traditional organizational boundaries of influence to provide alternative approaches to shared and renewed resources, the development of new resources, and the development of goods and services for greater social benefit.

Consistent Organizational Values imply a commitment to well-articulated and comprehensive standards for assessing strategic decisions in light of personnel, various publics, clients and markets, the present and future of our society as a whole, and the global future of this planet earth.

Public leadership involves *Future Modeling* by innovative organizations in their imaginative evolution of scenarios for their future beyond short- and immediate-term market analysis and public opinion. This involves assessment of long-term projections of demographics, environmental impact, global trends, and cultural influences which will shape and be shaped by our present organizational practices. Organizations with a commitment to future modeling continuously redesign and reinvent the organization in small ways in the present to respond to the future priorities.

Lastly, *Environmental and Social Analysis* is demonstrated by creative leaders and organizations who assess both the immediate and the long-term influences their decisions have on our local and global environmental resources; and our social and community concerns of neighborhood, institutional priorities, and employment.

Each of these four dimensions of public leadership—*Cooperative Partnerships, Consistent Organizational Values, Future Modeling,* and *Environmental and Social Analysis*—will be examined with local as well as global examples to stress the significance for future organizational priorities. As we deepen our understanding of these four dimensions of public leadership in the balance of this chapter, examples will be drawn from very specialized local institutions which transcend only one sector of society. While some of these local examples may seem at first reading to be mundane, they are purposely chosen. First, many books on leadership and organizational theory rely on sophisticated national and international examples to make their point. This often leaves the impression that there is little that can be done in our own institutions and organizations to achieve the same results. Second, these smaller examples of public leadership represent the efforts which are occurring in communities throughout this country, lending some hope and credibility to the belief that we are reawakening a commitment to public leadership as part of the fabric of all institutions, both in the public and private sectors.

Cooperative Partnerships

Those strategic alliances which enable our organizations to work in cooperation across sectors of society and with previous competitors in order to provide a new product, good, or service are examples of cooperative partnerships. Cooperative partnerships deliver not only a direct benefit to the bottom line and to the purposes of our organizations, but achieve a wider social good at the same time by maximizing our use of resources, both human and technical. These partnerships create greater opportunity, advancement, and care for the total social fabric.

In a recent study conducted for a regional association of chambers of commerce, Woolpert Consultants (a midwestern engineering, architectural, and urban planning firm) identified five models of cooperation among public organizations used throughout this country to advance our social agenda. These models of cooperation link both private and public sector institutions, especially government, with local businesses, in the advancement of the quality of life for society, especially in metropolitan areas. Their survey of the planning literature and experiments of metropolitan communities throughout the United States leads them to conclude:

> The recent planning literature is filled with descriptions of a variety of legislation, agreements, committees, and contracts local governments have developed to meet their regional needs for roads, utilities, and a sound economic base. The variety of solutions either demonstrates the truth of the old adage that says, 'The presence of multiple solutions indicates that none of them works,' or it demonstrates that each metropolitan's area problems are unique. Despite the variety of forms of cooperation, most metropolitan cooperative agreements fit into one or more of the following models of cooperation.[1]

The models of cooperation identified for public service agreements alone by Woolpert Consultants includes:

- Private Sector Agreements

- Councils of Governments

- Mutual Aid Agreements

- Special Service Districts

- Boundary Restructuring

Private sector agreements are those entered into cooperatively with private organizations to influence or express advocacy on a public issue, such as regional planning. Metropolitan "community progress councils" of top business executives are examples of these agreements.

Councils of governments are usually nonprofit corporations to provide a special forum for studies and recommendations concerning social issues of land use, zoning, and lobbying for specific legislation. These exist in many metropolitan areas linking central city and suburban officials into one organization to address regional issues of community development.

Mutual aid agreements consist of joint ventures between governments, and sometimes with private sector organizations, to achieve special purposes or to transfer or accept responsibility for a specific social agenda. These often have to do with issues of public safety, public works, and utilities. This can be as simple as a reciprocal agreement from one city jurisdiction to provide police services for a county in return for the county jurisdiction providing fire protection for a specific municipality. They also can include partnerships between governments and private organizations to address needs of community education, youth services, or mental health.

The fourth model of regional cooperation identified by Woolpert Consultants is special service districts which are formed under the authorization of voters, often to provide specialized services such as parks, hospitals, or irrigation. These districts may be administered by a separate entity which transcends local jurisdictions as well as county organizations.

The last example of public cooperation identified by Woolpert Consultants is the development of special boundary districts. This involves two governments working jointly on a common issue with the pooling of funds to develop special urban growth areas, planned communities, special research parks, or areas for unique opportunities for business development.

While not all of the cooperative partnerships which will follow fall neatly into these five categories, the research of Woolpert Consultants indicates that in the social sector of public service alone both governments and public organizations, are developing models of cooperation which are striving to enhance our commitment to public leadership. This modeling by public organizations may well foreshadow the way private organizations will link with one another as our globe shrinks in perception.

Cooperative partnerships exist not only in the public sector, but in all sectors of our society, including business, government, education, health care, and religious institutions. Following are several examples which indicate some of the commitments to cooperative partnerships that are emerging in communities throughout this country.

On a larger economic scale, we see cooperative partnerships among our major automobile manufacturers. The joint commitment of Ford Motor Corporation and Mazda to develop the 1991 model Ford Escort combines the benefits of Japanese production and technology with Ford's engineering designs and marketing breadth. General Motors' counterpart project with Toyota, the GM "Geo," is a similar venture between previous competitors.

Bergamo Center in Dayton, Ohio is a private nonprofit organization which had its roots in the conference and training industry. In ten years of leadership at Bergamo Center we evolved a dramatic shift in our organizational priorities based on the future of our strategic mission. The strategic mission simply put is "to educate people from all ages and all walks of life to appreciate their full human potential and their social responsibility to the human community."

As we charted our organization's future, we felt the compelling need to move beyond the traditional approach of a conference and training center dedicated to the pursuit only of professional education to a wider social agenda of education for community development. Within our strategic priorities we pursued several cooperative agreements which are illustrative of the kind of interventions even small agencies and organizations can make to enhance not only their organizational position but the social fabric of society at the same time.

In the past several years, we developed a partnership program with a municipal hospital for an older adult day care center. With a county board of mental health we developed a special program for public education for prevention of drug and alcohol abuse as well as therapeutic services for youth and families. We expanded a long-standing commitment to the religious and value education for youth, which began as providing retreats to local private high schools, into a larger commitment for youth education in the area of wellness, peer support, and leadership development for schools and school districts throughout the State of Ohio. We researched the development of a preschool serving both handicapped and culturally disadvantaged students in cooperation with a local city school system. The proposed program would mainstream children into an existing day care program, thus saving schools and taxpayers additional dollars in transportation and day care costs while providing maximum convenience and service to the children and their families. Also under consideration is a joint corporate wellness project for employees of several major corporations. For maximum efficiency they would be linked through a major research park foundation as partners with social service providers rather than individual company administered programs.

Focusing on physical resources we devoted underutilized space on a 150-acre campus to the housing of other nonprofit organizations in an attempt to share technology and human resources while reducing operating overhead, to enhance our common public commitment to the social welfare of other educational, human services, and arts organizations. These represent small initiatives of only one organization to expand its influence and impact the quality of life simultaneously.

Another example of cooperative partnerships, which involves the military and health care, is the rapid expansion of private and public partnerships to provide specialized health care services in military hospitals. Private providers now work in cooperation with major military installations to provide such specialties as open heart surgery and highly developed cancer surgery techniques previously unavailable to military personnel within their own health care systems.

In the local community surrounding metropolitan Dayton, the Miami Valley Research Park Foundation was created as a consortium of several universities with the State of Ohio to develop a separate private nonprofit corporation to attract international high technology businesses to revitalize a local economy through their cooperative efforts. In two large metropolitan cities in Ohio and Texas, regional city universities developed partnerships with several chambers of commerce to develop a strategic planning process for all of the municipalities, private businesses, and public institutions in multiple-county areas.

In southern Ohio, six chambers of commerce anticipated a dramatic change in the local economy, employment, health care, and residential neighborhoods due to a new interstate belt-line highway. They developed a consortium for regional planning, community education, and business development along this new interstate corridor.

Throughout the United States a variety of adopt-a-school programs are being developed by school districts and large local businesses. These "partner in education" projects provide an avenue for larger corporations to adopt a local school in order to provide management consulting, technical resources such as computer technology, and private funds to advance the special programs of their partnering school.

In Indianapolis, the Community Desegregation Advisory Council is an example of inter-governmental and inter-school district partnerships to provide for racial balance in metropolitan and county-wide schools which transcend local jurisdictions. This innovative separate nonprofit organization is represented by a board of municipalities and school districts, but has sufficient autonomy to implement one of the most successful programs of school integration in the United States.

Also within metropolitan Indianapolis, a unique project has begun involving several large corporations which joined efforts to set up their own private agency to work in an advocacy and partnership role with local school districts, improving educational services and the quality of life for all of their surrounding school systems. The long-term commitment of these businesses to develop more effective forms of educational service is an outstanding example of their commitment to public leadership and to their future work force which enhances the quality of life, the quality of work, and the quality of society for all of their present and future constituencies. This is an example of the growing response of private enterprise to support public services.

Organizations concerned with their commitment to public leadership demonstrate the flexibility to be involved in cooperative partnerships both to achieve the individual purposes of their organization, and to expand their social impact by working with competitors and complementary organizations across traditionally separate private and public boundaries.

Consistent Operational Values

In the marketing practices of many of our public and private sector organizations, we have witnessed the expression "value-added benefits." This terminology appears ironic, as if values had been previously factored out in the development of our goods and services during our production processes, our distribution systems, and our marketing efforts. Organizations committed to public leadership in the future will consider values as an equally valid part of the bottom line to support their immediate objectives of profitability, service, quality, reliability and dependability. The consistent expression of organizational values by upholding high standards and commitments to personnel within organizations, publics served by organizations, society as a whole, and the global community are characteristics of commitments to public leadership into the future.

Institutions, private concerns, public organizations, religious institutions, and social welfare agencies which demonstrate a high commitment to public leadership demonstrate the following three practices in their organizational behavior:

- **Treating Employees and Publics as Owners**
- **Understanding the Complementary Benefits of Competition**
- **Contributing to the Larger Mission of Customers, Clients, and Consumers**

These three expressions of consistency among our organizational values enhance the overall efforts of public leadership within our organizations and institutions.

Universal Technology Corporation is a national aerospace consulting firm working with both private sector contractors and the military in providing engineering, design assistance, and technical support for the highly specialized aerospace industry. In its thirty-year history, its founder Robert Guyton demonstrated a consistent organizational practice of treating his employees as owners. Recently upon his premature death, examples of his commitment to shared ownership of Universal Technology were revealed which explain the rapid success of this organization, which began as a private consulting firm in a two-room apartment and now is a multi-building facility of 160 employees. As Bob Guyton recruited new employees for Universal Technology, he identified those employees with the potential for making a lasting commitment to the organization. Individually, he invited them to join the corporation as stockholders. His gift to these employees was their first stock in Universal Technology Corporation. Not only was this stock not purchased by these select employees, it was a personal gift from him out of his own stock holdings within the company. Upon his death, his will specified that a portion of the private ownership of his stock be transferred to ownership by employees. This example of *commitment to employees as owners* is illustrative of a consistency of organizational values which strengthens our commitment to public leadership.

The second expression of consistent organizational values is the *willingness to view competition and our competitors as potential complements* to the future of our organizational mission. U.S. auto manufacturers and oil companies have anticipated the diminishment of fossil fuels as a source of automobile energy. They have set out to cooperatively exceed the advancing regulation by the Federal Government beyond the year 2000. Several of the major oil companies and automobile manufacturers have formed a consortium to jointly research the development of synthetic fuels from both the fuel production side and the automobile engineering side in order to beat the governmental deadline for such compliance. This uplifting example of a commitment by major corporate influence in this country to the issue of energy conservation demonstrates the benefits of viewing competitors as complementary to our individual business concerns and to the social welfare. It is in the best interest of all of these automotive manufacturers and energy-producing companies to collaborate, ensuring not only their individual survival but also the preservation of our environment at the same time. In this example, the consistency of organizational values demonstrated by these major U.S. corporations indicates a complementarity of their private concerns and the public agenda at the same time.

A third expression of consistent organizational values is the *contribution our organizations make to the wider mission of our customers, our clients, and our consumers.* Robert Berlon, a private consultant, was formerly a regional sales and field development manager for Hewlett Packard. Bob developed a distinctive sales philosophy based on his understanding of the importance of shared vision with customers, consumers, and clients. His vision-oriented approach to sales was inspired by the commitment of Bill Hewlett of Hewlett Packard to the social welfare.

> . . . Bill Hewlett had pledged 50 million to Stanford University. The significance for me was not the gift, but the reason for the gift. Bill was quoted, 'I want to see it (Stanford) strengthened for the future so that it will continue to benefit society, to educating promising young people, and performing research essential to the progress of mankind.' When had I heard this before? When I started at Hewlett Packard I heard similar statements from my colleagues and others. Wherever the corporate objectives were expressed, they were preceded by a statement of our vision. Wherever strategies were shared, they always were borne out of our vision. Vision had given birth to our objections and strategies. The vision I heard expressed was, 'Through technology we will make a contribution to all of society (not just HP, not just the United States, not just our stockholders) so that all of society will progress and benefit.'[2]

Robert Berlon applied this vision-orientation to sales at Hewlett Packard and went on to develop one of their leading divisions in the United States, specializing in sales to educational institutions, primarily universities. His model contends that the deeper the level of relationship an organization establishes with its customers, clients, and consumers, the less significant traditional variables of price, competition, and features become in the sales process. His fourfold model of deepening client relationships includes a commitment to *deliver good products and services; provide good service and support; contribute to the business issues of clients; contribute to the organizational issues of clients.* He contends that the greater our contribution to the higher levels of a client's organizational issues, the more we transcend the traditional influence and relationship between consumer and supplier. The lines between customer and supplier diminish, and we advance the vision of our client or customer so that their organizational development is directly impacted by the quality of our relationship. Bob Berlon indicates that this "hierarchy of contribution" to our clients and consumers at the first level is a sharing of technology or the basic good or service we provide. At the second level, it is a commitment to the application of our goods and services by providing necessary support to our clients' needs. Thirdly, as we contribute to the business issues of our clients, we enhance their effectiveness as a business or organization to run well internally. This level of commitment influences our client's business or organizational strategy. At the level of shared vision, Bob Berlon indicates that our ultimate contribution to our customer, consumer, or supplier is to improve their quality of life.

> What happens when we have developed our relationship on the basis of a shared vision? How do we impact our client when we contribute to their organizational issues? I believe that we impact the very *quality of life* of their organization. This can be measured. When we affect their productivity, we recognize this by such yard-sticks as: increased sales, increased production, decreased inventory, less down time, etc. The quality of life is determined in similar ways. Higher morale, less absenteeism, less turnover, etc. Any salesperson would feel proud to receive a letter from a president who is thankful for our contribution to his productivity. Imagine how the same salesperson would feel if a president expressed gratitude for impacting the quality of life of the organization. This would truly be the highest compliment given to a partner, the ultimate win-win result.[3]

Bob Berlon's sales philosophy indicates a fundamental commitment to consistency between business practices and organizational values, which represents an expression of public leadership. The willingness to influence our customers, consumers, and clients in ways that contribute to their own organizational health and vision is a strong indicator of our ability to provide not only for our immediate success but for the improvement in social quality of other organizations and of society as a whole.

Future Modeling

Organizations and their leaders, committed to public responsibility, model in the present what their organizations may be required to become in the future. These organizations are in constant pursuit of developing present examples in programs, products, services, and partnerships that indicate the contribution the organization may be required to make in the future as its services, economy, demographics, and global environment evolve. This "future modeling" approach to organizational development requires a high commitment to organizational risk. It means stepping out of the mold of expected performance in the present in order to create new expressions of services, products, clients, or markets to which we will become committed.

Future modeling requires a highly integrated view of emerging trends and economic forecasts, demographic and psychographic shifts, the environmental impacts of our products and services, and global trends and issues of cultural transformation. This universal integration is expressed by leaders who stand above all of the data at hand and make a leap of judgment into the future in order to determine future organizational priorities. This informed leap of action transcends product or service development which simply follows the traditional modes of marking trends in the marketplace in a reactive fashion.

United Theological Seminary in Dayton, Ohio is an organization committed to a future modeling approach to leadership. Through their planning in the past few years, they have examined carefully their role as a Methodist seminary within their religious denomination nationally, within the local community in which they reside, and within the global community. They have developed several new ventures expressive of this future modeling approach to organizational development. First, they have developed one of the most innovative third world educational experiences for seminary students within the United States. Based on their perception of a global world in the future, they have found it essential for ministers, who shape public perception and moral values, to have the experience of living and working in another culture with its economic, social, and political realities. They have become a national model for education in global concerns for seminary students.

Second, in their analysis of social trends and issues of the future, they have recognized the importance of technological communications and the implications of technology for the advancement of their religious mission. Their curriculum has been heavily shaped and influenced by advanced communications theory and the vehicles of electronic telecommunication, exposing seminary students to these resources as a fundamental ingredient of their future ministries in service of the church and the world.

Third, United Theological Seminary has become a local forum for public education on issues of racial equality and justice in the community in which they reside. They have developed strategic alliances and partnerships with minority organizations in order to promote a greater common understanding and shared approaches to community problem solving of very practical issues of public leadership in a racially segregated community. Their commitment to a future modeling approach to leadership evidences a comprehensive understanding of the role of public leadership for this theological seminary in the future.

Another example of future modeling approaches to organizational development is the cooperative learning opportunities of several universities throughout the United States through computer technology. Many colleges and universities now offer learning networks on computer and videotape for students throughout the country to develop their professional skills. Adult working students receive degrees and accreditation through "satellite learning opportunities" in the privacy of their own homes.

Antioch University has developed an Individualized Master of Arts Program serving students throughout the United States by means of such a cooperative learning network. In a nontraditional adult learning program, Shinook Learning Center in the State of Washington provides a computerized learning network which enables participants to pursue continuous dialogue and communication with instructors and other participants in their values, personal growth, and environmental education programs throughout the country. Anytime during the day or night through the use of a modem a student may enter into the "class dialogue" with other students and instructors, advancing their knowledge in these important issues of our social awareness.

Another emerging example of future modeling for organizations is the commitment of major defense industries and energy companies to environmental engineering. While the research dollars are still limited, and government supports and tax abatements are yet to come, these organizations are taking strategic risks by entering the new field of developing environmental products, technology, and services. They are creating future models of their organizational priorities, products, and services in light of a changing present reality. The commitment to a "future modeling" approach to organizational development is an essential ingredient of an advanced understanding of public leadership among businesses, school systems, government, health care, religious institutions, and social service agencies for the future.

Environmental and Social Analysis

Organizations committed to public leadership examine their organizational priorities in light of the social impact of their services and products. They are also committed to extensive environmental and social analysis. No doubt the environmental agenda, coupled with the proliferation of nuclear arms, has contributed more to an advancing understanding of globalization and the need for a comprehensive strategy for life than any other issue previously experienced in our history. Will Steger and Jon Bowermaster in *Saving the Earth* talk about this shift of consciousness in terms of our environmental agenda.

> Increased awareness of environmental problems has inspired a kind of 'ONE WORLD THEOREM' that is already flavoring international conferences no matter their initial agenda. Whether energy, economic, or even social summits are convened, heads of state have made environmental concerns a lead item. This makes perfect sense as no great leap is needed to recognize their importance. If environmental problems aren't addressed now by the world's leaders, they will never get the attention they need back home. Senator Albert Gore, who has taken the lead in the United States Congress on environmental issues, told one gathering of world leaders ('GLOBAL CHANGE AND OUR COMMON FUTURE,' May 1989) that environmental issues are already the highest priority on every nation's crowded plate. 'In the not distant future, there will be a new 'sacred agenda' in international affairs,' he prophesied, 'policies that enable rescue of the global environment. This task will one day join, and even supplant, preventing the

world's incineration through nuclear war as a principal test of state craft.[4]

Our organizational commitments to public leadership have much to do with our emphasis on environmental and social concerns as a primary agenda for assessing strategic priorities for institutional advancement. There are three expressions of environmental and social analysis that I believe are prevalent among organizations committed to public leadership. First, these organizations, despite the inconvenience to immediate production and distribution of their products and services, demonstrate a commitment to *monitor current practices of consumption, disposition, and acquisition of material and technical resources.* Secondly, organizations with a commitment to a public agenda for social leadership *assess the impact of their asset management on environmental and social concerns.* Thirdly, organizations committed to advancing the public agenda through environmental and social analysis *consider the systemic impact of their product and service on the present and future quality of life.* Each of these three dimensions of a commitment to environmental and social analysis strengthens our understanding of public leadership not only within our organization, but also for the benefits of society as a whole.

Several independent organizations, as well as the large consumer products company of Proctor & Gamble, are engaged in an investigation of the feasibility of recycling disposable diapers. Plastics from diapers, as well as other byproducts, are used for a variety of purposes in the recycling effort. This concern for the consumption, disposition, and acquisition of material and technical resources illustrates one corporation's commitment to environmental and social analysis in their product design and distribution.

It is popular to devalue the efforts of major corporations to address environmental concerns which are the result of the byproducts of their original production systems. However, it is also important to highlight the influence that large organizations and corporations can have on our local understanding of a consistent ethic for society of environmental analysis in the consumption of our material resources and their reuse. Recent efforts by McDonald's and Burger King Corporation to develop recycling processes for styrofoam represent a major effort of private industry in the advancement of this technology which may influence our use, our reuse, and our diminished reliance on styrofoam as a form of packaging in the future.

Another example of a consistent concern for the consumption of resources and its social impact was an effort of the Unocal Oil Company of California. For a period of time, Unocal offered to buy back for $500 all pre-1977 automobiles from their customers. The program was an enormous success and reduced the number of gas-guzzling automobiles which contributed to the heavy pollution of the environment in the State of California. This largely symbolic but also very practical effort demonstrates an organizational commitment to a *consistent ethic concerning acquisition, consumption, and disposition of materials* used in our organizational practices.

Several organizations now are switching from their commitments to heavy use of lawn chemical treatments on their corporate grounds to more organic approaches to lawn fertilization. This consistent commitment to examine our use of environmental materials applies not only to the workplace, but will transfer learning to our home environments as well.

In the area of paper waste alone, 35% of all trash in the United States is the result of waste paper and paperboard materials. In the workplace this translates to 1.2 pounds per employee per day. Efforts of corporate recycling can set a standard for our personal habits as well. One California-based corporation has developed a partnership with a social service agency by which the social service agency collects its recyclable goods and translates them into funding support for its own programs and services.

Future technologies such as electronic mail and the paperless office are being implemented in divisions of large corporations in order to examine their ability to diminish their reliance on consumable paper products, as well as to diminish their economic overhead in office supplies. A commitment to the responsible acquisition, consumption, and disposition of material resources is a responsibility of all organizations, not only those who require these for their production cycle. A growing consistency of environmental ethics among organizations in examining their use of resources is a fundamental example of public leadership and commitment to the quality of society for the future.

A second dimension of environmental and social analysis is the responsible management of our property and physical assets. A controversial, and still unsolved, social agenda which exemplifies the importance of environmental impact in the development of our assets is nuclear power plants. In this country, the enormously unpopular development and opening of the Seabrook Nuclear Power Plant on the Massachusetts/New Hampshire border still lingers as an example of our divided loyalties in the management of organizational assets. Nuclear waste, the byproduct of managing our energy assets through nuclear technology, looms as a frightening reminder of the threat to the quality of life and the impact which an inappropriate management of our assets can have. In her book *Earthright*, H. Patricia Hynes illustrates the potential environmental and social results of nuclear power as an asset.

> Another byproduct of modern civilization that continues to haunt the environment is nuclear waste. It is dumped into the ocean, buried in land, and shipped from country to country. While generally more tightly controlled than chemical waste, leaks of radioactive materials have occurred in many countries. The most horrific example of such accidental release in the past decade occurred in the Soviet Union at Chernobyl in 1986. Contamination from the accidental reactor meltdown spread over much of Europe, contaminating the food chain for many years to come. The long-term health effects remain uncertain, but estimates suggest that 5,000 to 50,000 additional cancer deaths may result over the next 30 to 60 years.[5]

Nuclear facilities represent a major example of the importance of clear thinking, not only in the immediate but also in the long-term future, for decisions on the development and disposition of our assets. However, governments and social jurisdictions are not solely responsible for assessing the impact of managing property and physical assets. This responsibility also falls to smaller private and social service organizations as well.

Historically within the State of Florida, a major religious denomination has made significant investments in the real estate market in several strategic areas. Initially, real estate was purchased to identify possible sites for the building of churches as the population centers expanded rapidly in this southernmost state. However, some jurisdictions of the denomination have established real estate development and speculation offices which have turned this management of the assets of land into a private business to support their religious mission. Opinions may be divided as to the appropriateness of religious institutions venturing into the real estate market for investment purposes. It does represent a significant question of public value which transcends traditional boundaries of private business, public enterprise, and religious institutions. How does the development of major population centers through shopping, retail, and condominium communities impact concern for local environments? And how does this religious denomination employ environmental analysis in the management of their real estate assets?

None of us are exempt in our organizational priorities from consideration of the use and impact of our major environmental assets on the future of society. The immediate short-term benefits, whether it be providing energy for our cities or income for our social missions, do not suspend the obligation our organizations to determine the impact of our asset management on the quality of life. Our decisions must transcend the present and the future of our unique purposes to include the larger public good.

A third and final expression of mature environmental and social analysis within organizational leadership involves a systemic consideration of the impact of products and services on the quality of life. One example of this systemic review of the public impact of our private habits and our product consumption is the automobile industry and its consumption of fuels. Small changes in the energy efficient use of transportation translate into large social benefits for our public agenda.

Transportation accounts for about 30% of CO_2 emissions. The average fuel efficiency is 26.5 miles per gallon (mpg) for new U.S. cars and 19.5 mpg for new light trucks. At this rate, cars pump their own weight in carbon into the atmosphere each year. Some cars now on the market, however, get twice as many miles per gallon as that average, emitting half the CO_2. Some foreign manufacturers have developed even more economical cars that are getting over 100 miles per gallon. Several innovative fuel efficient automobiles achieve over 50 miles per gallon; most are Japanese. In addition, the Volvo LCP 2000 is a four-passenger car that gets 63 miles per gallon in the city and 81 miles per gallon on the highway. Renault has recently tested a prototype vehicle that gets 124 miles per gallon.

Environmentalists call for the government to raise the fuel economy standards for new cars from the current

26.5 to 48 miles per gallon and for new trucks from 19.5 to 33 miles per gallon by the year 2000. This action would save more than five times as much oil as the Interior Department says might be found in Alaska National Wildlife Refuge. The Natural Resources Defense Council calculates that if new cars average 48 miles per gallon and new trucks 33 miles per gallon by the year 2000, United States CO_2 emissions could be reduced by four to five percent.[6]

In the one area of automobile transportation alone, a commitment to produce more fuel efficient autos and to drive them would make a major difference on the public health and quality of life in our cities. Considering the systemic impact of our distribution and use of products and services is an important priority for organizations committed to future public leadership.

Almost all organizations today involve the use of toxic materials directly or indirectly even in the simple cleaning of public restrooms and office suites. Consequently, concern for toxic waste disposal transcends not only organizations that systemically produce these materials, but those organizations who contribute to this systemic impact by their use, distribution, and disposal of toxic wastes. Responsibility for systemic issues like toxic waste transcends affixing blame only to major producing organizations since it also involves a commitment by all organizations who use these materials to be concerned for the public impact of our organizational practices.

To date, cleaning up hazardous waste has proven to be a difficult task, and banning the burial of wastes is really ineffective. If one state outlaws such burial (as California has), there's always another state (like Nevada), or a foreign nation that will gladly take it. Stiffer regulation helps; so do fines. But according to one EPA official, 'Sixty percent of major disposal facilities don't obey the laws and regulations anyway, nor pay the fines.' The increasingly common practice of shipping hazardous waste across state and international borders is perplexing. It is nothing more than a high stakes game of 'juggling the poison.' It answers none of the problems, just creates new ones. Americans generate roughly 275 million tons of hazardous waste each year, more than one ton per citizen. The United States is one of the leading exporters of toxic waste . . . most of the measurable mass is legally burned or buried. The rest, up to a third, is shipped and trucked to Canada, Mexico, India, South Korea, Nigeria, and Zimbabwe. 'Out of sight, out of mind.'[7]

All of our organizations, both public and private, contribute to the social problem of toxic waste and its disposition. A consistent ethic of considering the systemic impact of our production and use of products and services is a responsibility of all organizations concerned for public leadership. The capacity for our organizations to engage in this type of "systemic social analysis" is an important priority for leadership. Our public responsibility includes not only responsive and responsible approaches to our organizational success, but also our commitment to the social fabric of life.

Another example of the need for systemic social analysis is the disposal of solid waste. All of our organizations contribute enormous amounts of solid waste to our environment and to our world community.

The United States creates about 450,000 tons of residential and commercial solid waste each day. By the year 2000, this amount is expected to reach 530,000 tons per day. What happens to the half million tons of daily trash, today 80% of our waste is buried in landfills. The Environmental Protection Agency estimates that in the next five to ten years more than 27 states and half of the country's cities will run out of landfill space. Major cities, including New York and Los Angeles, will exhaust their landfill space in just a few years; Philadelphia and others have no more. Of the remaining 20% of waste that is not landfilled, 10% is recycled and 10% is incinerated.[8]

The responsibility for systemically reducing our production and use of solid waste materials is a universal responsibility for organizations within the public and private sector. In a disappointing vein, I was recently shocked to hear that a social service agency discontinued their program of recycling because the return on investment for recyclable materials had fallen short of the cost of the program. No longer can we be content with fingerpointing the responsibility to major corporations and public agencies to solve our social problems. The immediate responsiveness of organizations to the systemic impacts of our production and our distribution of services is an important example of our commitment to public leadership. Organizational recycling programs symbolize not only to our customers and suppliers but also to our employees a commitment to this wider social agenda through systemic analysis of the impacts and influences of our current business and organizational practices. In the area of recycling alone, the prospect can be hopeful and organizations can make a major difference.

> Much solid waste can be recycled and reused for the same or new purposes; some can be composted for gardens and landscaping, some can be repaired and resold. Recycling and reuse are a kind of modern alchemy in which one person's scrap becomes another's valuable raw materials. How much treasure is there in trash, the most optimistic estimate for government officials of how much of our waste can be recycled is about 60%. This calculation comes at a point when serious recycling programs are only two to three years old and the premier programs have so far achieved 30%. As recycling becomes a universal way of handling waste as markets are aggressively developed for recyclable products, and as people demand that new products and packaging be recyclable, the estimate of how much of our waste can be recycled will probably decline. Some environmentalists contend that 70 to 90% of our waste can be reused and recycled.[9]

Simply by recycling, organizations can have a major impact on our social agenda through creating a global awareness of the systemic impact of our production processes and service strategies on society.

This chapter has presented numerous examples of the commitment of organizations across several sectors of society to an active public agenda as a part and parcel of the purposes of their business or service. No longer can we be content with one-dimensional approaches to strategic planning and business analysis. The futures of our organizations individually and our society collectively are far more interdependent than we have come to acknowledge or realize in practice. Organizations committed to an active expression of their public leadership will consider the personal, global, and social impact that their business purposes have upon the social quality of life.

This social "quality of life" can be best exemplified in four expressions of public leadership: *cooperative partnerships with other organizations to provide for new resources of the future; a consistent expression of organizational values; the development of future models for productive and socially responsible organizations; and systemic environmental and social analysis within our organizations.* These four dimensions of public leadership are the active expression of a commitment to the future of society by integrating the impact of our organizations on the quality of our lives, the quality of our work, and the quality of our social systems. Organizations committed to this coextensive understanding of quality are more likely to transcend the economic trials of the next decade into a new century and millennium of opportunity and prosperity. They create true lasting value for themselves, their clients, their customers, and indeed for our global community.

Chapter VIII

Leadership in the Change Process

Leaders who seek to strengthen the quality of life, quality of work, and quality of society are familiar with the dynamics of change and resistance. Those who promote improvement through their role responsibility, their personal mission in life, or their current organizational situation encounter the two enduring questions for all leaders.

- **Why is change so difficult to accept for us and for those we serve?**

- **What personal and organizational strategies transform resistance to change into a positive force for growth?**

We expect that a positive change will enjoy the welcome support of our constituents: customers, employees, or clients. In fact, the opposite is often true. Change is very difficult for many to accept, and the inevitable consequence of resistance can often be deep and painful for everyone involved. We instinctively understand change as a change "from" something familiar, usually a change from past or present, rather than a change "to" a preferred future. If we would think momentarily about experiences of change in our lives—personal disappointment, changing leadership roles, loss of a key staff leader, forced transitions—accepting change for the sake of change is a foolish presumption. But we are equally limited if we discount even unwelcome individual, organizational, and social change as opportunities for growth. These provide a larger context for personal, organizational, and social, depth and integrity.

Orchestrating the process of effective change and the consequent experience of resistance requires personal, organizational, and public mastery. However, the practicing leader finds the dilemma of introducing, sustaining, and bringing to fruition effective change strategies to be a complex and difficult task. In his book, *The Path of Least Resistance*, Ken Hultman echoes these sentiments:

> There are many who would contend that change is about the only thing you can be sure of in life. That's perhaps too optimistic. I have come to believe that there is nothing quite as sure as resistance. Anyone who has ever tried to 'make some changes,' needs no introduction to resistance. Managers and supervisors are people who often find the need to change things—to try to make them work better—and just as often find themselves face to face with opposition . . . although the type of change may vary tremendously, it always seems like resistance is just around the corner, waiting for an opportunity to pounce on best-laid plans.
>
> I once spent hours being annoyed that I had to constantly contend with resistance. Then it finally occurred to me that my resentment wasn't getting me anywhere; in fact, it was greatly interfering with my ability to do anything constructive about resistance. I concluded that a more rational approach was in order and began to piece together ideas for dealing with it. After a few victories, battling resistance actually became somewhat enjoyable . . . also, when I look back on my career it seems somewhat ironic that resistance, the enemy of many, has provided direction and purpose to much of my professional activity.[1]

This chapter will present an overview of leadership in the change process. We will review three fundamental issues essential to a comprehensive approach to leadership involving ourselves, our organizations, and our publics in the process of effectively implementing change.

First, we will concentrate our attention on understanding the *dynamics of resistance to change*. Secondly, we will analyze and suggest helpful approaches to the *roles and relationships* necessary for constructive change processes. And thirdly, we will outline some *organizational strategies* for promoting growth and development through the change process.

These three ingredients of understanding the dynamics of resistance to change, effectively implementing the roles and relationships in the change process, and developing strategies for organizational growth through change are necessary characteristics of effective leaders capable of advancing individuals and organizations. It is through a comprehensive understanding and active approach to change and resistance that effective leaders will make a lasting contribution to the quality of life for their key publics, the quality of work for their organizations, and ultimately for the quality of society as a result of their efforts.

Understanding Resistance to Change

Psychologist James Zullo indicates that the capacity to resist is equal to the capacity to change. It requires the same ego strength to resist change as it does to accept and adopt the change process. Unfortunately, in the process of encountering resistance most leaders either back away from their intended change, re-examine their own priorities and strategies, or react negatively to those who direct resistance toward them as change agents. There are some learning psychologists who contend that resistance is a healthy indicator that effective change is occurring. Through our resistance the necessary disequilibrium of perception is occurring that allows us to look at new alternatives and reframe our assumptions in different and innovative ways.

Resistance, then, can be a positive force for growth if managed effectively. The skillful leader in the change process understands the importance of treating resistance as a symptom rather than a disease in the change process and its fundamental purposes. Looking at a few assumptions may be helpful as we transform our predisposition towards accepting resistance as a necessary part of the change effort.

It is important for us to understand that change in and of itself is not inherently helpful or not helpful. Many individual and organizational changes can precipitate unintended consequences which create circumstances far worse than the initial problem we were intending to address. Consequently, change in and of itself is not necessarily either good or bad. Unfortunately, many of us in the process of leadership equate our self-worth with the efforts or outcomes of our desired change. When we make such a close identification between our own personalities and priorities and the intended change, we may lose sight of the fact that change itself carries no inherent value. Our ego may become so closely associated with our purposes that we exercise reverse resistance due to a perceived rejection of ourselves as well as our ideas.

Secondly, the true value of change is often demonstrated in the long view rather than in the short term. The immediate perceived value on the part of our constituents—employees, clients, customers, or the community at large—is not always the full measure of the real value of our change efforts. It may take months or even years in some circumstances to fully realize the benefits of change. As a result of a more objective stance towards change, skillful leaders realize that resistance therefore is not necessarily a negative phenomenon. Resistance in fact may be protecting something very vital or essential to one's self-understanding or one's understanding of the organization or social climate in which one lives or works. Disassembling this present conception in order to accept and adopt a new, long-term change attitude often results in a great deal of anxiety and effort at the personal level. Consequently, effective change requires time.

Figure 10 outlines four levels of resistance to change. Each of these levels represents successively less complex forms of change for people and organizations to accept. At the most pervasive level of resistance to change, we find *personal and developmental change* as the most difficult to accept. The psychology of human development is clear that as human beings we grow as whole persons. We might adopt the image of a circle to understand this analogy with each part of our identity contributing its piece to make a whole image. Trends in developmental and learning psychology have researched and documented that our psychological maturity, our physical health, our relational integrity, our social stability, and our intellectual competence are all woven together in a continuous fabric of life.

Vince Dwyer, founder for the Center of Human Development at Notre Dame, uses the analogy of a tapestry. It's as if we spend most of our time behind the tapestry of our lives seeing all the threads and the knots tangled together. Yet, when we turn the tapestry around, we see a portrait much more integrated and coherent than we might have ever imagined. This composite or integrated identity evolves throughout our life in gradual stages of completion. In childhood and adolescence that circle which we call ourselves is permeable and able to be reformed and reshaped. Our experiences shape our inner identity and our self-perception. The psychology of learning indicates that children and adolescents learn by the accumulation of experiences and only later seek to interpret and understand them. A young child does not know a flame is hot until she/he first puts a finger in it. However, as we grow into maturity as adults we generate more judgments about our experiences, sometimes even before we experience them. You and I know that a stove is hot even before we touch it. Sometimes judgments can be prematurely formed, even inappropriate. Changing them, therefore, is difficult.

Levels of Resistance to Change

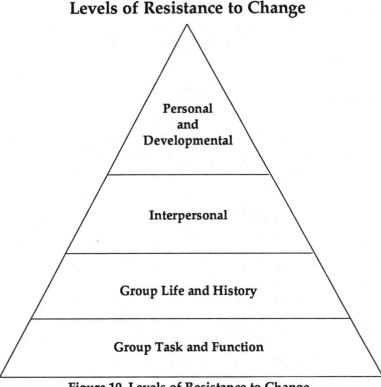

Figure 10. Levels of Resistance to Change

The process of personal and developmental change calls for ever-widening understandings of our self identity. New experiences require this circle of identity to expand. Yet in adulthood the expansion of that circle is no easy task because of what we believe we know. Let us use the image of a pie. If we were hosting a dinner for six people and sliced a pie into six pieces then suddenly discovered that we had a seventh guest and tried to put a seventh piece of pie into that ten- or twelve-inch circle, we would have to rearrange the entire pie. Assimilating change into our self-concepts can be an analogous experience. While it is very painful for us at times, our egos are called on to create a more expansive identity as we age and gain new experiences. This re-arrangement of the circle of our identity to accommodate new wisdom and experience can be a difficult process. Our identities resist that expansion. At the same time that our egos are called upon to expand and become more complex, we become more established in our views.

Maturity calls us to be more inner-directed or separate from our environments at the same time our experience requires us to become more universal in viewpoint. This two-polar drive, calls us to greater personal detachment while widening our circle of awareness in life. As we grow more complex in our detachment and separation from our environments and we expand our awareness and consciousness to be more universal, we find ourselves with increasingly fewer contemporaries of thought and experience. Consequently we resist this process of maturation.

During the course of life we sometimes get stuck and project or affiliate our identities on other people, organizations, institutions, roles, work settings, or personal relationships in an attempt to stay "attached." This is why resistance increases as we experience more value-oriented changes. Our identities resist the sometimes frightening process of becoming more inclusive of other perspectives and yet more distinct and separate from our environment. This process of becoming more universal yet differentiated is part of finding our particular life project, which for most of us is both liberating and terrifying. Individuals often arrest this process of self-discovery and transfer or subordinate it to other people, organizations, or systems. Authority, and therefore leaders, are often an easy target upon which to transfer this responsibility for personal change. Consequently, resistance is always present in a personal and developmental challenge.

Any type of change includes some change at the personal and developmental level. Indications of resistance among people in our organizations and systems is therefore a clue that the desired change is occurring. In fact, their self-perceptions, their priorities, and their personal understandings of the strategy and issue of change at hand is requiring them to reorient how they see and experience themselves. This process of inner reorientation necessarily generates resistance at the personal and developmental level.

At the second level of our model, we find *interpersonal change and resistance*. This layer of resistance to change deals with the needs and transactions among pairs or subgroups within a system or organization. These transactions often involve mutually beneficial relationships or at times destructive relational intimacies which exist within our organizational settings. When we initiate efforts of organizational or systemic change which require us to reposition our interpersonal relationships, it is likely that we will encounter resistance which originates from this interpersonal level.

Interpersonal change is heavily conditioned by our personal styles, our background, and past experiences. Many popular leadership development instruments concentrate on stylistic and temperamental approaches to leadership. A popular version of this approach to leadership style is represented by the Myers-Briggs Type Indicator. This instrument, based in concepts of Jungian psychology helps us understand our personal styles as either introverted or extroverted, as intuitive or sensate, as feeling or thinking and as judging or perceiving oriented. Someone who is highly introverted in their approach to working out new circumstances may disappoint someone who is very extroverted through their lack of communication concerning their appreciation of the circumstances of change at hand. This may not, however, indicate a lack of acceptance of the change process or an inability to comprehend it. It may simply be a difference in style. Our stylistic differences, therefore, often generate resistance in the process of change.

Similarly, somebody who is very intuitive, capable, and interested in large leaps of understanding and conceptual thinking may be very frustrated by somebody who wants all the details spelled out before accepting and adopting the change process from a sensate vantage point. A team member who assesses decisions based on relational impacts on others may be very feeling-oriented.

While another colleague may see the logic and concepts as the important factors for reaching decisions.

Somebody who is prone to make judgments based upon the assimilation of information quickly may have a high degree of impatience with someone whose approach is very perceptual-oriented, seeking to organize all of the necessary information without gaps of knowledge before reaching conclusions. Consequently, our personal styles exert a high degree of impact on the process of accepting change at the interpersonal level.

Our historical backgrounds can also bring baggage to the process of understanding resistance to change. We all have different values and varying experiences which condition our present circumstances. Introducing a new supervisor in an organization may strike somebody as a wonderful opportunity, based on past experiences of success with new supervisors. However, the employee whose past experience of new supervisors has been to lose stature in their current position or professional autonomy may experience a different reaction to this organizational change. In addition, the myriad of previous experiences, personal and organizational histories, and wide backgrounds we bring at the interpersonal level make this an important dynamic to consider in implementing change strategies.

While resistance often is expressed at the interpersonal level, it is rarely resolved in this manner. Accepting differences of style, background, and experience become part and parcel of a neutral approach to leadership and the change process. Leaders who get distracted by any of these three elements are unlikely to effectively move their organizations forward because these three elements—of style, background, and experience—are always present in advancing the change agenda.

At the third level of change, we encounter the dimension of *group life and history* as an element of understanding resistance. Like individual personalities, a group exists as a whole organism. Groups grow and develop as integrated units. Groups have capabilities and needs that are not reducible to individual members. We might describe a group as having a *gestalt* or a common field of consciousness. Changes that we introduce in organizations which upset the prevailing group life or history—even pleasant ones—often generate intense resistance.

I am reminded of a consulting assignment I accepted when a new leader transferred to a different organizational setting. He made the mistake of quickly replacing the existing management team. The mistake of this new leader upset the group life or history far more prematurely than he might have done with careful consideration. Even if the intended changes he proposed were ultimately good for the organization, he failed to take into account the prevailing life history of the group at that time. In addition, the leader who had exited the organization prior to the new leader's arrival was well-beloved and much appreciated by his colleagues and the different publics in which he interacted. It took this organization over ten years to work through its management dilemma to reposition a new group life history that was an effective support to the prevailing organizational priorities at hand.

Another example of upsetting the relational balance through change is introducing new members to a well-established group. We often assume it is the new member who must learn the "rules" of the prevailing organizational culture. However, those who have been responsible for introducing new employees to an organization realize that the entire work group or unit will have to change and incorporate the skills, expertise, and talents which the new member brings. Not surprisingly, there is often some resistance directed towards the new member of the organization, despite whatever benefits their expertise and skills may bring to the current circumstance.

The final dimension of resistance to change within an organization is on the operating level of *group task or function.* This is the functional and decision-making level of a group. At this level, the current perceptions of effectiveness and productivity that group members share and act upon is a key indicator to understand the process of resistance. Groups that understand themselves in a certain way, whether as very effective, or as ineffective, or as having relative strengths and weaknesses, may have difficulty in accepting a change in viewpoint even if that change of viewpoint brings them closer to a correct understanding of their capabilities.

One client organization was failing dismally in achieving the objectives set by its trustees and directors. Yet employees within the organization perceived themselves as a tightly-knit group with common values and principles and effective in their work. The difference was at the level of group task or function. The directors and trustees were looking at different priorities than the supervisors and line employees. Rather than engage in a debate as to which set of criteria was essential for success, it became important for this organization to assemble employees, board members, and directors together in order to project some common understanding or criteria for success in the future. In this process, a new level of group task or function was created rather than imposing one preexisting set of standards upon another.

The effectiveness of group task or function is evident by how well a group achieves and carries forward its goals and purposes in performing a task or a series of assignments. Groups who perceive themselves as successful at this level will be resistant to change even if those changes generate new opportunities and future growth potential. Changing the prevailing direction of group task and function often requires setting new standards for future excellence prior to moving ahead in an organization's development.

These four dimensions of resistance to change provide a high degree of complexity in introducing new assignments, new priorities, new activities, and new strategies to any group or organizational setting. In all change processes, it is likely that resistance to change will be present at all four levels. Consequently, a skillful leader or change agent will direct activities in the change process that seek to strengthen leadership in each of these four dimensions. Effective change strategies, therefore, develop individual competence through supervision, training, and development at the personal level in order to support and adopt new change efforts or interventions at the other levels.

Additionally, effective change strategies will support positive expressions of interpersonal dynamics in a work group and use them to carry forth new initiatives. When these dynamics are perceived as negative, or when subgroups are perceived as obstacles to the change process, the skillful change agent will be careful to assist subgroups in adopting new norms and values prior to moving them forward in accepting a new organizational strategy or agenda.

At the third level of group life and history, skillful change agents and leaders recognize that no matter how objective a strategy for change may seem (for example, something as simple as rearranging desks in an office area), there may be some underlying assumptions about group life or history that are relevant and must be addressed. I am reminded of a religious organization with which I consulted almost 15 years ago that attempted to reorganize and change their worship environment. The pastor was extremely frustrated after he had hired a prestigious architect who came out with a masterful design for the new church interior. He simply could not understand the resistance of his congregational members to changing the old array of religious artifacts in the church. During the consultation process, I took a tour with him through the worship space. I pointed out to him that all of the religious artifacts that he sought to change had family name plates on them with deep-seated memories for key members of his community. In a small-town, rural setting, this sense of family history and pride is a pervasive power in the fabric of life. Not only did he have to develop a new architectural plan for reshaping the church, he had to resymbolize and remythologize the meaning of family history for his congregation prior to successfully completing the remodeling process.

Lastly, at the level of group task and function, resistance to change can occur when groups perceive their existing standards of performance as effective despite the contrasting viewpoint of others. Consequently, the joint development of new standards for tasks and functions is often essential to minimizing resistance to change. This is particularly important when an organization attempts to introduce a new product or service. To the extent that employees, customers, and clients identify the organization and its skills in its previous service, they may have difficulty in accepting the new agenda as relevant. For example, a social service agency which has built a long-standing history in the community by providing individual and group psychological counseling may have a hard time effecting a shift toward providing training and consulting services in order to balance out their financial ledger. While these employees are already in the business of fostering growth and development, this change in service may seem to the staff or to the public like a radical shift of agenda at the level of group task and function.

Developing strategies to minimize resistance in the change process is the responsibility of effective leaders interested in advancing the quality of life, quality of work, and quality of society among their constituents. Taking into account these four layers of resistance to change is an important factor in that change process.

Appropriate change strategies, therefore, must include attention to the personal and developmental, interpersonal, group life and history, and group task and function levels to effectively complete a coherent approach to organizational change.

Resistance to change is proportional in intensity to its source depending on whether the resistance is generated from personal, interpersonal group life and history, or group task and functioning dimensions. The greatest resistance to change is that resistance which is generated from within ourselves. Resistance decreases in intensity to the extent that that resistance is focused interpersonally and relationally. Resistance is less intense at the level of group life and history and least intense at the level of group task and function. Positioning new change strategies to work effectively at the lower levels of intensity in resistance is an important element of a change agent's responsibilities. The skillful leader is mindful of this process of de-intensifying resistance to change in order to effectively implement change strategies. Consequently, in the face of resistance, the skillful change agents, or leaders, avoid over-personalizing resistance either within themselves or among others in order to move the organization forward. Strategies are kept at the level of group task and function or group life and history as much as possible to minimize focusing attention on the interpersonal and personal levels of change unless it becomes necessary.

Roles and Relationships in the Change Process

Daryl Conner, of O. D. Resources, Inc. of Atlanta, has developed a helpful model for understanding roles in the change process. He outlined a series of intervention tools which an organization can use to plan and analyze effective change strategies. Daryl Conner identifies necessary roles in the change process in the following ways:

> When an organization decides to initiate a change regarding its people, methods, or products, or is faced with adjusting to an unanticipated change in these areas, three roles are important to understand:
>
> • Change sponsor—the individual or group that uses their organizational power to legitimize the change.

• Change agent—the individual/group that is responsible for implementing the change.

• Change target—the individual/group that must actually change something about their knowledge, skills, behavior, or attitudes.

Often senior level management serve as sponsors, mid-level as agents, and lower level as targets. Although these roles are separate and distinct from each other, they are also overlapping. For example, sometimes sponsors serve as change agents as well as being impacted as targets; mid-level managers function as agents while also feeding the demands of the change and becoming targets, etc.[2]

Daryl Conner's model and consulting tools indicate that effective change strategies involve sponsors, targets, and agents together in a web of joint activities to effectively implement the desired change at hand.

Figure 11 is an expansion upon these roles and relationships in the change process, building on the fundamental concept of the roles involving sponsor, target, and agent. Specific skills characterize each of these relationships in order to minimize resistance to change and effectively implement a change strategy at hand. The effective execution of appropriate roles and relationships among

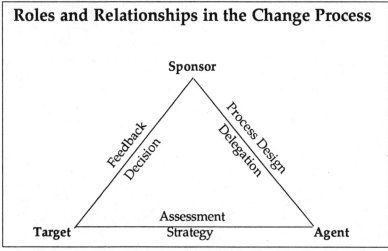

Roles and Relationships in the Change Process

Sponsor

Feedback
Decision

Process Design
Delegation

Assessment
Target Strategy **Agent**

Figure 11. Roles and Relationships in the Change Process

these primary roles will minimize confusion over the direction, priorities, and purposes of change. Each of these sets of players can effectively implement any successful change without inviting resistance among others. We will examine these roles and relationships in the change process by looking at three dynamics: first, the sponsor-agent relationship; second, the agent-target relationship; and third, the sponsor-target relationship. In order to examine these relationships concretely, we will use an example taken from a consulting client to clarify these relationships with more precision.

Our case study involves a personnel reorganization process among several departments of a multiple business unit organization.

Sponsor-Agent Relationships

The sponsor is the person or group with the authority to legitimize change. The agent is the group or individual with the responsibility to carry out and implement the change process. Effective sponsors relate to change agents by delegating responsibility for designing the change process. The sponsor's efforts are best directed towards the process of delegation, trusting the skills and expertise of the agent in effectively carrying forth the design of the change process. In return, responsible agents carefully orchestrate and gain advance sponsor approval to the process they will use in introducing change to the organizational system or environment.

In our current example, the senior executive for the organization and the Board of Directors are sponsors in the change effort. They call for the necessary changes in the organizational environment based upon their assessment of the future economic conditions of the organization. Their conclusion is that the organization will need to become leaner in professional program staff in order to address economic requirements for at least 2-3 years. They perceive available resources as being diminished for the future and insufficient to sustain the current size of the organization. The agent in this case is a management council of senior divisional heads for this social service agency. Their task, at the request of the board of trustees and chief executive (sponsors), is to design a change process to effectively carry forth the plan. Note carefully, however, that neither the sponsors nor the agents have decided upon which changes are necessary in order to effectively execute staff reductions in this social service agency. The sponsors have simply called for the change and delegated responsibility to the agents—in this case, a senior management advisory council—to implement the change process. The senior management advisory council in return has shared with the sponsor their organizational strategy for involving others in implementing the change process. Neither entity, the sponsor nor the agent, has taken the responsibility to specify which changes must occur in order to effectively implement the intended downsizing priority.

Agent and Target Relationships

Effective change agents are capable of enlisting the support of those who must change their behavior, skill, or experience within the change process. All people, no matter how close or how distant from organizational priorities, seek to have influence over the changes that govern their behavior. In our case study of downsizing a social service agency, the various department directors and key employees would benefit by being involved in the change process even though some of them may lose their positions and "personal" project priorities in the eventual results. These staff members are the targets in our change process, the ones who will be required to make actual changes.

Effective change agents conduct an initial assessment of target needs and wants prior to implementing any change strategy. As a result of this assessment of the targets' relative strengths and limits, their preferred priorities, and their skills and abilities, agents then involve the targets in effectively participating in the change strategy. In the case of our social service agency, the senior management advisory council developed an assessment tool in conjunction with all of the department heads whose employees would be affected by the proposed downsizing in the organization. Next, the assessment process was conducted by the department heads to involve them in the change strategy directly with their employees. Finally, the change agents and the targets were both involved in analyzing the results of this assessment process. Once this assessment process was completed, the change agents and the targets—in this case, all department directors and key employees— were involved in developing alternatives to respond to the concerns of the sponsors about limited resources and reduced program priorities for the future. As a result of this carefully balanced assessment and involvement process in the strategy of change, the agents were able to minimize unnecessary anxiety and the inevitable fear of losing one's position or one's territory that accompanies downsizing processes.

In this change effort, fewer positions had to be lost than initially anticipated, and some new markets were developed for this social service agency which shifted job responsibilities from some departments to others and involved other departments in working jointly to create new programs and priorities for their local publics. It also meant that some employees who would have lost their positions under a single-focused downsizing program were given the opportunity to participate in the development of new markets over a longer timetable, avoiding the immediate loss of their jobs. Had the sponsor in this case called for a downsizing with specific positions to be eliminated, this participation process would have been eclipsed and a great deal of resistance would have occurred.

Sponsor-Target Relationships

Often in the process of organizational change key leaders responsible to legitimize the change keep their distance from those who are effected by changes, especially unpleasant changes. In our example, it was not uncharacteristic for key members of the Board of Directors or the chief executive to avoid sustained or routine contact with employees who would be outplaced as a result of a downsizing effort. The appropriate role between sponsor and target in an effective change process is one of preliminary feedback and discussion prior to the final implementation of a decision. Effective sponsors take the time to assess the final impact of proposed solutions through advance consultation with representative groups from the targets, prior to execution of change strategies. In this way, employees are given the opportunity to give feedback on these decisions prior to the implementation process. Their views, even unfavorable ones, often have some subtle influence over shaping the timeframe, the cost, or the direction of the ultimate change process.

In the case study of downsizing our social service agency, the sponsor took the opportunity to meet with interdepartmental groups of employees to review the proposed changes that had been developed in the organizational plan by the Directors and the senior management advisory council. The sponsors painstakingly took time to explain why the downsizing had to occur, which new opportunities and markets would be explored, and how long these markets had to mature. They indicated their commitment to minimize the loss of jobs for the employees affected, then discussed all the attempts that had been made in the process to allow employees to identify new opportunities for service which would minimize the number of positions lost. They also indicated that some new interdepartmental priorities would be established which would provide for more efficient ways of managing the organization and might eventually increase service requirements so that employees could be called back to work in the future.

Obviously, a certain amount of resistance still took place in the downsizing of this organization. Some employees, in fact, did lose their jobs. However, employee groups were given an opportunity in small intimate circles to express their viewpoints and their concerns and to have a dialogue with the sponsors before ultimate decisions were effected. By taking upon themselves this act of leadership in being available for structured feedback processes, the sponsors effectively conveyed to the targets (employees) that their views counted in the eventual decisions. The timing of these meetings was prior to final implementation of decisions, and some minor modifications were made to the original plan based on these feedback sessions.

There is ultimately no perfect way to introduce change in an organization so as to eliminate resistance. However, this dynamic of balanced and symmetrical relationship between sponsors, agents, and targets can minimize unintended resistance and unnecessary changes. Involving sponsors, agents, and targets in the appropriate participation in the change process fosters a greater atmosphere of teamwork and shared contribution.

Since most leaders are involved in the change process at the level of change agent, a few tips for introducing change strategies would be helpful in managing both targets and sponsors. Change agents are most effective in dealing with target customers, clients, and employees when they review their change strategies with these groups in advance. The characteristics of effectively reviewing a change strategy with targets includes the following:

1. **Announce the reasons for change**

2. **Identify clear channels to give input to the change process**

3. **Identify the desired consequences and potential unfavorable consequences to the change process**

4. Identify expected timeline and points of review in the change process

5. Acknowledge dissent while not always responding directly to it

6. Practice complex decision-making

7. Don't abdicate the change process.

Skillful change agents are clear about the reasons for a change. They don't avoid the fact that organizations experience adverse conditions and require unpleasant changes in order to conduct their affairs. Direct, honest, and open expressions of the reason for change are greatly appreciated among those whose behavior and experience will be required to change as a result of organizational efforts.

Secondly, skillful change agents identify in advance the clear channels of communication for targets to influence the change process. Often unintended anger, frustration, or hostility is generated in change efforts because clear channels of communicating dissent are not made available to targets. When real opportunities for communicating dissatisfaction, approval, and disapproval occur, employees, clients, and customers are more likely to respect the process of change. Most people feel valued when they have a means of influencing change through expressing their considered opinions.

For most targets in the change process, their greatest fear is that the others who have control over their destiny do not understand the impact upon them. It is important for agents to *identify in advance both the desired consequences that will occur in the change process and also those unfavorable consequences that may occur.* In our previous example of the client organization that was downsized, it was important to anticipate the desired consequence of saving the organization's funds and resources in order to maintain quality service in the future as well as to acknowledge that this would involve some loss of employment. Resistance was further diminished by identifying how that unfavorable consequence would be managed with the employees affected.

Fourth, one of the sources of greatest frustration things for targets in the change process is to be left unaware of the expected timeline for closure of a change strategy. They also benefit by knowing the points of review and evaluation in assessing the impact of change. One organization whose board of directors had

decided that it would hire an outside consultant to review its overall effectiveness extended their timeframe three times during the
process, with the final evaluation process taking over eighteen
months. This seemingly endless postponement eroded confidence
among key managers in the ability of the board to establish priorities in the organization's evaluation process. *A clear, realistic, and
firmly held timeline for completion of the change process is appreciated by
most targets.*

*Fifth, most targets who will be influenced by a change process greatly
appreciate being able to express their dissent.* Most customers, clients,
and employees realize that their viewpoints may not always be
adopted and followed, but they do appreciate the opportunity to
express them. It is not necessary for change agents to respond to
every objection in the change process, but it is important for them
to be available to hear them. Leaders can acknowledge the
feedback without necessarily acting on it directly or immediately.

*Sixth, effective change agents understand the nature of complex deci-
sion-making.* Complex decision-making involves sequential and
planned decisions which do not rule out other options until abso-
lutely necessary. Consequently, effective change strategies take
into account multiple levels of decision-making prior to adopting
ultimate decisions that have dramatic or pervasive consequences.
It is a rare organizational change strategy that cannot be broken
into several levels of decisions prior to implementation of the final
outcome. For example, an organization that seeks to downsize its
employees based on market conditions can often develop some interim strategies of testing new markets, re-examining current sales
and communication practices, and developing some training opportunities for their employees to strengthen their motivation in
reaching new customers and clients, all before implementing the
ultimate change. These interim decision-making practices often
make the ultimate and inevitable changes, which may be unpopular, more palatable and effective.

*Lastly, effective change agents are aware that ultimately they them-
selves are responsible for managing the change process.* Sometimes in
the middle of change efforts, either sponsors or targets seek to influence the steps and procedures that have been outlined in the
change process. This may be as simple as modifying a timeline by
a sponsor, to something more complicated such as changing the
levels of consultation within an organization amidst an unfavor-

able change. Skillful change agents hold fast to their authority to manage the process and refuse to alter ongoing processes despite any dissatisfaction of targets or sponsors in the middle of a change effort. Not all change processes are well-defined, but they are rarely improved in design while still in the midst of the strategy of change. Most effective change agents maintain tight control over the change process and allow sponsors and targets to concentrate their efforts on giving feedback to the content and direction of change itself, rather than focus on the process itself.

There are also innovative strategies which change agents can adopt to strengthen sponsor effectiveness during organizational change. Effective strategies by change agents to strengthen their sponsors include:

1. Meticulously identifying a common goal and vision

2. Carefully agreeing on a timeframe and cost (human and technical)

3. Previewing the change strategy

4. Providing regular written analysis and progress reports

5. Staying focused on strategies for problem-solving

6. Providing solutions for review in advance

7. Developing prototypes for future action

Skillful sponsors who do not seek to control the change process can be at a disadvantage in not having their agendas well represented in the midst of organizational change. Skillful leaders and change agents take the time and the care to respond to the concerns of sponsors by including them in key decisions that are important in developing an effective change strategy. *These change agents collaborate with their sponsors to meticulously identify the common goal and vision for the change effort.* Before any change strategies are announced, the scope and direction of intended change is clear among both sponsors and agents. With mutual clarity on the goal, greater resourcefulness can emerge. Rather than to specify the scope of the change as to downsize an organization, for example, the focus of the change effort might be to conserve $100,000 in the annual budget. This more neutral statement of goal or vision provides for maximum freedom for options to be generated during the change process.

Secondly, skillful agents carefully negotiate with their sponsors the timeframe and the human and technical cost anticipated in the change effort. Nothing is more frustrating in an organization than to embark on a change process and run out of funds, or to unexpectedly incur unacceptable costs of human and technical resources in implementing the change. This quickly erodes confidence in the ability of key organizational leaders to manage effective change in the future. Consequently, the advance definition of acceptable timeframe and human or technical costs for change processes is an essential element of the sponsor-agent relationship.

Thirdly, skillful change agents preview their change strategy well in advance with sponsors. They are flexible in their process design *until the change strategy is begun.* In previewing strategies, they are willing to modify their approach to introducing and evaluating change, based on the feedback of sponsors. There is a delicate balance between allowing the sponsors to control or direct the efforts of change and engaging them in a consultation on how the change process should be managed. Generally, key leaders in an organization should not manage change processes too closely; rather, the effective delegation of these processes to skillful change agents brings about the most satisfying change. It allows for more flexibility of feedback in the organization and less fear of displeasing the boss than might ordinarily occur. This allows for the best and most creative solutions to emerge. Consequently, skillful change agents involve sponsors in previewing their change strategy, avoiding last-minute changes of plans or redirection of the strategy based on some priority which a sponsor failed to mention.

Fourth, effective change agents provide regular written analysis and progress reports to sponsors during the course of change efforts. Frequently, sponsors who delegate the responsibility for implementing change are concerned about the progress of organizational change, especially when some aspects may be unpopular. Written summary reports are helpful reminders to sponsors that their quiet and one-step-removed participation is an important part of the process. It also provides a regular vehicle for communication between sponsors and agents, keeping them mutually accountable for one another's agenda.

Fifth, careful change agents stay focused on the strategies for change with sponsors and avoid isolated problem-solving in that context. Problem-solving in change strategies is part and parcel of the relationship between the change agent and the targets for change. However, the content of change strategy is best solicited from those most influenced by its results. Consequently, those who are one or two steps removed from the change efforts should not be directing the content or recommendations for change. In an organizational downsizing process, for example, it is generally not helpful for top executives to determine which positions and program priorities should be modified or eliminated. This is better done by those closer to the action or the ultimate impact on the local client. However, communicating the methods and strategies for solving problems with sponsors is an important part of a change agent's responsibilities.

Sixth, creative change agents provide their sponsors with a range of solutions for review in advance. Change agents who review proposed strategic changes in an organization with the targets prior to consulting with sponsors simply set up all of these roles for failure. A range of solutions, including those which may be more or less acceptable, must be reviewed with sponsors prior to any announcement or public communication of the implementation of a change process.

Lastly, successful change agents develop future prototypes for actions in the present. This involves developing new models or examples of relationships, roles, program priorities, and market strategies in order to demonstrate a broad approach to organizational changes. In the process of change constricted mindsets take over and we become plagued with limited options, particularly in the midst of change that is unpleasant. The more unpleasant the anticipated organizational change, often the more constricted our viewpoints. Future-oriented change agents maintain their flexibility by developing new models for actions and services, to broaden the perspective of key sponsors in the midst of complex change processes.

Effective change strategies involve the artful interplay of the relationships between sponsor, agent and target. All three roles have a vital responsibility for implementing an effective change strategy. Change strategies in organizations which minimize the responsibility of any one of these roles will generate more resistance than necessary. A balanced plan of communication and strategy among these three essential players can make a lasting impact on the health of their systems by involving sponsors, agents, and targets in the responsible implementation of organizational change.

Strategies for Growth Through Change

Despite the necessary experience of resistance which we encounter—personally, interpersonally, and within our organizations—change has enormous potential to precipitate growth. Balanced leaders understand that even unpleasant change can provide experiences for individuals and organizations to expand their capabilities, enlarge their vision, and strengthen their perspectives to serve their organizations and their publics more effectively in the future. Proactive leaders have learned ways to maximize the benefit of change, even unwelcome change, and to diminish resistance among those they serve. Most people in an organization take their cues on how to respond to the change process from the tone, the direction, and the strategies set by these designated leaders.

There are a few key change intervention strategies that are helpful in order to maximize the learning experience among individuals and with organizations in the process of change. Leaders attentive to the personal, organizational, and public dimensions of change keep one eye focused on the purposes and direction of change, and the other on the developmental opportunities that change presents. If well executed, change expands our capacities as human beings to be more personally and professionally competent—strengthening ourselves, our organizations, and our public service as a result of our efforts.

To conclude our chapter, we will review six strategies that if effectively employed can strengthen the developmental learning which occurs personally, organizationally, and publicly as a result of change processes.

Skillful leaders focus the direction of change as moving toward the future rather than as departing from the past.

Often in the change process employees, customers, clients, participants, and other publics are very conscious of the present established order, irrespective of its long-term value for the organization. It is incumbent upon leaders in the change process to focus people's attention on the intended future direction of change. Comparisons or references to past behavior or performance and its successes and failures are not nearly as helpful as outlining a positive image of future goals and directions which represent the expected change effort. For example, rather than focusing on an organization's past history of decline in serving a particular customer, market, or client base, it would be more effective for the CEO to describe future markets and priorities that the organization seeks to attract as a result of change. Repeated referencing of past problems or difficulties taint the change process as a reactive effort controlled by the past rather than directed by future priorities.

Skillful leaders relate facts in the current environment to their future goals for change.

Often in the midst of change, the temptation is to emphasize strong and polarized feelings concerning the relative merits of the change process. Inevitably employees, customers, and clients share deeply held opinions about whether or not change is a positive contribution to the organization from their perspective. They are also prone to focus on signals of decline or departure from their current status quo. The skillful leader in the change process knows how to concentrate on the facts of the current situation which require a need for change. This strategy is further enhanced by relating the facts of the present situation to future goals and priorities that are essential for the change effort. For example, in a stalled fund raising campaign for a nonprofit organization, rather than focusing on the mistake of an overambitious capital plan, it may be more helpful to focus on the reasons in the current situation which require a strategic change of viewpoint. The skillful leader might indicate that "last year's contributions to our capital campaign declined by 15% over the previous year. This was after a string of steady increases of at least 5% for the past ten years. During last year's capital campaign program, we announced what may have been an over-ambitious approach to expanding and remodeling our facilities at a 5% growth rate. We will reexamine that approach in light of these declining contributions to test whether or not that expansion plan meets the desired goals of our contributors." Rather than focusing on the past error, this approach to documenting the reason for future change—in this case, a diminished capital program—will bring employees, clients, and customers a common background of information necessary to understand the reason for future changes. This strategy is focused on responsibility for the future rather than blame for the past.

Skillful leaders treat resistance objectively.

Since all change in an organization involves "attitude adjustment" among clients, customers, employees, and sponsors, it is important for those directing the change effort to stay as objective as possible when experiencing resistance. We know that resistance is engendered by personal, interpersonal, group life and history, or group task and group work priorities. Whenever there is change, resistance is a logical correlation to people's feelings about these four dimensions of organizational life. The skillful leader is able to remain detached by separating his or her ego and self-esteem from the resistance experienced. Unfortunately, resistance in the change process is often expressed directly towards the leader of the change effort. Most people resent the fact that there is a need for change itself and are quick to criticize the process of change as being unfair or biased as a convenient expression of anxiety. They also may not have the skills or the background to understand their underlying and often unconscious fears about the expected changes. Those who are in the forefront of directing change efforts therefore may be the recipients of the full measure of people's negative feelings. Clients, customers, and employees may not really object to the strategies of change nor to the agents of change themselves, yet often these become the initial focus for the expression of resistance. The skillful leader understands these dynamics in the change process and realizes that objections expressed towards the strategies and activities of change, and toward him or herself as an agent of change may be convenient ways to express uneasiness with the fact that there is a need for change itself. Skillful leaders do not allow themselves to become personal issues in the change process or to identify themselves too closely with the outcomes or the strategies of change.

For example, in the midst of an outburst of criticism during an annual meeting for an organization's strategic plan, the detached CEO is able to step back from the criticism at the moment with a response similar to the following. "I'm sorry that some of you, as stakeholders in this organization, believe I have been remiss in some of my past duties concerning clear priorities for the organization. It is true that we did not achieve two out of the seven goals we had projected for last year. However, our experience on the successful five goals has far transcended the economic and public benefit to the organization that we anticipated for all of the past goals. I will keep your criticism in mind for future priorities and take seriously your concerns, while I don't share your viewpoints." That type of ego detachment is characteristic of leaders who are able to treat resistance objectively.

Skillful leaders encourage participation in the implementation of change strategies.

All leaders realize that participation increases motivation and ownership for a particular activity or priority. Often people need involvement to express strong opinions with respect to a particular change effort as a reflection of their need to exercise some control over the environment that expects them to change. Thoughtful leaders realize that people usually do not have a choice as to whether or not the organization or the system will make the necessary changes. These leaders also are skillful at realizing that people can have access to how the change is implemented even if they do not have influence over whether or not the change will occur. Involving people in the implementation of change strategies can allow them to focus their dissatisfaction and keep them more satisfied with the overall need for change, by helping them avoid evaluating change as universally right or wrong in terms of its personal or organizational impact. For example, the president of a small electronics manufacturing group may recognize and determine a need to reposition their products and services to new markets. However, she should allow the sales force to be involved in determining the relative priorities and investments necessary to shift positions. She may state that the organization needs to reposition itself to respond to new markets in light of the competition of foreign investors in small electronic components. However, the best strategy for adopting that change will be developed by involving customers, suppliers, and salespeople in the effort. This strategy of extensive participation in the implementation of change often allows those impacted to influence the pace, the tasks, and the implementation of change. This involvement further moderates their concerns and their expressed resistance to organizational change efforts. Only a few may influence the need for change, but all can influence how change is implemented.

Skillful leaders develop a change team.

The role of any leader involves many complex tasks, issues, and priorities, particularly amidst the process of organizational change. In today's diverse and variable organizational environments within even small organizations, the burden of implementing change cannot rest successfully with only the single individual or leader, no matter how skillful or talented. The development of a team of respected peers and constituents, including customers, suppliers, and employees within an organization, is a helpful model for managing the change process. In essence the role of change agent is expanded to include a change team rather than an individual person or single representative. These change teams often can serve to introduce the change process to their peers in ways that convey a sense of confidence and assurance that all perspectives will be represented in assessing the scope of change. For example, the quality assurance manager of a large metropolitan hospital had a fairly good idea of the changes she wanted to make in the employee system of quality work teams. However, rather than making these changes herself within the organization, she sought senior management's approval to convene a task force to review past performance of the various work teams and outline some future directions for their improved performance. This participation of employees, managers, and senior executives in evaluating the current and future course of quality work teams produced more shared values and more lasting results in the organization than an isolated administrative decision would have done.

Effective leaders evaluate the results of change, not the need for change itself.

Often when change requires adaptation in the organization's culture, its means of participation, its manner of treating staff, constituents, or publics, there is a temptation to focus closely on the immediate perceived value of change itself. The skillful change agent maintains attention and focus on the benefits of specific outcomes and activities of change in their component parts rather than on the total process of change itself. In addition, more positive results can be achieved from the change process if the leader keeps the strategy and the activities of change in the forefront as "provisional," able to be modified based on future evidence that comes into the organization's picture. Consequently, careful attention by leaders to the results, the strategies, and the activities of change in their individual elements becomes a positive force for monitoring the progress of an organization's change efforts. Focusing too much attention on the wider dimension of whether or not an organization's change strategy was globally effective or ineffective dilutes the capacity to learn from the change effort. Invariably in change processes, certain aspects of our plans and priorities go awry. Unanticipated consequences occur. Unexpected delays, setbacks, and disappointments derail our timeframe. Focusing on the concrete results of change can be an important aspect of managing and leading in the change process.

One organization executive was recruited to lead a turnaround situation at the request of the board of directors. Once in the position of CEO, he quickly realized that the current management team required an almost total reorganization, and perhaps even outplacement, in order to effectively move the organization forward. He carefully developed a strategy of individualized training, coaching, and counseling with existing managers to help them make the transition to the new organization's future. In the end, however, three-quarters of the existing managers were not able to make the transition and their outplacement was required. This was a dramatic for an organization which had always placed a high value on longevity and loyalty to employees. In the face of global criticism by his board of trustees, the CEO laid out the individual positive benefits that had resulted in employee morale as a result of this change. Without denying the fact that it was distasteful but necessary to outplace three-quarters of the existing management team, he focused on the improved performance and attitudes of employees within those departments as evidence of the benefits of continuing the change effort. He was able to acknowledge the undesired consequences of change, but also to highlight the positive results of individual change strategies. Ultimately he empowered the directors to be more patient with the change process.

Leaders recognize that the collective mission of leadership is not to be what we are now, but to become what we are not yet. A friend who is an organizational consultant is fond of saying, "Because we are limited by what we know, we are unable to comprehend what we do not know." The challenge for all of us as leaders is to evolve a more complete and more complex understanding of ourselves, our relationships, our organizations, and our contribution to the social good. The purpose of leadership is not to follow the prevailing conditions, but to be in the forefront of initiating change as an opportunity for individual, organizational, and social transformation. This tendency to be in the vanguard of change processes, however, often makes leaders prone to experiencing resistance, disappointment, and discouragement. As leaders, we are called to recognize and realize the transformative and humanizing influence that change can have on our lives both individually and organizationally. Effective leaders possess and promote an expansive attitude among people and organizations as a necessary complement to the changes they introduce. This attitude towards healthy change is represented by a Shaker hymn that expresses this humanizing quality of change in poetic form:

'Tis a gift to be simple, 'tis a gift to be free.
'Tis a gift to come down where we ought to be.
And when we are in the place just right,
we will be in the valley of love and delight.
When true simplicity is gained, to bow and to bend
we will not be ashamed.
For to turn to turn it will be our delight,
As it's by turning, turning, that we come round right.

(Shaker Hymn, "Simple Gifts")

It is our ultimate task as leaders in the change process to empower others and our organizations to become more right for the tasks, responsibilities, and conditions which lie ahead.

Chapter IX

Strategic Leadership

Organizations and systems have enormous power and influence to shape the quality of our lives, the quality of our work, and the quality of society. The quality of our life in our families and communities is heavily influenced by public service organizations, social service agencies, educational systems, and the workplaces in which we earn our livelihoods. The quality of our organizations is largely shaped not only by the internal management and leadership systems in which we are involved, but also by external organizations such as competitors, governments, and social agencies which regulate and monitor our individual businesses and services. The quality of our society is also heavily influenced by the organizational structures which make key decisions concerning our environment, our health, our safety, our educational systems, and the distribution of economic resources on a national and global scale.

Chapter VI outlined the benefits to a process-intensive approach to organizational leadership which is focused on strategy. These two characteristics of process intensity and strategic focus are essential in developing organizations with the fitness to respond to the quality of life, the quality of work, and the quality of the social fabric necessary for our futures. However, organizations can be often limited in the necessary inner vision required to manage them with a propensity towards strategy and a focus on process. This chapter will outline a model for strengthening organizational systems with these two variables of strategic focus and process intensity in mind. This chapter may be used as a planning process over an extended time frame to develop a new strategic agenda within an organization. This particular approach can be helpful when repositioning an organization, making a change in key strategic leadership, or assessing the impact of outside variables on the organization. These variables could include assessing new markets or new competitors which will significantly change the internal vision and external strategy of an organization's plans and priorities.

This chapter may also be used as a guide for individual planning episodes within an organization. Each one of the elements of strategic leadership woven throughout this chapter may be used at key points in an organization's history to clarify strategy and strengthen its process. For example, an organization primarily concerned with its mission development may have rapidly broadened its base of products and services to the point where its fundamental focus or its primary mission seems unclear. At another time an organization may focus on its strategic action planning. It may find that it has developed some effective products and services, but that these seem to be waning in their responsiveness to its consumers, customers, and clients.

However elements of this strategic leadership model are used, it is important that they are understood as helping organizational leaders distinguish long-term strategy from immediate plans and priorities. Often in organizations, key strategic leaders get mired and overwhelmed in the management systems required day to day, leaving little time to focus energy in a process intensive way on their future strategy. The model outlined in this chapter is helpful to disengage from the demands at hand in order to develop a convergence of organizational focus. Earlier in the book we mentioned that strategic planning consists of focusing energy and attention on one's primary internal and external constituencies in the same direction at the same time. Dwight Eisenhower once said, "the plan is nothing, planning is everything." Developing this convergence of perception and energy is difficult but essential. This refocusing of energy and attention is largely a matter of inner perception and revisioning. This inner perception requires a new "Zen," or way of seeing an organization's internal and external environments in light of its past, present, and future requirements. The process of strategic leadership, then, consists of reframing a commonly held vision and viewpoint about an organization's priorities and plans. This proactive view of integrating an organization's past experience and its desired future in light of its present realities is contingent upon having the necessary process skills to shape consensus on new strategy. This is the substance of strategic leadership.

Our model for strategic leadership includes five elements:

- **Developing a Strategic Position**
- **Mission Development**
- **Success Factor Analysis**
- **Strategic Action Planning**
- **Organizational Restructuring.**

These five processes are the essential ingredients of strategic leadership necessary to move organizations forward. Balance and diversity among these elements will help organizations be attentive to the quality of life for their internal and external constituents, to the quality of their organizational work and productivity, and to the lasting public impact they have on the quality of society. Attention to each of these strategic processes is an important indicator of an organization's ability to address a new future in light of present opportunities, challenges, and complexities by evolving and developing a global mindset.

Developing a Strategic Position

A *strategic position* is a present statement of a favorable or preferred organizational future in light of changing internal and external environments, which is shaped by key decision makers, planners, managers, and implementers. Developing a future strategic position is largely an artful process of proactively engaging one's internal and external publics in *assessing present communications, building future scenarios,* and *analyzing available strategic options* for an organization's future. A strategic position will succinctly represent the organization's vision in a concise description such as, "By the year 2000 (name of organization) will be recognized for. . . ." This statement of a favorable strategic position is the central point of focus, energy, and intensity for all organizational efforts. The future strategic position should be the phrase and the memorable point of identification with which all internal and external constituencies are thoroughly familiar. For example, if one encountered an employee of an organization in the hall and asked what the organization does, ideally the employee would answer with the statement of the favorable strategic position. Likewise, if one were to contact one's outside vendors, customers, clients, or consumers and ask them how they understood the purpose of one's organization, ideally they would answer in light of the basic elements of one's strategic position.

Some examples of strategic position statements include a major health care institution which states that, "By the year 2000, Methodist Hospital will be known as the center for research in medical technologies for incurable diseases throughout the midwest." Another example of a strategic position statement for an international training center is, "By the year 2000, Developmental Resources, Inc. will be known as the state-of-the-art leaders in training and educating nonprofit executives." A third example of a strategic position comes from a local municipality, "By the year 2000, the City of Pleasant Heights will be known as a regional arts, cultural and recreational community strengthening an appreciation of the quality of life in its metropolitan area."

While the statements of strategic positions should be quite simple and easily communicated, they require intensity, deliberation, and extensive process to articulate. I have found it helpful to engage organizations and their leaders in three separate steps to develop their strategic position.

Step number one is comprised of a *communications audit* interviewing in small groups key representatives of internal and external publics concerning their perception of the organization's contribution to the quality of life, quality of work, and quality of society. Once a *communications audit* is complete, organizations often find it helpful to engage in a *scenario building* process to develop alternate futures based upon the assessment of their key internal and external constituents. Thirdly, once a preferred strategic position is developed (which often is a composite of various scenarios outlined in this planning activity), it is helpful for organizations to evaluate their work through *strategic position analysis*. Each of these steps will be outlined in some detail to give some flavor of the process design necessary to formulate an effective strategic position within an organization.

Communications Audit

The *communications audit* is the first step in engaging one's customers, employees, suppliers, vendors, and various publics in assessing the organization's contribution to themselves as well as to one another. This is best achieved by involving internal and external constituents in a discussion of the organization's contribution to leadership and the quality of life, organizational leadership, and public leadership. A model for each of these focus group consultations follows. Each of these small group focus sessions reviews the organization's ability to communicate its various contributions. These sessions are best conducted in an informal setting. These groups consist of internal constituencies, such as employees and executive leaders, as well as external groups of customers, suppliers, vendors, and various publics. If an organization has a board of advisors, a board of directors, or a board of trustees, their inclusion in this process is also vital. Participants in these consultation sessions are best served when given the opportunity to respond to questions privately and in writing, as well as to share their feedback in a group setting convened by a facilitator. Each of the three sets of questions below can be used in this fashion. Imagine convening a small group of no more than 10 to 15 participants to engage in each one of the following three discussions based on their prior written input after receiving these questions in advance of a meeting.

The first two consultations which follow are best completed with groups of internal constituencies, such as employees, board members, trustees, key stockholders, and directors.

Leadership and the Quality of Life Consultation

1. *Part of the strategic planning process for (name of organization) in the year 2000 will focus on strengthening the quality of life for its constituents. What supports, resources, or services could (name of organization) provide that would contribute to the quality of life for yourself and other constituents of our organization?* (Please list 3 or 4 key ones below)

2. *Strengthening the quality of life is a shared process in any organization. What supports, resources, or skills do you have to contribute to strengthening the quality of life for other constituents in this organization or its future?* (Please list them below)

3. *What obstacles exist, if any, to the effective contribution of this organization to the quality of life for its internal and external publics?*

Organizational Leadership Consultation

1. *You have heard some key priorities for (name of organization) from our previous organizational studies and planning processes.* In view of these and your insights, what elements of organizational leadership would you like to see strengthened through this strategic planning process? (Specifically, respond to the following points)

- *What 2 or 3 key improvements would you like to see incorporated into the organization's structures, programs, products, or organizational plans for the future?* (Please list)

- *What 2 or 3 key improvements would you like to see in the quality of organizational leadership both among staff and executive members of our organization?* (Please list)

- *What 2 or 3 key improvements would you like to see in the quality of team leadership to strengthen our external communication and network abilities as an organization?* (Please list)

The final consultation model is most effectively completed with external constituencies or publics, such as customers, suppliers, vendors, donors, or other people outside of the formal organization which contribute to or are influenced by its mission.

Public Leadership Consultation

The year 2000 signals a new century. It may be a new era in human history in many organizations which contribute to the future. The complexities and interdependence of all organizational systems will be challenged by the requirements of fewer, but also shared, resources. What role do you see for (name of organization) for its responsible expression of public leadership in the future? (Specifically)

- *What 2 or 3 local community issues, initiative, or needs would you like to see (name of organization) champion within our greater metropolitan community to respond to consumer, social, political, business, or environmental concerns?*

- *What 2 or 3 national issues or trends in our industry or service would you like to see (name of organization) make a contribution to through its products and services by the year 2000?*

- *What 2 or 3 international or global issues of strategic importance would you like to see (name of organization) work with other systems to influence by the year 2000?*

These three assessments—of leadership and the quality of life, internal organizational leadership, and external public leadership—are the three most important inputs for determining an organization's effective strategic position. These elements comprise a communications audit which is the first step in developing an effective future strategic position for an organization. A summary of trends, issues, and strategies identified by this audit would be prepared by key leaders for use in the following leadership processes.

Scenario Building

Once an organization and its leaders have crystallized key themes and issues through the communications audit process, it is important to cross-reference the information for developing strategies for an organization's future. This *scenario building* exercise is best done with a matrix work team comprised of internal and external publics of an organization. A cross-section of organizational leaders, including a diversity of skill and expertise also involving a wide range of commitments to the organizations (such as both salaried and hourly employees), is an important contribution to this process. The ability of these internal publics of an organization to engage in the following *scenario building* process with the external publics of the organization, such as customers, suppliers, vendors, and board members, is a dynamic to effective scenarios for the future of an organization.

The process of *scenario building* involves a cross-matrix work group of 20-25 people. The process benefits from working off-site in a secluded place with dedicated time to develop three to four alternate scenarios for the future of the organization. These future scenarios are often best formulated in smaller work units allowing more intimate discussion among no more than seven participants at a time. This *scenario building* process is comprised of leading these small groups through the following future scenario questions. A briefing by key leadership on the communications audit sets the stage for these scenarios.

Future Scenario (name of organization)   Year _____

1. *Describe the optimum primary mission of your organization at the end of the timeframe for our scenario.*

2. *Describe changes expected in the major internal and external constituencies of our organization in the timeframe of our scenario (roles, demographics, markets, geographic considerations, psychographic considerations).*

- Internal Constituencies:

- Major External Constituencies:

- New Constituencies:

3. *Describe the human resources and their preferred organization in the future scenario for (name of organization). Include an outline of the future structure, function, expertise, and major positions this organization will require.*

4. *Describe the economic base of our organization at the end of the timeframe for our future scenario. List all sources of expected revenue and expenses (in relative proportions by percent).*

5. *Describe and outline the major product lines, business services, or public services of our organization by the end of the timeframe of our future scenario.*

At the end of this *scenario building* process, participants in this scenario development retreat would have an opportunity to evaluate and critique each of the scenarios developed. Some common themes in each area of mission, future constituencies, human resources and organizational design, economic base, and primary product or service should be apparent. These common themes should be synthesized by key leadership and converge on a direction expressed in a preliminary statement of strategic position. The statement of strategic position would clearly express, "By the year _____, (name of organization) will be recognized as. . . ."

Strategic Position Analysis

Warren Bennis and Burt Nanus in their book, *Leaders, The Strategies for Taking Charge,* describe an environmental scanning process which has some common elements to our strategic positioning discussion here. They discuss an environmental scanning process conducted for a major airline by a management consultant. At the end of that process they provide several indicators to evaluate an organization's strategic position. They identify these evaluative issues as an assessment of the risks, rewards, resource requirements, and impacts upon various stakeholders within the organization.[1]

A *strategic positioning analysis* includes these elements for critiquing a future organizational strategy outlined by Warren Bennis and Burt Nanus. This *strategic positioning analysis* is best facilitated at a later time, after the *scenario building* process. A select group of representatives is to be chosen from the internal and external organization's constituencies who participated in the *scenario building* process. A group of no more than ten should be involved in this *strategic position analysis* which is outlined below. Leadership would clarify its proposed strategic position with the group assembled searching for critical refinements.

Strategic Position Analysis

Strategic Position Description:

_____

_____

1. *List the alternatives to this strategic position for your organization.*

2. *Identify the risks in assuming this strategic position for your organization.*

3. *List the anticipated rewards that could be expected in this strategic position if it were adopted.*

4. *List the internal and external resources that will be necessary to accomplish this strategic position if implemented.*

5. *Identify the expected favorable and unfavorable impacts on key internal and key publics as a result of adopting this strategic position in the future for our organization.*

Once these elements are analyzed for the preferred strategic position of an organization, a final shaping and redevelopment will occur, sharpening the critical focus for the organization's strategic position. An organization's strategic position is the present statement of their response to future environments. It is the heart of the strategic leadership process.

Mission Development

The second qualitative ingredient of successful strategic leadership is the capability of leaders within an organization to engage in successful *mission development*. Many organizations begin their planning process with the development of a mission. However, this neglects the fundamental point of entry an organization seeks in influencing its internal and external publics based on its past history and future goals. Consequently, mission development is most effectively done once the strategic position is clearly identified. Whether consciously stated or left dormant, an organization or group functions under a fabric of meaning that gives both cohesion and division to its parts. This is an organization's mission. A mission links the organization's strategic position with the present needs and interests of its diverse publics.

The *mission development* of an organization should reflect the principles and conditions under which a group and organization exists. It should answer the question, "Why are we here now?" All organizations, whether in the public or private sector, are under constant scrutiny from competitors, collaborators, and other systems within society to justify their existence. The mission development process is a way to sharpen an organization's perceptions of itself in order to continually re-evaluate its purpose for existence and make clear choices about its future markets, products, services or intended goals for itself and its various publics.

A mission for an organization is contingent upon a comprehensive understanding of the needs and interests of its preferred external constituencies and its internal members or employees. It also defines the relative role the organization seeks to play in addressing them. The mission development of an organization is based upon a conscious articulation of the level of vision or dream that serves as the basis for an organization's primary existence. An adequate expression of *mission development* within an organization should include a statement of:

- **Clear identification of the organization's primary public.**
- **Why an organization exists.**
- **The values and principles one's service or product intends to achieve (goal values).**

- The values or beliefs that shape an organization's philosophy of service (means values).

- What is unique or "particular" to this organization that is not present in the same way elsewhere (distinctive character).

- In an ideal image, what this organization would be.

An organization's *mission development* is best accomplished with a small strategic group of internal and external constituents who are familiar and comfortable with an organization's strategic position. This is often done in the context of a planning retreat or over several sessions spanning several months. Typical participants in a mission development process would include board members, directors or trustees; employee groups from across the separate sections or divisions of an organization; and key external publics and their representatives (suppliers, vendors, or customers of an organization).

The *mission development* process is largely comprised of a two-step assessment. First, the small group of participants is engaged in an assessment of the following mission development questions. These mission development questions consider an organization's constituency, purposes, and values. Once this discussion and the ensuing notes are collected, usually a small work group of one or two individuals is established to draft the statement of mission. The statement of mission is then fed back to the primary work group for further critique. Once an agreed-upon statement of mission is developed, it is widely shared internally and externally with an organization's constituents in order to gain further feedback before adoption. A final adoption process in a *mission development* phase is important. This final adoption process should include ratification of an organization's mission from its board of directors, trustees, or major stakeholders.

The following outline represents some of the discussion questions necessary for a core group to consider in the process of *mission development*:

Mission Development

I. Constituency

A. How would you describe the primary, secondary, and auxiliary constituency (markets) you intend to serve? (demographics, roles, geography, social profile, etc.)

B. What types of direct service or products should your organization provide to each of these constituencies?

C. What public identity or public perception of your organization would be desirable to achieve and maintain among other organizations with a similar purpose or product?

II. Purpose

A. In a phrase or one-sentence headline, why does your organization or service exist?

B. What is unique or particular to your service or your product that may not be present in the same way elsewhere?

C. In an ideal image, what would your group or organization be known for?

III. Values

A. What values and principles do the services of your organization seek to promote?

B. What values or beliefs shape why you serve and how you serve internally within your organization?

Once these questions have been addressed and analyzed in a small task force, the comprehensive statement of an organization's mission is issued. This statement of mission becomes a public expression of an organization's key values, commitments to its constituencies, and purposes. The statement of an organization's mission serves to galvanize a common strategy and focus for its primary products, services, and communication vehicles, both internally and externally. Prominence of an organization's mission statement in public vehicles such as newsletters, flyers, brochures, and promotional materials as well as in internal communications is an important means of strengthening an organization's commitment to its mission. Convergence of focus across an organization's internal and external publics is perhaps the most fundamental ingredient of an organization's strategic leadership. Therefore, convergence on an organization's strategic position and in its statement of mission are the two primary ingredients of effective strategic leadership.

Success Factor Analysis

Most organizations engage in some form of goal setting or development of objectives as part of their strategic planning. However, little common ground or understanding seems to be prevalent among goal setting or objective setting processes. This confusion over nomenclature and concepts often makes it difficult for organizations to convene internal and external groups of their key publics in order to effectively accomplish this end.

Price Waterhouse, Inc., a financial and organizational consulting firm, has introduced the helpful concept of critical *success factor* analysis. Critical success factors are those elements within an organization that must go right for the organization to function as desired. Success factors help an organization identify which fundamental abilities it requires to achieve its task or primary purpose. Price Waterhouse contends that no organization can be successful in the current glut of available information and options unless it can strategically focus its attention and direction on no more than six critical success factors. They describe their critical success factor concept and its origin as follows:

> The concept of critical success factors (CSFs) was developed by Dr. John Rockart of MIT. He observed that most information systems produce an extensive amount of information. Very little of the information, however, appear useful in assisting managers to better perform their jobs. CSFs attempt to overcome this traditional shortcoming. The approach assumes that the designers of an information system should be discriminating and focus on 'success factors', those key areas where 'things must go right for an organization to flourish'.[2]

Assisting an organization identify what must go right in order to succeed is an effective way to get around the typical dilemmas in goal setting and the establishment of objectives. The use of critical *success factor* analysis is helpful in three modes of organizational development. First, it is helpful to assist an organization to identify how it intends to position new developments, such as products and services, in light of a past organizational history. Secondly, critical *success factor* analysis can be helpful to help an organization reassess the feasibility of a product or service if the past outcome has been less than anticipated. Thirdly, a fundamental use of critical success factors is to discriminate primary purposes as a focus for future planning amidst multiple demands and priorities. Critical success factors then become the fundamental vehicles for discriminating among operational, strategic, and tactical decisions within an organization. The concept of *success factor* analysis can apply to individual business units or divisions within an organization or to an organization as a whole.

In the context of our discussion of strategic leadership, we will focus on developing success factors for an entire organization. Successful organizations and their strategic leaders and managers use these success factors for day-to-day operational decisions concerning priorities, programs, and services.

Price Waterhouse, Inc. indicates that there are four prime sources of critical success factors. Their model of developing critical success factors is taken from an analysis of:

- **The structure of the particular industry (service)**
- **Competitive strategy, industry position, and geographic location**
- **Environmental factors**
- **Temporary factors**[3]

I find it helpful in working with organizations in *success factor* analysis to expand upon their five types of success factors for their future planning.

The first type of *success factor* that an organization considers is related to their internal organizational structure and their major product development. This involves organizational and product or service development.

The second type of *success factor* organizations are encouraged to focus upon is their external communications and marketing. In this area, organizations review their direct public communications through print, telecommunications, and other forms of media, as well as indirect communications that are done through their informal networks and sources of influence in the community. For example, one way to evaluate this type of indirect external communication is to look at the various memberships and affiliations that executives and managers hold within an organization. This often is a good measure as to how effectively they communicate their public message through their personal presence. Through *success factor* analysis organizations may develop a more intentional plan of indirect communication through the memberships and affiliations of its leaders.

The third type of *success factor* addresses the expected needs and interests of their external constituents. The perceptions and expectations of their suppliers, vendors, customers, or clients for present and future needs or interests is an important source of *success factor* analysis.

The fourth element of *success factor* analysis focuses on internal and external environmental conditions which influence organization or which it seeks to influence. Internal environmental impacts involve the geographical location of the organization, the time in its organizational history, and its available human and technical resources to accomplish the mission. The external environments of an organization address the current social, cultural, and political milieu. These influences have a major impact upon an organization, although the organization has little corresponding ability to influence these factors in return without careful planning.

The last type of *success factor* analysis an organization considers is its competitive and cooperative position. This assesses various organizational networks such as other businesses and service providers with which the organization has to either compete or cooperate in order to achieve its objective. This analysis includes consideration of the current costs of products and services, current benefits of products and services, and the features that are unique to the organization's products and services which its competitors and collaborators may not focus on with the same intensity.

Success factor analysis is accomplished with a small group of strategic planners within an organization. This often involves key members of the board of directors, trustees, or stockholders, as well as the executive staff and representatives of the management team. These individuals are in a unique position to evaluate the strategic strengths and limits of an organization in relationship to its internal and external environments. *Success factor* planning is often best accomplished outside of the workplace in a secluded setting where participants can engage in a thorough analysis and investigation of the following *success factor* analysis questions.

An example of a *success factor* analysis meeting is outlined below through a series of questions which would assist an organization to develop and evaluate its critical success factors.

Success Factor Analysis

1. *Describe the current strengths of the organization's position, mission, products, and services.*

2. *What key limitations or weaknesses could our external and constituents perceive in our products, services, organizational structure, or public communication?*

3. *What, or whom, do we perceive our internal and our external competition to be?*

4. *What key elements of our external or internal competition could we turn into potential opportunities for new projects, programs, products or services?*

5. *Are there any other direct or indirect competitors to our products or services? (psychographic, demographic, cultural, social)*

6. *In presenting the products or services of our organization as a valued resource to our customers, suppliers, vendors, and clients, what qualitative values do we seek to be recognized for?*

7. *What fundamental abilities will our organization be required to demonstrate in order to succeed?*

8. *Recast these abilities in four to seven statements of critical success factors beginning with the phrase, "(name of organization) requires the ability to . . . in order to succeed."*

Once this *success factor* planning group has met and reviewed the eight questions, they are in a position to develop the key success factors for an organization. The acid test, however, of the effectiveness of *success factor* planning is the organization's subsequent ability to make decisions about the information it uses, the products, programs, and services it develops, and the new ventures in which it engages based upon these factors. Success factors, if used properly, become the primary decision-making tools within an organization to recast its present in light of a preferred future, assisting the organization in achieving its strategic position.

Action Planning

Once an organization has clearly identified its preferred strategic position for a future timeframe, its future mission development, and its success factors, it is well suited to engage in formal *strategic action planning*. *Strategic action planning* involves key employees of an organization in projecting the future development of programs, products, and services which will be directly communicated and marketed to their major publics. This product or service phase of organizational development is accomplished in established primary work groups where colleagues regularly engage in the distribution, evaluation, and development of new products, programs, and services.

Effective *strategic action planning* is done in short timeframes of one to three years. It is also accomplished with the active participation and involvement of key service providers within an organization. These teams are primarily responsible for the production, distribution, and development of an organization's products and services. These work teams should be thoroughly familiar with an organization's strategic position, its mission development, and its success factors for the future. They also should have access to and communication with an organization's external publics in order to assist them to better shape their products, services, and programs.

Action planning is only meaningful in light of an accurate understanding of the needs and interests of an organization's external public and a key success factors to translate them into effective practice. Programs, projects, products, and services are best developed under the examination of one particular success factor at a time. For example, an organization that intends to engage in strategic action planning should be certain that each new product, program, or service and its existing resources are able to be justified in terms of their ability to support a primary success factor of the organization. Consequently, the basis for evaluating strategic action plans is their long-term effectiveness in assuring the organization's ability to succeed based on its stated success factors.

Strategic action planning should also engage work groups and teams in addressing causal, rather than symptomatic, issues. This involves moving upstream in terms of an organization's client or customer base to understand their core needs as opposed to their changing habits, desires, or wishes. For example, automobile dealers in upper Minnesota might perceive a desire or an interest among buyers for convertible tops. Practically speaking, given the harshness of the winters and shortness of the summers, this is not an effective product line. Center city school districts may perceive a desire or interest among the local community for adult continuing education courses in the evening, but their proximity to a major metropolitan community college may prohibit their ability to develop them successfully. They may, however, focus on issues of family education and parenting which builds on their direct link with an adult population through their school children. Consequently, organizations that focus on causal, rather than symptomatic issues are more likely to address primary issues of their organization and their clients.

Program and *action planning* is best done when it is based on external needs rather than internal resources. It is not atypical for an organization to develop new product lines, programs, and services simply because it has the available resources. However, the external need-based criteria for new programs, products, and services is an essential ingredient for action planning success.

Action planning teams can often be standing work groups within an organization which exist to continually evaluate, monitor, reorganize, and develop new programs, projects, priorities, and services. These action planning teams are often helped by a clear organizational focus on the fundamental ingredients necessary to evaluate the feasibility of an action plan. These evaluative criteria are the organization's success factors.

Figure 12 describes a typical *action planning* process for successful work teams. This *action planning* method, when standardized throughout the organization, provides a coherent way to review and evaluate current and future projects and services against the criteria established during the success factor phase of organizational development. The questions which follow are a narrative expansion of this *action planning* worksheet. The first few questions of our *strategic action planning* discussion focus on general characteristics of the organization. Often, this is a helpful introduction and a way for a work team to focus its energy on the immediate task at hand.

Strategic Action Planning Discussion

1. *Please identify the key achievements of our organization in relationship to the success factor we are addressing.*

2. *What obstacles or impediments have at times hindered our progress on priorities or our expectations in achieving this success factor?*

3. *In what ways can we best utilize and invest our time and attention in the future to achieve excellence in this success factor?*

4. *What 10 to 12 key actions, priorities, decisions, or products in the next one to three years should we focus our primary energy upon for implementation?*

(For each of these key actions, decisions, or priorities, complete the action planning worksheet [Figure 12] delineating the following information.)

5. *Describe the operating objective for this action plan.*

6. *Which members of the action planning team or other personnel will be responsible to champion and accomplish this objective?*

7. *What series action steps will be necessary to formulate the strategy to fulfill this action plan?*

8. *What completion dates and timetable should correspond to the individual tasks on our action steps?*

9. *What expected results, both qualitative and quantitative, should indicate our success in the implementation of this action plan?*

10. *What internal and external communication network will we be required to rely on to successfully implement this action plan?*

11. *What further information is required to assure that this action plan is implemented as projected?*

In an overall strategic planning process for an organization, a work team focused on one success factor at a time would engage in the action planning process. A work team would be assembled for each critical success factor in order to review the above questions. If an organization had six critical success factors, it would have six work teams, corresponding to each of the success factors. Each work team would then develop 10 to 12 actions or priorities to implement the success factor within the timeframe of the plan. These would be combined to form 5-7 major initiatives per work

Action Planning Worksheet

Operating Objective_____

Expected Results

Project Champion_____

Action Steps (Strategy)	Completion Dates/ Timeline

Communication Network

Information Required

Figure 12. Action Planning Worksheept

team. Each work team would then develop an action planning worksheet to correspond to each one of these individual plans and priorities. Consequently, the sum total of the strategic plan should result in approximately 25-40 action plans for the entire organization.

This *action planning* process can be helpful for short-term annual planning within work groups or divisions of an organization. It is essential, however, that action planning be grounded in a clear understanding of an organization's strategic position, a comprehensive appreciation of an organization's mission (including its constituents, its purposes, and its values), and a fundamental commitment to the basic success factors necessary for an organization's success.

Organizational Restructuring

Often organizations seek to implement new plans or priorities and redirect their current efforts or attention through the process of reorganization or restructuring. However, many organizations engage in restructuring processes prematurely. Without a thorough understanding of the current best use of an organization's resources in light of its preferred strategic position, organizations often replicate the same problems or engender new problems with restructuring efforts. Structure is not a substitute for strategy.

The fundamental purpose of restructuring is *to reorient existing resources and to develop new resources in light of changing priorities.* Restructuring itself does not reorient priorities. Restructuring is a commitment to an established strategy for an organization's priorities based on its need to reallocate, reorganize, and adjust its present and future resources. If an organization is not clear on its fundamental strategic position, its mission development for the future, its success factors, and the basic product, services, and priorities it intends to promote, then it is not prepared for a restructuring process. If an organization seeks to restructure in order to accomplish a more fundamental purpose, such as developing a new strategic position or developing new programs and services, the restructuring process is likely to be unsuccessful.

Restructuring, then, has the simple and singular benefit of reorienting an organization's resources in order to achieve specific goals related to projects, programs, products, and services following upon some clear statement of success factors. In order to engage successfully in *organizational restructuring*, two elements are necessary.

First, an organization must be clear about the prior building blocks or ingredients for its strategic leadership. An organization must have a clear sense of its strategic operating position. As a result of its strategic operating position, an organization must be satisfied with its current approach to mission development and share it with a high degree of congruence throughout the organization both internally and externally with its publics. As a result of a clear sense of mission development, the executives, managers, and leaders within an organization should have some common understanding about the fundamental success factors it is seeking to accomplish. These success factors should work to move the organization's mission closer to the direction of its ultimate strategic position. Once these success factors are in place, then an organization must have a well-established process of strategic action planning in order to reevaluate existing programs, services, and products, and develop new ones to achieve the desired success factors.

The second element which is essential for successful restructuring is the involvement of key staff and employees in the restructuring process. Many times *organizational restructuring* is done at the corporate, divisional, or management level which eliminates some important data necessary for the restructuring process that the involvement of additional employees and staff could provide. Organizations always run the risk of prematurely scaring people into reactive modes of behavior when they announce restructuring plans. This is the primary fear of short-sighted executives when an organization involves its employees or its staff in the restructuring process. However, the benefits of involving representative people in the restructuring process far outweigh the liabilities to an organization, because employees and staff are treated as primary resources for the restructuring process. Successful reorganization or restructuring plans are based on the perceived interests, priorities, and perceptions of an organization's staff and employees about its success. This important base of information is a helpful tool with which to build restructuring processes. Successful restructuring in large organizations is often done by a task force involving a matrix of potentially affected employees throughout the organization.

The questions which follow are examples of an employee audit given to representative employees within an organization prior to a restructuring process. This audit is accomplished by inviting individual employees who may be affected by the restructuring to share their feedback and views on each of these questions. This process is often done in a written format which is conducted individually with employees, giving them every opportunity to influence the restructuring based upon their needs, interests, priorities, and perceptions of the organization's success and limitations. It may also be followed up with a representative sample of interviews. Rarely do organizations fail by involving employees in the restructuring of their positions and services. The shared participation in restructuring activities provides the maximum input, information, and resources for senior level leaders to make key strategic decisions. The input of those affected by these decisions greatly strengthens the quality of the results, as well as the morale necessary to make restructuring plans succeed. As one executive was told recently in the midst of a restructuring process, it can be too costly for an organization to be "overly correct" in its reorganization plan. What is important in an organization's restructuring is not the correctness of the structure as much as it is the impact the structure has on facilitating a new level of strategy and commitment to the priorities at hand. There are many ways for organizations to restructure their existing plans, products, and services. Restructuring in itself rarely achieves this end. The purpose of restructuring is to reorder human and technical resources in order to accomplish some higher purposes.

The questionnaire below is an example of an employee audit given as part of a restructuring plan.

Employee Planning Interview

This questionnaire is designed to help your organization, and you, better assess your goals for the future and its requirements for leadership. Answering each of these questions will help you and your organization prepare for subsequent discussions and planning which may result in the redistribution of responsibilities and roles. Please bring a written copy of these ideas for the meeting to share with your facilitator. Thank you.

1. Please describe in summary fashion your key position responsibilities.

2. *Please evaluate how challenging you find your responsibilities in:*

- *variety and innovation of tasks*
- *intensity of attention they require*
- *repetition and frequency of task completion*

3. *Which aspect of your present position and responsibilities do you find most satisfying and why?*

4. *Which aspect of your present position and responsibilities do you find least satisfying and why?*

5. *If you had the opportunity to redesign your position in order to be more effective, what would you include and why?*

6. *If you had the opportunity to redesign your position in order to be more effective, what would you eliminate and why?*

7. *In looking at a desired future model for your position in relationship to your work group, what tasks and responsibilities would you feel best suited for?*

8. *In order to assist your organization achieve its future goals, what new knowledge, skill, or experience would you seek to improve upon?*

9. *Who do you consider your external constituents, clients, or customers to be?*

10. *Who are your internal clients, constituents, or customers (other members of your organization)?*

11. *What aspects of your effectiveness do clients and customers or internal colleagues most frequently comment on, positively as well as critically?*

12. *Please add any other suggestions you would offer regarding your position and the overall improvements sought through this personnel planning process.*

Once potentially involved members of a work group have completed this questionnaire, selected group interviews are helpful to reframe the key issues concerning a restructuring plan. These issues should be condensed to four or five priorities to be addressed in restructuring. These priorities then can be shaped by the leaders of a restructuring process to develop a more effective organizational model to reorient and reorganize an organization's resources and its personnel.

One division of a large client corporation recently engaged in a massive reorganization of the entire division. They expanded the work force by 300% and seven out of ten employees in the division received new job responsibilities. It took them almost two years to re-establish the morale and enthusiasm which had existed prior to the reorganization process. While ultimately this reorganization was successful, the lack of involvement by line staff and employees in the restructuring plan bore negative consequences for their morale and enthusiasm for the effort. All organizational structures are potentially either effective or ineffective in assembling human and technical resources. What gives organizational structures lasting value is their ability to efficiently galvanize people's energy, enthusiasm, knowledge, and skills in the appropriate direction to achieve crucial strategic priorities. In order for restructuring plans to be successful, those strategic actions must clearly reflect an organization's strategic position, its future mission, its critical success factors, and the immediate priorities at hand.

Restructuring, while often an apparent solution to an organization's problems, should be the last element of strategic leadership to be undertaken. It is best done only when there is convergence and consensus among the other elements of strategic leadership outlined in this chapter.

Strategic leadership is a largely dynamic process involving conceptual, tactical, and operational decisions and priorities within an organization. The strategic leadership process outlined above is a reflection of these three elements in practice. Conceptually, an organization must imagine a preferred future and have it clearly represented in terms of its strategic operating position. Tactically, an organization must have a clear sense of how to develop its mission and what success factors are essential in order to reorient an organization's resources to achieve those goals. Tactically, an organization must also have in place strategic action plans to evaluate existing products, services, and programs, as well as to develop new ones, in order to respond to changing demands of their internal and external environments. Operationally, an organization must be capable of reorganizing its current material and human resources in order to achieve its conceptual and tactical objectives.

Strategic leadership in the end, however, is far more a process than it is a product. In all of the five elements of strategic leadership—*developing a strategic position, mission development, suc-*

cess factor analysis, strategic action planning, and restructuring—a fundamental commitment to reorienting people's perceptions and mindsets is more important than the detailed analysis of these planning activities. Unfortunately, in many strategic leadership processes we focus more on the plan than on the process of planning. It is the shared development of a strategic vision throughout an organization, including both its internal and external publics, which constitutes its strategic leadership.

We have avoided calling this process strategic planning for a very important reason. It is not the product of a planning process (usually a document) that is essential to its success. It is changing perception and adopting commonly held new ways of seeing, which represent an organization's effectiveness in strategic leadership.

Orchestrating a common "Zen" of seeing within an organization is the goal of this model of strategic leadership. Unless leaders within organizations can engage their colleagues in seeing the present with a new vision, then our dreams for the future will go unmet. It is this capacity to reorient our sense of the present in light of future values and priorities that constitutes successful strategic leadership. Models, tools, processes, and exercises are intended only to assist us in this essential, yet elusive, process of being mindful in a new way. The fundamental elements of strategic leadership maintain both process intensity and strategic focus which assist our organizations and our publics in being mindful and focused on future priorities in light of more comprehensive visions.

Chapter X

Spirituality and Leadership

Chief Justice Oliver Wendell Holmes is reported to have said, "What lies behind us and what lies before us are tiny matters compared to what lies within us." Certainly the task of leadership requires careful attention to the lessons of experience which lie behind us. No responsible practitioner of leadership would abdicate responsibility for making proactive decisions and careful choices about the organizational, personal, and public matters which lie ahead of us. Yet, we are often hesitant in the literature and the practice of leadership, to ponder the ultimate questions which lie within us.

The challenge of leadership includes development of an inner consciousness or spiritual awareness that sustains us through the fundamental dilemmas of leadership: between the person and systems, among people, and within ourselves.

This chapter will describe three masteries which are essential for a comprehensive understanding and full awareness of the relationship between spirituality and leadership. The three masteries of spirituality through leadership involve:

- **Personal Mastery: Finding Strength Through Limits**
- **Relational Mastery: Achieving Wholeness Through Diversity**
- **Public Mastery: Creating Meaning Through Organization.**

Before we detail each mastery, discussing the linkage between spirituality and leadership will be helpful.

Spirituality is the full inner awareness of the meaning and values which govern the outer roles and responsibilities of leadership. There is no effective outer mastery of the practice of leadership that is not fundamentally grounded in a solid inner spiritual mastery. The spiritual dimension of leadership is not necessarily a reflection of the formal religious beliefs or confessional practices which we hold, although these often serve as a convenient vehicle, helpful framework, and public expression of our inner values, hopes, aspirations, and struggles. The content of our spirituality, while related to our religious beliefs and practices, is rooted in a more fundamental understanding of the person within himself or herself, in relation to others, and in service to the organization. Spirituality expands our inner consciousness of the meaning of the various roles, responsibilities, and dilemmas of leadership.

There is an integral link between the outer paradox of success and failure in leadership and the inner personal struggle for wholeness. A seminary professor who teaches the spirituality of leadership uses the medieval mystics as his original sources. At first, I was confused as to his choice of sources, considering the enormous modern literature available in the fields of leadership, spiritual development, and the psychology of consciousness. However, he explained that the medieval mystics all developed their inner mastery of the spiritual life based on their experience of leading and managing organizations and systems in a time of complex social change.

Inevitably, those who assume the task and responsibilities for leadership quickly realize that the ultimate dilemmas of human life which face us personally, relationally, and organizationally transcend our immediate grasp and our short-lived powers to achieve full success. Finding new meanings, new awareness, and satisfaction in the dilemma of leadership challenges is a spiritual process. Yet, we are hesitant to claim spirituality as an essential ingredient in the process of leadership. Rarely would a business school in this country consider teaching such a course. We are more likely to dismiss this connection between spirituality and leadership as a confusion over the duality of the sacred and the secular dimensions of life. We may fear that we are abandoning our political practice of the separation of church and state. But the purpose of a spirituality of leadership is not to link specific religious practices with our organizational behavior. The goal is to achieve the essential state of mind and inner detachment necessary to function effectively, live comfortably with ourselves, and create meaningful work and organizations with others. This inner detachment or spirituality of leadership is represented in the relationship between Zen Buddhism and Japanese management. Japanese management systems are well-known for their integration of the higher purposes and spiritual values with their organizational practices. However, in the West we have adopted two fundamental organizational spheres of influence that keep our reflective dialogue on spiritual values and our organizational practices in two separate worlds. Business and government are supposed to care for worldly and temporal affairs; faith and religion are intended to shepherd the spiritual life.

The paradox we have accepted is that there are separate, sacred and secular realities. We have been weaned from early childhood to believe that the purpose of business has to do with making profits, developing organizations, and satisfying customer needs. We have learned that the purpose of government is to provide for the social welfare and protect our common freedoms. We have given our social agencies the purpose of caring for the disenfranchised, the weak, and the homeless. And lastly, we have adopted the assumption that our religious institutions care for our spiritual well-being, somehow distant and apart from the other dimensions of life. This parceling out of the sacred and the secular is a world view which polarizes the fundamental ingredients which comprise human meaning. This compartmentalizing has further played itself out in the demarcation and segregation of many human systems serving different dimensions of human needs and social good. Rarely will we find training programs which present leadership practices across public, private, nonprofit, and religious organizational contexts. It is as if somehow we believe that these separate institutions require distinct and diverse forms of leadership.

We are slow to grasp the common nature of our work, the common purposes of our endeavors, and the integrated function of our different disciplines. We are quick to point out our distinctiveness, our differences. Yet it is precisely in adhering too closely to our distinctive disciplines and these differences that we often fail. We have isolated the purpose of doing business from the purpose of making meaning and value.

In the book, *The Art of Japanese Management*, Richard Tanner Pascale contrasts the difference in our western view of organizations and personal development with the Japanese perspective.

Japanese executives assume it is their task to attend to much more of the whole person, and not to leave so much to other institutions (such as government, family, or religious ones). And they believe it is only when the individuals' needs are well met within the subculture of a corporation that they can largely be freed for productive work that is in larger part outstanding. U.S. executives conditioned by a society for which good reason firmly separated church from state and later the corporation from both, perhaps naturally assumed in the early years of this century that the mandate of the corporation was much more narrowly economic. Such a view, especially given the later technologies of mass production epitomized by the assembly line led easily to an engineered view of individuals as primarily interchangeable parts and units of production.[1]

Yet as the boundaries of our world view expand and we grow into the consciousness of a global mindset, we recognize that the differences between personal and organizational values are transparent and largely perceptual. When shared with other systems, the distinctiveness of our varied organizational systems and our leadership practices can be a source of common energy and renewal not only for individual organizations, but for society and the human spirit as well. Development of an integrated consciousness of leadership, however, requires a level of inner reflection and detachment resembling the spiritual disciplines. The Japanese have a proverb for success and prosperity which teaches, "In your work be mindful, and in your family be present." This adage of mindful presence in both work and family describes the fundamental task of leaders in achieving a personal sense of integrity within themselves and creating humanizing organizations and public systems which create this kind of harmony between the individual and society, among organizations, and within institutions.

This quest for unity of organizational purpose and spiritual values is rooted in an inner quest for spiritual integrity. It will require us to put aside for the moment some of the standard assumptions and practices we hold about the differences between organizations. It will require us to set aside the belief that management and leadership somehow are task-oriented functions developing only the productive side of the human spirit apart from the personal meaning and relational side of life. We will need to understand, as some Japanese business executives have learned, that it is through the inner satisfaction of our needs and wants and the fulfillment of our human desires for meaning that we feel motivated to greater sources of productivity.

It is no accident that Japanese culture and organizations have developed such a unified spirit between the inner values and their public behavior. Business was the social force which united the country's self-respect and self-esteem after the devastation of World War II and the atomic destruction of Hiroshima and Nagasaki. It was Japanese business, not government, that inspired the consciousness of their nation and rallied them once again to a sense of their rightful meaning and purpose in the world.

Our purpose is not to extol the virtues of Japanese management; certainly they have their shortcomings in organizational practice, as do our systems. Our purpose is to explore the essential unity between our organizational life, our relational integrity, and our personal values under the theme of spirituality. Spiritual leadership is born through the struggle of leaders to balance the complex tradeoffs of people and systems. Spirituality is evident in the creation of human meaning while satisfying our need for production. It is precisely in the midst of these experiences of adversity and hardship that true leaders find their spiritual home. Spirituality is a tool for reconciling encounters with disappointment and tragedy in the carrying out of responsibilities by developing an alternate vision of life. Recently the tragic dimension of leadership was again portrayed when another Indian democratic president was assassinated, ending a long line of family rule in that nation. Making sense of the limits of human perception to find significance in such tragedy is part of a spirituality of leadership.

Leadership is no stranger to the experience of disappointment, adversity, and hardship. Yet it is precisely through the struggle with these fundamental dilemmas of leadership that our spiritual strength and consciousness emerges. Richard Tanner Pascale and Anthony Athos put it this way:

Any human organization must inevitably juggle internal contradictions—usually between the imperatives of efficiency and the countervailing human tradeoffs. Perhaps the phenomenon of 'spirituality' evolved as a means of making sense between this inescapable dilemmas—between the individual and society, between man and efficiency.[2]

The evolution and development of a mature inner consciousness provides us with a resiliency, a joy, and optimism of life. This inner mastery enables us to assume the tasks of leadership by responsibly inspiring hope and confidence among others that the right path will emerge and we finally shall succeed. Spiritual writer Anthony DeMello, in his book *Awareness*, begins with this parable:

> A man found an eagle's egg and put it in a nest of barnyard hen. The eaglet hatched with the brood of chicks and grew up with them.
>
> All his life the eagle did what the barnyard chicks did, thinking he was a barnyard chick. He scratched the earth for worms and insects, he clucked and cackled. And he would thrash his wings and fly a few feet into the air.
>
> Years passed and the eagle grew very old. One day he saw a magnificent bird above him in the cloudless sky. It glided in graceful majesty among the powerful wind currents, with scarcely a beat of its strong, golden wings. The eagle looked up in awe. 'Who's that?' he asked.
>
> 'That's the eagle, the kind of the birds,' said his neighbor. 'He belongs to the sky. We belong to the earth—we are chickens.' So the eagle lived and died a chicken, for that's what he thought he was.[3]

The spiritual task of leaders is to develop the consciousness of eagles within themselves and others. It is to enable and empower themselves and others to achieve the personal mastery, the relational mastery, and the organizational mastery to create systems which serve to strengthen the human spirit, allowing us to soar beyond our current perceptions and awareness.

In his book, *The Seven Habits of Highly Effective People,* one of the habits discussed by Dr. Steven Covey is putting first things first. I suggest to you that spirituality is the first task of leadership. It is mastering the inner game of life so that our outer behavior and our organizational practice instills a consistent spirit of achievement, prosperity, satisfaction, and meaning among those we serve.

Personal Mastery: Finding Strength Through Limits

Many leaders have evolved their wisdom of leadership in the complexity of organizational responsibility. They recognize the importance of taking stock of their personal strengths and, further, learn how to lead through their limits. This first expression of a spirituality of leadership requires us to understand that our limitations are not necessarily weaknesses, but opportunities for others to succeed with our encouragement and our presence. It is precisely in avoiding the temptation to over-extend our strengths that we find the true inner strength to lead with courage and integrity.

Spiritual writer Henry Nouwen tells a story in his book *Compassion* which relates to finding strength by encountering limits. The story describes an old man sitting along a stream, watching a scorpion trapped within a forked branch in the stream. As the scorpion struggles to free itself from the entanglement of the branch before it drowns, the old man repeatedly puts his hand into the water to free the scorpion. Each time the old man touches the scorpion, the scorpion stings him. Finally, a passing stranger queries the old man. "Old Man," he says, "why is it that you continue to try to free the scorpion after he continues to sting you?" The old man replies, "Just because it is the nature of the scorpion to wound, it does not change the nature of a person to save." Through adversity he finds greater inner strength.

In our responsibilities of leadership, we encounter experiences of disappointment, hardship, and struggle. Through them we learn the limits of our egos and find the strength of character to push our organization, our system, or our task at hand forward. This is the personal mastery of finding new strength in the limits of our personality. The old man found the strength of compassion through the pain inflicted by the limits of his external circumstances. In his failed attempt to free the scorpion he found his true nature as person, to be compassionate.

For many leaders, the experience of discovering our limitations and our weaknesses is a painful process. Books, articles, and seminars on success rarely teach us about the process of pain and suffering and its value for personal mastery. Yet for many the task of leadership involves not only the joy of success in leading, but also the recognition of pain and suffering in our own limits and in the limits of our organizations and society as a whole to consistently achieve our purposes and our potential. An inner disposition which recognizes the wisdom of finding strength through limits is a fundamental quality of the spirituality of leadership.

Many current leadership development programs use diagnostic testing instruments to assess relative personal strengths and limits for their participants. There are several popular instruments on the market which are used by a variety of organizations and consulting firms to help assess these leadership capabilities. The *Myers-Briggs Personality Inventory* is based in Jungian psychology and helps us recognize our strengths as well as our limits which can be applied to varied leadership challenges. In their *Situational Leadership* model, Drs. John Blanchard and Paul Hershey describe different approaches and styles of leadership that are effective in different circumstances. The *Personal Profile System* developed by Performax, Inc. is another popular leadership instrument used throughout many corporations and organizations.

These and other personal leadership tools recognize the importance of understanding our strengths and limitations as essential to the process of leadership. However, few of these tools take the necessary last step to situate the concept of personal strengths and limits within a spiritual base of understanding. Conventional wisdom holds that we succeed in leadership by exerting our strengths and expanding upon them. However, it is precisely in moments of trial, adversity, complexity, hardship, and failure that the over-extension of our strengths can be our undoing in leadership.

The Center for Creative Leadership in Greensboro, North Carolina contends that one of the major reasons for executives derailing is their inability to learn from hardship and adversity. It is precisely this ability to let go of our egos and suspend the exercise of our strengths which leads to the spiritual mastery of finding strength through limits. It seems incongruous to imagine that it is when we let go in the face of complexity, disappointment, and hardship that the true solution or alternative can emerge to be personally, organizationally, and publicly successful. It is, as the Christian scriptures indicate, through our weaknesses that we find our greatest strengths.

The concept of ego-detachment is well-documented as a fundamental principle of spiritual wisdom. Writer Thomas Merton discusses the differences between Eastern and Western views of human personality and the ego in a letter to John C. H. Wu, an Eastern colleague in the field of spirituality.

> I know of no one in the West who has treated of person in such a way as to make clear that what is most ourselves is least ourselves, or better the other way around. It is the void that is our personality, and not our individuality that seems to be concrete and defined and present, etc. It is what is seemingly not present, the void, that is really I. And the 'I' that seems to be 'I' is really a void. But the West is so used to identifying the person with the individual, and the deeper self with the empirical self (confusing the issue by juggling around a divided body and soul), that the basic truth is never seen. It is the NOT—I that is most of all the 'I' in each one of us. But we are completely enslaved by the illusory 'I' that is not 'I' and never can be 'I' except in a purely fictional and social sense.[4]

Thomas Merton touches on a fundamental experience of leadership. It is precisely in detachment from our egos that we find the true courage, conviction, and strengths to lead with success amidst adversity. It is when we are fearless of the consequences of our actions and the personal pain, difficulty, or disappointment they may cause which frees us to discover new ways of thinking, new approaches to moving our organizations forward, and new strategies for effective living and work.

This concept of the ego-less understanding of the person is firmly rooted in Jungian psychology, which contends that there are two major dimensions to the human person. The first is the persona, the primary driving force or strength of our egos or personalities. It is the full extension of our gifts and talents, the public, external, and active expression of what we appear to be. However, Jungian psychology also discusses the dark side of the human personality. Rather than endowing this with a sense of evil or weakness, it discusses the concept of the "shadow." The shadow is the undeveloped side of our personalities. It is the ego-less dimension of who we are. It is the what-we-are-yet-to-become dimension of life. In the shadow we find our greatest inspiration and creativity. It also represents the most primitive, childlike, and fearful expression of the hidden resources within ourselves. This shadow has a fundamental and practical merit for the task of leadership. It is often in the experience of adversity, complexity, and challenge that the skillful leader will of necessity develop or exercise her undeveloped side. The assertive leader who becomes more passive and more responsive to his constituents often makes the breakthrough of consciousness necessary to change the circumstances and the dynamics at hand in order to succeed. It may be the consultative leader who exercises a decisive viewpoint far from her natural course of action who makes apparent a new opportunity for changing mindsets. It is the intuitive, inspiring leader who, in the face of ambiguity, conflict, and difficulty, needs to rely on a strong understanding of data and information to succeed in addressing the organization's next challenge. In essence, it is when we let go in leadership and trust our inner spiritual wisdom by expressing our shadow side that we become more fully the person we are called to be and exercise the broadest extension of our capacities to lead.

It is rarely in the expression of our more natural gifts and abilities that we find the completeness of leadership. It is rather in the expression and exercise of our undeveloped sides that we find the wholeness of our human person which gives other people the courage of their convictions to lead responsibly in any given situation. We become more comprehensive and complex persons by exercising our hidden selves, when other alternatives have failed us.

A colleague who is a Jungian psychologist once described the process this way: our persona, our strengths, are those things with which we are endowed from birth. They are natural to us and an essential part of our personalities. Yet, it is by exercising our undeveloped side that we often find the hidden strength which is the essential ingredient of leadership. This "selfless" concept of leadership is noted by Richard Tanner Pascale and Anthony Athos in Japanese organizations.

There are a few concepts as deeply imbedded in the
Western mind as the concept of "self." Our philosophy,
language, and psychology are filled with it. We see our
'selves' as distinct entities, separate from all others in
most important respects, with separable beliefs, talents,
and experiences. In Japan, each person is believed to
possess a unique spirit, soul, mind, and heart—but his
'self' or 'self concept' is seen as an impediment to
growth. People are regarded less as individuals than as
collaborators in the context of their roles. One's separate 'identity' is not singled out as the primary sign of
personal development throughout the life cycle as it is
in the West.[5]

This selfless concept of leadership is not without its personal
consequences. Many leaders, skillful in exercising this sense of
selfless leadership, experience an aloneness in their higher levels of
self-understanding and consciousness. They stand apart more
often in the complexity and sensitivity of their decisions. However, a mature appreciation of aloneness is an integral component
of the personal mastery of leadership. It is as simple as Harry
Truman's clear imperative, "The buck stops here." This selfless
sense of aloneness is an essential source of finding a true spirituality of leadership. For it is through aloneness that we find a greater
sense of communion with a transcendent, value-oriented completeness which some call the presence of God.

Dr. M. Scott Peck, in his book, *The Road Less Traveled*, discusses
this relationship of aloneness with the experience of power in leadership.

There is another problem with power: aloneness. Here
there is a similarity in at least one dimension between
spiritual and political power. Someone who is ap-
proaching the peak of spiritual evolution is like someone at the peak of political power. There is no one
above to whom to pass the buck; no one to blame; no
one to tell you how to do it. There may not be anyone
on the same level to share the agony of the responsibility. Others may advise, but the decision is yours alone.
You alone are responsible. In another dimension the
aloneness of enormous spiritual power is even greater
than that of political power. Since their level of awareness is seldom as high as their exalted position, the po-

litically powerful almost always have their spiritual
equals with whom they can communicate. So presidents and kings will have their friends and cronies, but
the person who is evolved to the highest level of awareness, of spiritual power, will likely have no one in his or
her circle of acquaintance with whom to share such a
depth of understanding . . . this kind of aloneness is
'shared' by all who travel the farthest on the journey of
spiritual growth. It is such a burden that it simply
could not be borne were it not for the fact that as we
outdistance our fellow humans our relationship to God
inevitably becomes correspondingly closer. In the communion of growing consciousness, of knowing with
God, there is enough joy to sustain us.[6]

Those of us who seek to lead would be foolish to seek out this
experience of aloneness and distance; through selfless leadership, it
finds us. We are equally foolish to avoid it, since it provides an
opportunity for further self-understanding and access to the true
spiritual dimension of leadership. It is precisely in the experience
of aloneness and the experience of our personal limits that we
come to recognize the wisdom and the insight of the divine in our
lives. This wisdom and insight moves us to new levels of consciousness, and provides not only an inner spiritual benefit, but
also a corresponding clarity of viewpoint which allows us to lead
with greater wisdom, compassion, and understanding.

Perhaps few leaders are truly capable of, or interested in, the
fundamental personal mastery of finding strength through limits.
Yet the greater our capacities to lead, the more likely we are to find
ourselves in the experience of aloneness in the face of adversity,
complexity, difficulty, or hardship. The more we make the right
choices about the role and responsibility we have as leaders, the
more likely we are to be misunderstood by those we lead. It is
fundamentally in this experience of aloneness that we find the
spiritual wisdom which Scott Peck discusses.

Renowned biologist Dr. Jane Goodall discusses her understanding of this aloneness of leadership in a book entitled *The Courage of
Conviction.*

For me, the very fact that one person can have such a
tremendous impact is a source of hope. It means that if
the right leader appears he—or she—could do so much

to alleviate the desperate muddle and anguish of our troubled times. But there is another note of hope, too, for despite the despair and pessimism that surrounds us man has, nevertheless, come a long way.... The trouble is that only a few people understand the importance of that most difficult choice of all—to sink comfortably deeper into the selfish materialism dictated by our biological instincts, or to struggle upward toward a way of life dictated by human values, following an ethical code of behavior we sincerely believe to be right.

I'm aware of the importance, for myself of this choice, yet I have traveled pitifully few steps along the upward trail. I have met a handful of people who have traveled far, who have crossed the bridge to a level of existence in which spirit dominates matter. They are easy to recognize for they have a special stillness, like a quiet smile, even in adversity. Mostly they and their like through history, live apart, at peace in their vision. Only a few have tried to lead their fellow men across the gulf. For they know the price: disbelief, ridicule, contempt. The outstretched hand of the greatest of them was seized and pierced with nails. Today more than ever before we need their help.[7]

It is this inner strength of character to lead through our strengths and the discovery of new strengths through limits that is characteristic of exceptional leaders. However, this mantle of exceptional leadership does not come easily. The price is often adversity, complexity, and difficulty. The reward is a spiritual wisdom and insight that comes through greater understanding of oneself by finding both one's strengths and one's limits.

One of the most effective tools I have used with client for developing this capacity for spiritual self-reflection is keeping a journal. Leaders in the midst of "boundary experiences" may find new wisdom and insight through regular entries in their journal. Boundary experiences may be critical issues or points of challenge we encounter in the leadership process. Boundary experiences may also include the limits in our current experiences, wisdom, and knowledge necessary to realize a needed breakthrough for action. Some boundary experiences may be exhilarating when they are moments of enormous excitement, challenge, opportunity, and enthusiasm within an organization or a system. Skillful leaders can develop this capacity for spiritual reflection as a practical tool to mature their spiritual mastery. In these boundary events and challenges we can discover our limits as sources of new strength, uncovering new opportunities to lead and new ways of serving others previously untapped by our human experience.

The process of journal keeping involves four steps:

- Describing the boundary experience
- Asking the question, "What am I called to learn from this experience?"
- Asking "What am I called to do differently?"
- Asking "What wisdom for life have I gained for future challenges?"

This journal exposes to leaders new dimensions of their personalities which call on their abilities to master the spiritual disciplines. This process of inner reflection can promote a sense of resiliency, detachment, and inner calm in the midst of a challenge or crisis, enabling the leader not only to catch his or her breath before moving forward, but perhaps to tap an alternate source of wisdom.

The formula for this journal is a simple one, since the day-to-day demands of life do not leave unlimited time or energy to commit to the process of extensive inner reflection. Making a journal entry often takes no more than fifteen to twenty minutes. Some leaders report that their journals have become such an integral part of their personal mastery that they keep it on a daily basis.

A brief summary of the four elements of a journal entry may be helpful to the reader.

Describe the Boundary Experience

In the midst of a difficulty or an exhilarating opportunity, it is often helpful to externalize our inner experience. This externalization may come through conversations with others. But it is also helpful to dialogue with oneself by describing in as much detail as necessary the current leadership challenge. An executive managing a complex takeover situation from a larger organization may describe all of the demands, priorities, issues, and challenges he or she is facing in the midst of that dilemma. The social service agency director who receives massive budget cuts from the state may record the past, the present, and the future experiences that impinge upon her, restricting her options in the midst of this challenge.

Ask "What Am I Called to Learn from This?"

Each boundary experience presents us with a new opportunity for learning. So often our learnings through difficulties or challenges occur in hindsight, after the fact. The process of keeping this spiritual journal allows us to move this insight process into foresight. It is in the immediacy of the moment when we are most present to understand the meaning of a situation. Asking the question in the midst of a challenge, "What am I called to learn from this now?" may generate some interesting and creative new ways of viewing the situation previously unavailable to us through conventional means of organization and management.

Ask, "What Am I Called to Do Differently?"

The full measure of spiritual wisdom is the grace of acting upon our insight. The wisdom of our inner faith is measured in the actions of love. Behavior is the fullest expression of our inner values. Thoughtful consideration of alternative ways to act or to respond in the midst of challenging situations is an important expression of spiritual leadership. Effective leaders' concern for a comprehensive and integrated approach to their lives and their work are not content to stop at the point of insight alone. They recognize the importance of identifying and moving forward to new behaviors. This challenges them to move beyond their existing strengths to discover new opportunities for personal growth as well as organizational advancement.

Ask, "What Enduring Wisdom for Life Have I Gained for Future Challenges?"

So many of us travel through life with experiences which are unreflected upon. One spiritual adviser noted in a lecture that "experience unreflected upon is violent." At the time this seemed an inordinately strong statement to make about the lack of awareness most of us bring to our lives and work. Yet thinking through that observation makes clear that each experience allows us new opportunities for insight, for growth and for greater understanding of ourselves, our relationships, and our workplaces. The last step of maintaining a spiritual journal is to explore the wisdom we have gained from an experience which may benefit us in other circumstances in life. One of the true insights of an integrated leader is the ability to apply personal insights to their organizational behavior and to cross-reference insights from relationships into both personal and their organizational contexts. This "whole life" concept of leadership is a strong indicator of the presence of a deep spiritual foundation for the practices in which we engage as leaders.

Relational Mastery: Wholeness Through Diversity

If personal mastery of a spirituality of leadership involves discovering our strengths through limits, it becomes apparent that a necessary ingredient for achieving success is reliance upon the skills and abilities of others. The second mastery of a spirituality of leadership is to learn to discover and achieve wholeness through diversity. A corresponding lesson to the recognition of our personal limits is to realize that through the strengths and diversity of others we become more complete within ourselves, and in this way our organizations and systems achieve their full potential. While this insight is easy to adopt and recognize in concept, it is very difficult in practice. Group and organizational differences and diversity can contribute to competing egos, conflicting agendas, and chaos. Yet all successful leaders know that in circumstances of change and challenge we benefit by finding alternate strengths beyond ourselves and utilizing diverse approaches to situations and problems in order to find new meaning and insight. This practical reality is rooted in a fundamental spiritual understanding of human wholeness. It is precisely through our diversity and our differing gifts that we achieve a sense of completeness and fulfillment, personally, relationally, and within our organizations.

In the boundary experiences of organizational life, when our own strengths fall short of the goal, reliance upon and encouragement of the talents and abilities of others is the means through which we find relational mastery as well as organizational competence. In an article entitled "Business Leadership in a Creative Society," Abram T. Collier puts the paradox of wholeness through diversity this way:

> Because the society in which we live is a creative one, the task of leaders is to further their creative ideal in their organizations. To do this, they need to recognize

the power and strength that an organization can derive from the differences among people. To maintain order amidst the chaos that diversity can create, executives need to foster understanding and respect for one another among individual members, as well as show them that the right to be creative carries obligations with it. Finally, as a creative society derives its power from its members' beliefs in the importance of their individual growth, leaders need to epitomize that growth.[8]

Abram Collier indicates that the source of creativity or wholeness is in our recognition and acceptance of diversity as a fundamental principle for human fulfillments. This principle is not foreign to organizational systems. In fact, it has been the foundation of our nation itself. However, as we recognize through our political systems, the comfortable integration of diverse viewpoints and different talents and experiences causes us disequilibrium and imbalance. This sense of disequilibrium and disharmony is due less to the differences which keep us apart than it is to the realization that differences highlight our individual limitations. In this way, our personal mastery of finding strength through limits and our relational mastery of discovering wholeness through diversity are interrelated. We find our personal, relational, and organizational wholeness with others rather than independently.

It is the experience of diversity and the alternative understandings which we encounter from others that cause us disequilibrium within ourselves, as they underscore our limitations of viewpoint. None of us in the end is capable of achieving complete solutions to any human dilemma of consequence by ourselves. The measure of mature leaders is their ability to assimilate increasingly complex and sophisticated human paradoxes within themselves, their relationships, and their organizations. In essence, the most masterful leader has met no challenge that he or she cannot address. However, masterful leaders recognize the inherent spirituality of this process of addressing enormous challenges by relying upon the strengths and skills of other people. Full appreciation of diversity in viewpoint and perspective is largely a matter of inner attitude or consciousness. We must go beyond mere clinical, organizational, or human relations skills to convey a deep, inner belief that wholeness and integrity are achieved through relationships with others who bring diversity to our immediate circumstances. The search for wholeness through diversity anchors our sense of what is right, what is authentic, and ultimately what is true. Successful leaders are less prone to claim the banner of truth, wisdom, or knowledge. In fact, educational psychologist Paulo Friere indicates it is often the mark of oppressors to define reality on their terms. His world view contends that reality is rooted in the collective understanding of wisdom. Detecting and following this collective wisdom is largely a spiritual discipline. It implies a recognition that if I rely only on my own skills and abilities of leadership, I am greatly limited in my capacity to succeed. Long-term success, satisfaction, and wholeness as people and as organizations will be achieved only with the full contribution of the talents and abilities of others, and the expression of diversity among these talents. Leaders who have achieved this relational mastery seek to empower others by calling forth their additional talents, knowledge, and skills to address present circumstances more comprehensively.

This sense of wholeness through diversity has its parallels in the spiritual concept of presence. It is only when we are fully present to a circumstance and able to hear the full measure of others' viewpoints, wisdom, and knowledge that the limitations of our own ego becomes apparent and opportunities to evaluate circumstances in new ways become clear. In the process of abandoning our egos and maintaining an openness to the diversity of the skills, abilities, and knowledge of others, we all become more whole and complete in the process. This spiritual presence includes a broad sense of appreciation and respect for others. This regard for others is not based simply upon the expediency of their knowledge, skill, or experience. It is fundamentally rooted in the deeper recognition that through the contributions of others we all become more whole. This may seem to be a rather naive or simplistic insight for the process of leadership. Yet current researchers and writers in organizational development pay tribute to the fundamental virtue in this relational viewpoint of achieving strength through diversity.

Peter M. Senge, in his exciting book *The Fifth Discipline*, discusses this concept of diversity and openness by reviewing the philosophy of Hanover Corporation executive Bill O'Brien. Peter Senge describes this process of wholeness through diversity as an inner spirit of openness.

> While reflective openness benefits significantly from reflection and inquiry skills, and from systems thinking

knowledge and skills, openness is more than a set of skills. As O'Brien says, "We should be careful not to prescribe a clinical treatment of a spiritual subject. Openness goes beyond a personal quality. It is a relationship you have with others. It is a change in spirit, as well as a set of skills and practice."

It is most accurate to think of openness as a characteristic of relationships, not individuals. At some levels it makes no sense to say, "I am an open person." The same person will experience genuine openness with some people and not with others.

. . . If openness is a quality of relationships, then building relationships characterized by openness may be one of the most high-leverage actions to build organizations characterized by openness. This is precisely what I and many of my colleagues have observed time and again— that "learningful" relationships among key members of the organization have an extraordinary impact on the larger organization . . . .

The impulse toward openness, as O'Brien says, "is the spirit of love." Love is, of course, a difficult word to use in the context of business and management. But O'Brien does not mean romantic love. In fact, the type of love that underlies openness, what the Greeks call agape, has little to do with emotions. It has everything to do with intentions—commitment to serve one another and willingness to be vulnerable in the context of that service. The best definition of the love that underlies openness is a full and unconditional commitment to another's "completion," to another being all that he or she can and wants to be.[9]

Peter Senge comes remarkably close to assessing a spiritual dimension for leadership. Discovering wholeness through diversity is a commitment to the recognition and fulfillment of the gifts and talents of others. Not only does he describe a viable organizational practice of openness to another's skills and abilities, he also describes a fundamental human value of the spiritual life. Our individual and corporate completion comes from our learning from the diversity and distinctive contributions of others.

Public Mastery: Meaning Through Organizations

All of us find our human development either enriched or diminished by the organizational systems in which we work or live. Human beings are conditioned by systems in the nature of our world, the dynamics of our human relations, and the structures of the social system which comprise the fabric of meaning in our lives. Organizations do not have neutral impacts. They strengthen or hinder our growth. At times, they do both. Organizations shape human meaning. Yet so often in organizations we become lost in the immediacy of producing our goods, providing our services, and distributing our products in ways that are unreflective of the capacity to create meaning.

The final spiritual mastery of leadership is a public one. The highest expression of leadership is the capacity to manage and administer organizations in ways that create meaningful systems for others which strengthen and enhance their individual and collective human development. This creation of meaningful organizational systems provides for the immediate motivation to succeed in the tasks of increasing profits, promoting a mission, providing services, and keeping customers and clients satisfied. It has also the higher benefit of enriching the fabric of our lives, strengthening the development of our personalities, and enriching the social fabric of our communities in the process.

This third dimension of public and organizational mastery involves creating meaning through organizational systems. The process of establishing meaning in organizations is not limited to the immediate interpersonal skills of executives and leaders. So often the process of making meaning is relegated to an evaluation of our transactional or communications skills in organizational life. Creating meaning is more than improving our methods of communicating. This practical ingredient is important and may produce a net increase in our product, goods, and our services, but it misses the spiritual element of public leadership. Public mastery strengthens the system of meaning internally in our organizations and externally for the publics which we serve.

The spiritual mastery of creating meaning through organizations has both an internal and an external expression. Internally, the creation of meaningful environments is apparent to employees, staff, and associates of our businesses and our services. Meaningful work environments provide for the public expression of our individual talents and abilities in ways that allow us to complete ourselves as human beings by exercising Sigmund Freud's dictum of succeeding at both work and love.

The process of creating meaning through organizations extends far beyond the inner circumstances of our businesses and our systems to include expressions of meaning to our customers, clients, suppliers, and the various publics we serve. A meaningful social contribution is an important expression of our organizational commitments. Max DePree, president of Herman Miller Furniture Company, describes an internal commitment to the creation of meaning within an organization.

> What is it most of us really want from work? We would like to find the most effective, most productive, most rewarding way of working together. We would like to know that our work process uses all of the appropriate and pertinent resources: human, physical, and financial. We would like a work process and relationships that meets our personal needs for belonging, for contributing, for meaningful work, for the opportunity to make a commitment, for the opportunity to grow and be at least reasonably in control of our own destinies. Finally, we'd like somebody to say, Thank you.'[10]

Max DePree cogently illustrates the significance of creating internal systems of meaning within our organizations. Organizations not only have a productive function for their employees and their constituents, they also have a spiritual function of serving as the focus and the vehicle for a collective expression of human meaning through work. This spiritual awareness of creating meaningful work systems is an important dimension of mastery for a committed leader. Committed leaders do not use the latest techniques in organizational psychology and human relation skills only for the immediate organizational benefit of improving the bottom line. They recognize the importance of staying focused on the longer term bottom line, which includes a vision of creating meaning and allowing for the expression of meaning among employees and colleagues within their organizational systems. To the extent that our organizations become a common expression of productive values among our employees and staff, then our organizations transcend their immediate historical circumstances of providing a product or developing and producing a good or service. They stand apart as a contribution to human consciousness, strengthening the capacity of the human spirit to produce, to expand its horizon, and to accept new challenges which enhance our public good in the future. Organizations and institutions are collective expressions of human meaning. They serve as vehicles for people to express the productive side of shared human potential.

This final mastery of a spirituality of leadership is the recognition among leaders of a commitment and a responsibility to create meaning for their internal publics by leading organizations in ways that express the collective concern for the quality of human work.

The external expression of creating meaning through organizations is shared with our customers, our suppliers, our vendors, and external collaborators to our organizational systems. In this way, business leadership has a wider social purpose of strengthening the social fabric and the capacity for social productivity among the organizations with which we compete and collaborate. This final integrity of leadership requires that we deal with our competitors as well as our collaborators as co-creators of a social fabric rooted in a belief that together we contribute to public mastery by succeeding in our organizational tasks both separately and together.

In his discussion of the value of capitalism, Max DePree illustrates this public mastery of leadership as a radical departure from our established way of thinking about organizations and systems. He discusses his concept as inclusive capitalism.

> Inclusive capitalism requires something from everyone. People must respond actively to inclusiveness; naturally there is a cost to belonging.
>
> • Being faithful is more important than being successful. If we are successful in the world's eyes but unfaithful in what we believe then we fail in our efforts at insidership.
>
> • Corporations can and should have a redemptive purpose. We need to weigh the pragmatic in the clarifying light of the moral. We must understand that reaching our potential is more important than reaching our goals.
>
> • We need to become vulnerable to each other. We owe each other the chance to reach our potential.

- Belonging requires intimacy. Being an insider is not a spectator sport; it means adding value; it means being fully and personally accountable; it means foregoing superficiality.

- Last, we need to be learners together. The steady process of becoming goes on in most of us throughout our lifetimes. We need to be searching for maturity, openness, and sensitivity.[11]

Max DePree outlines the function of organizations to create meaning through the public exercise of responsible leadership. This social purpose, the public agenda for leadership, is the responsibility of all organizations irrespective of the sector of society in which they serve.   This public responsibility for leadership makes colleagues of competitors and creates new networks among public service organizations, corporations, small businesses, religious institutions, and health service agencies.   It calls all of us to transcend the immediate circumstances of leadership: to focus not only on the relationship and impact of our internal bottom lines but on an assessment of our contribution to the bottom lines of our social well-being.

This final spiritual mastery of leadership—developing meaning through organizations—forces us to redefine our standards of success.   Fundamentally, comprehensive leaders are motivated by broadening the understanding of success which they hold for themselves, their organizations, and the people whom they serve. This expression of public mastery in leadership strengthens the human capital of life as well as the economic capital which contributes to organizational viability.   It is fundamentally a spiritual recognition that in the end there is no effective contribution to leadership that does not strengthen us, our relationships, our organizations and society simultaneously. There is no separate exercise of leadership which is truly successful if it does not contribute and add quality to our lives, to our work, and to our society.

The prevailing definition of leadership in this book has been that leadership is a commitment and a contribution to the quality of life, the quality of work, and the quality of our society. Those who would settle for any less have settled for a more constricted understanding of the call and commitment to leadership to which we are all challenged.   This challenge pervades the personal, relational, and organizational circumstances of our lives.   In the end, leadership is a simple task of making a contribution to all things and making all things better. Yet we recognize with wisdom, age, and experience that simple tasks often require a great deal of complexity. In the words of Chief Justice Oliver Wendell Holmes, "I would not give a fig for simplicity this side of complexity, but I would give my life for simplicity on the other side of complexity."

As leaders, we recognize that the challenge to strengthen the quality of our lives, the opportunities to strengthen the quality of our work and organizations, and the responsibility to strengthen the quality of society present us with many questions which remain. Our attitude must call us to recognize the spiritual wisdom of leadership. While the challenges lie before us, the wisdom lies within us, the strength lies in others alongside of us, and true opportunity lies in our expanded awareness and ability to link our spiritual values with our public and organizational behavior.

The core of dedication to this comprehensive life of leadership is spiritual in nature. In this process, we become transformed by becoming more of who we are through acceptance of our limits. In this process we empower others to find wholeness in our shared experience of diversity. Through this process we create meaning by leading organizations to serve the social challenges of our times.

We earn the right to be called leaders only through a passionate devotion to unify the personal and the productive sides of our lives, and to create organizations which provide unity and meaning to our social fabric as well as to our organizational agenda. This book was written for those who dare to claim this right as their commitment and contribution of lasting value. For these leaders, there are no limits to true success as there are no limits to the challenges they address.

Leaders live by a pervading understanding that all they do either contributes to, or detracts from, the fabric of life for everyone. In their spiritual wisdom they have internalized the grace of leadership of Indian Chief Seattle, who wrote these words to President Benjamin Franklin Pierce upon the purchase of the State of Washington from his tribe. His enduring words are the soul of leadership. "This we know. All things are connected. Whatever befalls the Earth befalls the children of the Earth. Man did not weave this web of life. We are merely a strand in it. Whatever we do to this web we do to ourselves."

Endnotes

Chapter I

1. Dag Hammarskjold, *Markings* (London: Faber & Faber, 1964), pp. 16-17.

2. Konosuke Matsushita, *Quest for Prosperity* (PHP Institute; Tokyo, Kyoto, Singapore), pp. 202-203.

3. Morgan McCall, Michael Lombardo, and Ann Morrison, *The Lessons of Experience* (Lexington: Lexington Books, 1989), pp. 92-94.

4. Ibid., p. 93.

5. Sherry Cohen, *Tender Power* (Reading: Addison-Wesley, Incorporated, 1989), p. 35.

6. James O'Toole, *Vanguard Management* (New York: Berkeley Books, 1985), p. 49.

7. John W. Gardner, *On Leadership* (New York: The Free Press, 1990), p. 182.

8. Phillip Berman, *The Courage of Conviction* (New York: Dodd, Mead & Company, 1985), p. 179.

Chapter II

1. Robert Ornstein and Paul Ehrlich, *New World New Mind* (New York: Simon and Schuster, 1989), p. 63.

2. Ibid., pp. 8-9.

3. Ibid., p. 63.

4. Richard Tanner Pascale and Anthony Athos, *The Art of Japanese Management* (New York: Simon & Schuster, 1981), pp. 28-29.

5. Ibid., p. 310.

Chapter III

1. Elliot Jacque, "Executive Vision: A Matter of Time," *Small Business*, June 1985, p. 8.

2. Walter Kiechel, III, "How Executives Think," *Fortune*, February 4, 1985, p. 128.

3. Hammarskjold, *Markings*, pp. 16-17.

4. Thomas Merton, *The Hidden Ground of Love* (New York: Farrar, Straus & Giroux, 1985), p. 594.

5. Fernando Bartolomé and Paul Evans, "Must Success Cost So Much?", *Executive Success* (New York: John Wiley & Sons, 1983), p. 77.

6. Cohen, *Tender Power*, p. 201.

7. Ibid., p. 159.

Chapter IV

1. Max DePree, *Leadership is an Art* (New York: Doubleday, 1989), p. 28.

2. Pascale, Athos, *Art of Japanese Management*, p. 35.

3. Marsha Sinetar, *Do What You Love, The Money Will Follow* (New York: Dell Publishing Division of Bantam Doubleday, 1987), p. 196.

4. Erik Erikson, *Childhood and Society* (New York: W.W. Norton Co., 1950), p. 267.

5. Allen Tough, *The Adult's Learning Projects* (Austin, Texas: Learning Concepts 1979), pp. 45-62.

6. Warren Bennis and Burt Nanus, *Leaders, The Strategies for Taking Charge* (New York: Harper & Row Publishers, 1985), p. 205.

7. James Fowler, *Faith and the Structuring of Meaning*, Unpublished Manuscript, Candler School of Theology, 1977, p. 1.

8. James Fowler, Stages of Faith and Adults' Life Cycles, in *Faith Development in the Adult Life Cycle*, ed., Kenneth Stokes (New York: Wm. Sadlier, Inc., 1982), p. 193.

9. Sinetar, *Do What You Love*, p. 191.

10. Ibid., p. 208.

Chapter V

1. Donald A. Schon, *Educating the Reflective Practitioner* (San Francisco: Jossey-Bass Publishers, 1987), pp. 25-26.

2. Ibid., pp. 35-36.

3. Peter M. Senge, *The Fifth Discipline* (New York: Doubleday, 1990), p. 11.

4. Ibid., p. 25.

5. Dr. Martin Luther King, Jr., "I Have a Dream," *Testament of Hope*, ed., James Washington (New York: Harper Collins, 1982), p. 219.

6. Abraham Lincoln, "The Gettysburg Address," *The World Book Encyclopedia* (Chicago: World Book, Inc., 1990), Vol. 8, p. 177.

7. Bennis, Nanus, *Leaders, Strategies for Taking Charge*, p. 214.

Chapter VI

1. "Interview with Jorgenson Honda," conducted by Organizational Resources International, 1990, p. 2.

2. Ibid., p. 4.

3. Ibid., p. 4.

4. Ibid., p. 2.

5. St. Vincent Hotel Mission Statement, p. 1.

6. Donald L. Runkle, "General Motors/Hughes Technology Exchange," November 7, 1989, p. 4.

7. Ibid., p. 5.

8. Ibid., p. 3.

9. Ibid., p. 3.

10. Donald L. Runkle, "In Search of the Perfect Car," November 1989. p. 1-2.

Chapter VII

1. Woolpert Consultants, "Models of Cooperation," Unpublished Manuscript (Dayton, Ohio: October, 1989), p. 4.

2. Robert Berlon, "Vision, Mission, Vision: A Diagram of Relationships," Unpublished Manuscript (Cleveland, Ohio, 1988), p. 2.

3. Ibid., p. 2.

4. Will Steger and Jon Bowermaster, *Saving the Earth* (New York: Knopf Publishers, 1990) p. 267.

5. Ibid., p. 147.

6. H. Patricia Hynes, *Earthright* (Rockland, California: Prima Publishing and Communications, 1990), p. 185.

7. Steger, Bowermaster, *Saving the Earth*, p. 147.

8. Hynes, *Earthright*, p. 47.

9. Ibid., p. 41.

Chapter VIII

1. Ken Hultman, *Paths of Least Resistance* (Austin, Texas: Learning Concepts, 1979), p. vii.

2. Daryl R. Conner and Charles L. Palmgren, "Building Synergistic Work Teams" (Atlanta: O.D. Resources, Inc., 1983), p. 1.

Chapter IX

1. Bennis, Nanus, *Leaders*, p. 182.

2. "Critical Success Factors," Document R-25 (Price Waterhouse, Inc., 1984), p. 2.

3. Ibid., pp. 4-5.

Chapter X

1. Pascale, Athos, *Art of Japanese Management*, pp. 132-133.

2. Ibid., p. 72.

3. Anthony DeMello, *Awareness* (New York: Doubleday, 1990), p. 3.

4. Merton, *Hidden Ground of Love* , p. 627.

5. Pascale, Athos, *Art of Japanese Management*, pp. 190-191.

6. M. Scott Peck, M.D., *The Road Less Traveled* (New York: Simon & Schuster, 1978), pp. 288-289.

7. Dr. Jane Goodall, in Berman, *The Courage of Conviction*, pp. 82-83.

8. Abram T. Collier, "Business Leadership in a Creative Society," *Executive Success*, ed., Eliza Collins (New York: John Wiley & Sons, Inc., 1983), p. 169.

9. Senge, *Fifth Discipline*, pp. 284-285.

10. DePree, *Leadership is an Art*, p. 21.

11. Ibid., p. 61.

Bibliography

Barthelemy, Robert. *High Performance, Getting the Best Out of Our Organizations, Our People, Ourselves.* Dayton, Ohio: IDEA, 1984.

Bennis, Warren. *Leaders, The Strategies for Taking Charge.* New York: Harper, 1985.

Bennis, Warren, et. al. *The Planning of Change.* New York: Holt, Rinehart, and Winston, 1969.

Bennis, Warren. *Why Leaders Can't Lead.* San Francisco: Jossey-Bass, 1989.

Berman, Philip L. *The Courage of Conviction.* New York: Dodd, Mead & Co., 1985.

Blake, Robert and Mouton, Jane. *The Managerial Grid III—The Keys to Leadership Excellence.* Austin, Texas: Scientific Methods, Inc., 1984.

Blau, Peter and Scott, Richard. *Formal Organizations.* San Francisco: Chandler, 1962.

Brome, Vincent. *Jung, Man and Myth.* New York: Athenaeum, 1978.

Burns, James MacGregor. *The Power to Lead.* New York: Simon & Schuster, 1982.

Burns, James MacGregor. *Leadership.* New York: Harper Row, 1978.

Burns, Tom and Stalker, G.M. *The Management of Innovation.* London: Tavistock Publishers, 1961.

Cohen, Sherry. *Tender Power.* Reading, Massachusetts: Addison Wesley, 1989.

Collins, Eliza (ed.). *Executive Success, Making it in Management.* New York: Wiley and Sons, 1985.

Covey, Stephen. *The Seven Habits of Highly Effective People.* New York: Simon & Schuster, Inc., 1990.

DePree, Max. *Leadership is an Art.* New York: Doubleday, 1989.

Donaldson, Les. *Behavioral Supervision: Practical Ways to Change Unsatisfactory Behavior and Increase Productivity.* Addison-Wesley, 1980.

Drake, John. *Counseling Techniques for the Non-personnel Executive.* New York: Drake, Beam, Morin, 1974.

Drake, John. *Selection Interviewing.* New York: Drake, Beam, Morin, 1976.

Drucker, Peter. *Innovation and Entrepreneurship, Practice and Principles.* New York: Harper Row, 1985.

Drucker, Peter. *Managing the Non-Profit Organization.* New York: Harper Collins, 1990.

Drucker, Peter. *The New Realities.* New York: Harper & Row, 1989.

Egan, Gerard. *Interpersonal Living: A Skills/Contract Approach to Human Relations Training in Groups.* Monterey: Brooks Cole Publishers, 1976.

Egan, Gerard and Cowan, Michael. *People in Systems,* a model for development in human service professions and education. Monterey: Brooks Cole Publishers, 1979.

Erikson, Erik. *Childhood and Society.* New York: W.W. Norton & Co., 1963.

Fisher, Roger and Ury, William. *Getting to Yes.* New York: Penguin Books, 1983.

Furlong, Monica. *Merton, A Bibliography.* San Francisco: Harper & Row, 1985.

Gael, Sidney. *Job Analysis.* San Francisco: Jossey-Bass Publishers, 1983.

Gardner, John. *On Leadership.* New York: The Free Press, 1990.

Gardner, John. *Morale.* New York: W.W. Norton, Inc., 1978.

Gardner, John. *Self Renewal, the Individual and Innovative Society.* New York: W.W. Norton, Inc., 1981.

Gardner, John. *The Heart of the Matter.* Washington: Independent Sector, 1986.

Gardner, John. *Leadership and Power.* Washington: Independent Sector, 1986.

Gardner, John. *The Nature of Leadership.* Washington: Independent Sector, 1986.

Gardner, John. *The Tasks of Leadership.* Washington: Independent Sector, 1986.

Glaser, Rollin and Christine. *Building a Winning Management Team.* Bryn Mawr, Pennsylvania: Organizational Design & Development, Inc., 1980.

Glaser, Rollin and Christine. *Team Effectiveness Profile.* Bryn Mawr, Pennsylvania: Organizational Design & Development, Inc., 1984.

Helgesen, Sally. *The Female Advantage, Women's Ways of Leadership.* New York: Doubleday, 1990.

Hersey, Paul and Blanchard, Ken. *Management of Organizational Behavior* (4th edition). Englewood, New Jersey: Prentice Hall, 1982.

Hultman, Ken. *The Path of Least Resistance, Preparing Employees for Change.* Austin: Learning Concepts, 1979.

Hynes, H. Patricia. *Earthright.* Rockland, CA: Prima Publishing and Communications, 1990.

Kirkpatrick, Donald. *A Practical Guide for Supervisory Training and Development.* Addison-Wesley, 1983.

Kotter, John. *Power and Influence.* New York: The Free Press, 1985.

Kouzes, James and Posner, Barry. *The Leadership Challenge.* San Francisco: Jossey-Bass, 1988.

Levinson, Harry and Rosenthal, Stuart. *CEO Corporate Leadership in Action.* New York: Basic Books, 1984.

Mager, Robert & Pipe, Peter. *Analyzing Performance Problems, or You Really Oughta Wanna* (2nd edition). Belmont, California: Pittman Learning, Inc., 1984.

McCall, Lombardo and Morrison. *The Lessons of Experience: How Successful Executives Develop on the Job.* Lexington, Massachusetts: Lexington Books, 1988.

McLagan, Patricia, et.al. *Models for Excellence.* Washington: American Society for Training and Development, 1983.

Merton, Thomas. *The Hidden Ground of Love.* New York: Farrar, Straus, Giroux, 1985.

Morgan, Henry and Cogger, John. *The Interviewer's Manual: Fair and Effective Interviewing.* New York: Drake, Beam, and Morin, 1980.

Morin, William. *Successful Termination.* New York: Drake, Beam, and Morin, 1981.

Morrison, James. *The Human Side of Management.* Addison-Wesley, 1971.

Mott, Michael. *The Seven Mountains of Thomas Merton.* Boston: Houghton, Mifflin, 1984.

Oates, Stephen B. *Let the Trumpets Sound, The Life of M.L.K. Jr.,* New York: Harper & Row, 1982.

Ornstein, Robert and Paul Ehrlich. *New World New Mind.* New York: Simon & Schuster, 1990.

O'Toole, James. *Vanguard Management.* New York: Berkeley Books, 1985.

Pascale, Richard and Athos, Anthony. *The Art of Japanese Management.* New York: Simon and Schuster, 1981.

Peters, Tom. *Thriving on Chaos.* New York: Alfred A. Knopf, Inc., 1987.

Pohly, Ken. *Pastoral Supervision.* Center for Supervisory Studies, United Theological Seminary, Dayton, (revised manuscript in progress), Texas Medical Center, Houston, 1977.

Robbins, Anthony. *Unlimited Power.* New York: Fawcett Columbine, 1986.

Ross, David and Hersey, John. *Counseling in Action,* a handbook on counseling techniques for managers, Ross and Associates, Norwalk, Connecticut, 1977.

Sargent, Alice. *The Androgynous Manager.* New York: American Management Association, 1983.

Schon, Donald. *Educating the Reflective Practitioner.* New York: Jossey-Bass, Inc., 1987.

Seaman, Don. *Working Effectively with Task-Oriented Groups.* New York: McGraw-Hill, 1981.

Senge, Peter. *The Fifth Discipline.* New York: Doubleday, 1990.

Sinetar, Marsha. *Do What You Love, The Money Will Follow.* New York: Dell Publishing Division of Bantam, 1987.

Sinetar, Marsha. *Ordinary People as Monks and Mystics.* New York: Paulist Press, 1986.

Stokes, Kenneth. (ed.) *Faith Development in the Adult Life Cycle.*New York: W. H. Sadlier, Inc., 1982.

Toffler, Alvin. *Powershift.* New York: Bantam Books, 1990.

Tough, Allen. *The Adult's Learning Projects.* Austin, Texas: Learning Concepts Press, 1979.

Washington, James. (ed.). *A Testament of Hope, The Essential Writings and Speeches of Martin Luther King, Jr.* New York: Harper Collins, 1986.

Wolch, Jennifer. *The Shadow State: Government and The Voluntary Sector in Transition.* New York: The Foundation Center, 1990.

Yorks, Lyle. *Managing: Performance Appraisal Process Workbook,* New York: Drake, Beam, and Morin, 1983.

Zaleznik, Abraham. *The Managerial Mystique.* New York: Harper Row, 1989.